The Angelica Home Kitchen

The Angelica Home Kitchen

*recipes and rabble rousings
from an organic vegan restaurant*

Leslie McEachern

RECIPE DEVELOPMENT WITH Chef Peter Berley
PHOTOGRAPHY BY John Bigelow Taylor

TEN SPEED PRESS
Berkeley / Canada

A Kirsty Melville Book

Ten Speed Press
P.O. Box 7123
Berkeley, CA 94707

Cover and interior design by Betsy Stromberg
Illustration on page 17 by Tom Donald

SECOND EDITION

Library of Congress Cataloging-in-Publication Data
McEachern, Leslie.

The Angelica home kitchen : recipes and rabble rousings from an
organic vegan restaurant / Leslie McEachern.
      p.   cm.

ISBN 1-58008-503-2

1. Vegetarian cookery.   2. Angelica Kitchen Restaurant.
TX837 .M476 2000
641.5'636—dc21   00-021910

PRINTED IN CHINA

ON RECYCLED PAPER WITH SOY-BASED INK

1 2 3 4 5 6 — 06 05 04 03

Contents

PART I ❖ Building a Foundation

History ❖ 2

Philosophy & Principles ❖ 10

If You Don't Chew Your Food, Who Will? ❖ 23

Appetizers and Condiments ❖ 108

Soups ❖ 129

Salads and Dressings ❖ 142

Breads, Spreads, Muffins, and Sandwiches ❖ 156

Entrées: Daily Seasonal Creations ❖ 170

Sauces and Marinades ❖ 200

Desserts ❖ 214

Beverages ❖ *244*

Profiles

**Behind the scenes of Angelica Kitchen and
people whose work is essential to ours**

Angelica, the Herb
(Angelica archangelica)—Our Namesake

Angelica is a magnificent, queenly herb that really stands out in the wild; it grows up to eight feet. In the plant's first year, angelica is a rather large clump of attractive bright green foliage that resembles celery. The flower stalk appears in the second year, a wonder to behold since it grows so fast you can almost watch it reach toward the sun. The tiny white or greenish, honey-scented flowers grow in globe-shaped compound umbels. They produce many seeds, which readily germinate, providing plenty of new plants for the next year when the cycle starts over.

Angelica has a long, interesting history. It was named after St. Michael the Archangel and was considered to be an angelic plant with magical powers of protection and healing. Peasants used it to ward off evil spirits and witches, and they made necklaces of the leaves for their children to wear to protect them. So highly regarded were angelica's healing powers that special laws were drawn up in the twelfth century to safeguard it in home gardens.

During the Middle Ages, angelica was used as protection against the plague. According to legend, an angel, appearing to a monk in a dream, revealed that the magical plant would cure the plague. Thereafter it became an ingredient in an official remedy published by the College of Physicians in London called "the King's Majesty's Excellent Recipe for the Plague." Nutmeg, treacle, and angelica water were mixed together and drunk twice a day by those afflicted with the plague. Angelica was also used for rabies, colic, coughs, and other lung diseases and as a digestive aid.

Today the roots, leaves, and seeds are all used medicinally, most often for digestive and bronchial ailments. The fresh leaves can be macerated and used as a poultice to help relieve chest congestion. A decoction of the fresh root is considered to be a useful treatment for chronic bronchitis (one to two tablespoons three times a day and again at bedtime).

Angelica has a sweet, licorice flavor that permeates the whole plant. Fresh leaves can be added to salads, soups, and stews or used as a garnish. The dried leaves or dried, ground root can be added to baked goods. Commercially, angelica root and seeds are used to flavor herb liqueurs such as Benedictine and Chartreuse as well as gin and vermouth. And candied angelica stems are a traditional treat that has been enjoyed for centuries.

In her book *Medicine of the Earth,* Susan Fischer-Rizzi details angelica's overwhelming ability to strengthen a person's resistance to many toxins and weaknesses. We are fortunate to share the angelica name, and it is with loving pride that we strive to evoke its healing tradition and the radiance associated with it.

Acknowledgments

I realize I have been preparing to write this book for at least twenty-five years, so acknowledging all the influences, helpers, and players has been a sweet, private affair. Publicly, I would like to recognize David Leslie, Claire Watson, David Gibbons, Roger Vergnes, Ken Jordan, Peter Cervoni, John Chapman, Nina Reznick, and Julia Hill Gignoux, who have all made essential contributions. For their inspired creativity I thank the artists John Bigelow Taylor and Diane Dubler (photographers), Beck Underwood (graphics), Laurie Dolphin (book design), and Judy Ross (textile design). Writers who generously contributed to this work are Annemarie Colbin, Marion Nestle, Ph.D., and especially Susan Meeker-Lowry, who wrote the section "Now, Industrial Agriculture" in the third chapter. And for their constructive, thoughtful input on the text, I thank readers Michael Ableman, Ellen Goldsmith, Michael Colby, Lu Ellen Huntley, and Allan and Maura Balliett.

To present and past staff members, a strong, diverse, and diligent assemblage of very special folks, I bow to your daily effort to make Angelica Kitchen the best it can be; and to Peter Berley who infused the Angelica Kitchen menu with his superb culinary creativity. Heartfelt thanks especially to Shannon Traynor for her support and encouragement as I made my way through this project.

To each of the farmers and suppliers who deliver their vitality to Angelica Kitchen in addition to the vital ingredients they provide, you remain my main inspiration.

To Wendell Berry, whose writing keeps me rooted, I am ardently grateful.

To my friends, who knew I was up to the task and bolstered me spiritually throughout this extraordinary experience, grazie e te amo.

And finally, deeply, I thank the Angelica family of guests. You motivated this project and encouraged me to complete it through your loyalty, your patience, and your love. I dedicate this book to all of you.

Addendum to the Second Edition

Thank you Chandler Crawford, friend, agent, and instigator for reaching out to make this edition come true.

To Liana Hoodes, who helped immeasurably sorting out the new text about organic standards, I look forward to our next project.

To Kirsty Melville at Ten Speed Press, I truly appreciate the respect shown to the first edition, and thank you for giving me this opportunity.

And to Annie Nelson, the project editor at Ten Speed Press who midwifed this edition, you have made this job a joy.

Introduction

I'll give you the recipes, but cooking is just like religion.
Rules don't no more make a cook than sermons make a saint.
—from *I Dream a World*

I was an outdoors gal all my life, until I met Angelica Kitchen. Since then I've brought my love of the outdoors indoors by feeding people the freshest, most beautiful ingredients I can find.

Over the last twenty-two years as owner and operator of Angelica Kitchen, I have been asked repeatedly when I will be opening more restaurants—this book is my answer. The dilemma of whether to build more locations, and thereby feed more people, and even more importantly build a strong support network for the independent ecological family farmer has been constant. I continue to choose to stay small, finding satisfaction in our home on 12th St., maintaining a sense of place.

You could say I'm a reluctant restaurateur, since I believe we need to invite family, friends, and neighbors into our homes to prepare and enjoy meals made fresh from ingredients grown and gathered locally. This daily act in our kitchens will do more for our individual health, both physically and spiritually, as well as our collective health, culturally and globally, than any well-intentioned restaurant could dare dream.

My part in fulfilling that dream has been to open the recipe archives of Angelica's and to speak my piece about ecological agriculture and cultural responsibilities through this book. The first edition, released in autumn of 2000, was self-published and took five years to make. I was determined that the look and feel would have my mark on it throughout. Interest in the original book was overwhelming; readers were making favorite Angelica recipes at home and reading about why supporting local, sustainable, self-employed farmers is a benefit for us all. That first edition sold out in two years—just through the front door of the restaurant and some direct mail orders. It seemed time to send the book out into the wide world and the good folks at Ten Speed Press have stepped up to make that happen. This second edition has a great new look as well as updated information. Note the new text in the section titled "The Complexities of 'Organic'" with comments from farmers about how these changes affect their farming future. The recipe section is now laid out in a more practical format, and this new binding is called "lay flat"—most helpful when following the chocolate cake recipe!

I hope through this book you will be inspired in your cooking and in your relationship to the foods you are handling. My wish to you is for satisfaction in the choices made for your health and for the earth's health, which are of course one and the same.

♡ leslie

PART I

Building a Foundation

History

The Early Years

My first visit to Angelica Kitchen, in 1978, is etched in my memory. I was visiting New York City from North Carolina and was to meet some friends at a restaurant in the East Village. Arriving a little early, I sat down at a booth by the window and looked around. I felt as if I knew this place, as if I'd been here before . . . yet I knew I hadn't.

The East Village in the seventies was an exciting scene, an eclectic, tolerant neighborhood that attracted all kinds of interesting people. Among them were three free spirits who had come of age in the sixties, Jack Albert, who ran Angelica Herb & Spice Shop on St. Mark's Place, and two of his friends: Eden Ferengul, who fashioned flowers out of colored tissue paper and shared them with others in the streets and parks of Manhattan, and Allan Margolies, who, along with Eden, worked across the street at Bethlehem Bakery. When Jack decided to expand the herb shop into a kitchen, Allan and Eden joined in. In 1976, Angelica Kitchen was born.

The original Angelica Kitchen was a cozy brick-walled place at 42 St. Mark's Place—a former beauty shop that Jack, Allan, and Eden had renovated into a restaurant. The space was tiny, seating only twenty people. It was a business built on generosity and the cooperative spirit. Prices were kept near cost and the modest profits were split among everyone who worked there. For those who couldn't afford to pay, barter—washing dishes, waiting tables, or even artwork for the walls—was always an option. "There were ten or fifteen people living off of that little hole-in-the-wall restaurant," Eden recalled. "Our saving grace was that we operated from the heart. Follow your heart—that's the most important thing."

Jack and his partners built an open kitchen for all to see, a legacy that has survived to this day. Several dishes from the original menu also remain, including the Angelica Cornbread, Miso-Tahini Spread, the house dressing, and the Dragon Bowl—rice, beans, tofu, veggies, and sea veggies priced close to cost.

It wasn't long before there was a loyal customer following from all over—London, Japan, and Brazil, not to mention New Paltz, Poughkeepsie, Wall Street, and Hell's Kitchen. More often than not there would be a line of people waiting for takeout that snaked through the middle of the restaurant. People who wanted to dine in the restaurant waited in line outside. We often served two hundred meals a day out of our tiny kitchen.

One of Angelica's regular lunch customers at that time was Frank Simons. An art director at a computer graphics company on Madison Avenue, he was also a restless adventurer. Creative, curious, enthusiastic, and inventive, Frank loved theater and performance art and made several successful short experimental films. He also collaborated with his mother, a yoga teacher in Boston, on an instructional yoga album.

Frank happened to be at Angelica's one day about five years into the restaurant when Eden, Allan, and Jack were talking about calling it quits. They were burned out and ready to shut the place down in a month. Overhearing their conversation, Frank said, "I'll buy it." The three partners hadn't even considered that option. What would they be selling anyway? How would they come up with a fair price? He'd be buying the name, Frank explained, the concept, and the good will and integrity developed over the past five years. He promised to "extend the legend." The partners let Frank figure out a price and in March 1981 the deal was done.

Eden, Allan, and Jack bought a used van and headed to the Ozarks in northern Arkansas. Jack and Eden still live in Eureka Springs, and Jack has opened a restaurant called The Oasis, which features "Ark-Mex" cuisine. Eden teaches art in a local grade school and still makes paper flowers to sell at fairs. The original Angelica Herb & Spice store eventually moved to First Avenue and Ninth Street. Although ownership has changed hands over the years, we share common roots and similar philosophies: respect for purity, for whole ingredients, and for the healing power of plants.

After my first visit, Angelica Kitchen soon became one of my favorite places to eat whenever I was in New York. I had no idea during those years that I would one day be its owner. Like the restaurant's founders, I too was a child of the sixties. My college years began in 1967, the height of the sixties revolution. As the anti–Vietnam War movement grew, I joined in. During this time, I had the privilege of working with the lawyer for the Black Panthers, William Kunstler, to organize a protest. As I embraced the passion, the camaraderie, and the group spirit uniting us in this cause, I discovered a drive within myself to work for social change. These years also set a precedent for my determination to support however I could the laws of nature.

After moving to the mountains of North Carolina in the spring of 1981, I was working for Edward and Sons Trading Company, a business that manufactures and imports healthy products from Japan and Europe. In New York City on a public relations tour for the company, I was conducting a tasting of miso products in a health store on First Avenue. Frank came in to buy supplies for Angelica Kitchen. We caught each other's eye and chatted briefly. We met again the next day at Angelica's. Meeting Frank changed my life. That summer we fell in love and in September I moved to New York.

Frank was diagnosed with cancer, and by the next spring he was spending most of his time and energy battling the disease. No longer able to manage the restaurant, Frank asked me to step in. The first day I went to work there the place was obviously wanting. "What do you need?" I asked the staff. "Sponges!" they replied. I went out and returned with sponges. "What else?" "Rice" was their answer. The rice supplier couldn't deliver right away so I hopped in a cab, picked up a fifty-pound bag of rice, and hauled it back. It's been like that ever since. I've worn many hats—manager, waitress, dishwasher, plumber, you name it. Necessity turned me into a living advertisement for the entrepreneurial commitment.

Frank died in August 1982. His parents asked me to stay while they decided the fate of the restaurant. One of the conditions of the lease was that it had to be run by a hands-on owner. Carlton Midyette, a dear friend with extensive business experience and a big heart, became my adviser on a day-to-day basis, which helped me keep it going. I knew I had to take over, otherwise Angelica's would close forever. So with Carlton's help I made an offer to Frank's parents, which they accepted. By 1984 I had become the proud owner of Angelica Kitchen.

Taking the Organic Road

During the early eighties, we did our best to serve as much organically grown food as possible. In 1984 I set the goal for Angelica's to be 100 percent organic. The accountant was appalled. "You can't do that! It costs too much!" I remember thinking, "Oh yeah? Watch me." In those days, finding organic food wasn't easy. You had to network with the few people who knew where to get it. One of the best sources was a couple named George and Tilly who trucked produce from their farm in New Jersey to a little storefront on East Sixth Street off Bowery. People from all over the city came to them, among them Angelica's founders. I continued the tradition. When George was unable to deliver my order to the restaurant, I would run back and forth from East Sixth Street to St. Mark's Place with the hand truck hauling cider, kale, squash, daikon, lettuce. . . . Their wonderful produce was worth all the trouble.

At the St. Mark's Place address we had no refrigerated storage space, no walk-in cooler. I convinced Bruce at Prana Foods on First Avenue and Ninth Street to share their cooler space with Angelica. Getting many of our key ingredients became quite labor intensive because the cooler was two blocks away and in the basement. We got used to making ten or twelve trips with the hand truck each day regardless of the weather. We'd literally run over on St. Mark's to Prana, race down the stairs, back up loaded with cases of produce, buckets of tofu, or cases of cider, and push the hand truck on the avenue. In 1986, we finally built a small walk-in refrigerator in our basement. When the restaurant moved to Twelfth Street we took it with us, and it's still in service today.

Although George and Tilly were our major source of organic vegetables, we also purchased from large suppliers like Erewhon, Lundberg, and Organic Farms, an organic wholesaler in Maryland, and smaller suppliers including Morse and Barry from Windfall Farms, Macrobiotic Wholesale out of North Carolina, Bruce Mac-Donald of Commodities in Tribeca, Carl from Genesis Farms on Long Island, Bruce from Prana Foods, and the MacDonalds of Ithaca. At that time we were not too concerned about organic certification. Trust was the key. Angelica Kitchen and the organic industry grew up together in the 1980s.

Stay or Go?

In 1986, I was notified that Angelica's lease wouldn't be renewed in 1988. I felt sure the community would continue to support the restaurant in a new location, yet I was torn between relocating the business and my simply leaving New York City.

I opted to stay. It took me a couple of years to find just the right place. After many false starts in the commercial real estate world, I looked at a vacant space on Twelfth Street. The minute I walked in and stood in the raw, rundown space, I had a vision of the restaurant as it is now, alive and thriving. It's been fifteen years since that day and I can say that my vision was more than fully realized.

The new lease was signed in August 1988; then the work of demolition and construction began. Finally, on January 3, 1989, Angelica Kitchen reopened at its new location. Opening night was a great success. I had expected that after the move to Twelfth Street I'd be able to take a breather. How wrong I was! We needed twice as much inventory as before and a larger customer base and staff. There had to be new schedules, new ordering, more quality control and preparation routines, and new systems of bookkeeping and taxes. The work had just begun.

One of my favorite features of Angelica Kitchen in its current location is the community table—I call it our family table—a natural outgrowth of the communal spirit of the restaurant's early days on St. Mark's Place. The table seats eight and is available for those who want to sit and meet with other diners over a meal. Wide-open interactions have taken place at the community table over the years. It's been a barometer of social and cultural change, a sounding board for economic and political discussions, a forum for dissent, a pick-up spot. I'm sure romances have been kindled there, and some have probably been extinguished as well. Musicians have started bands, campaigns were launched there, good food enjoyed. Of course on occasion someone will get too rambunctious or bring their bedroom talk to the table, in which case they'll be asked to leave. On the whole, the table is companionable but runs the gamut from delightful to annoying. All the interactions that take place there reflect the full, lively community of which Angelica's is a part.

In the spirit of establishing a friendly guideline for dining together, I had cards printed to hand out to rowdy customers with this quote from Paul Pitchford's *Healing with Whole Foods:*

> Set aside a special time and place for meals in a clean environment, surrounded by pleasant sounds, aromas, colors, and conversation. Relax and get comfortable. Perhaps undertake self-reflection about your condition. Eating is a time to receive offerings in the form of food to nurture and revitalize your body. Nurture your thoughts as well.
>
> Consider your manners insofar as they represent your intention toward others. Give attention to the unique qualities of each food and the work involved in bringing it to you.
>
> AVOID:
> - *Emotionally charged subjects and confused, scattered talk or thoughts.*
> - *Eating while tired, too hot or too cold, worried, angry, standing, or watching TV, reading or before bathing.*
>
> These activities make food hard to digest.

Good Cookin'

Over the years, Angelica Kitchen's menu has undergone many changes as vegetarian food evolved from the early days of dense, bean-and-grain-based meals. In the mid-1980s, Pam Williams was a pivotal chef in the restaurant's history. She created a lighter, more balanced and varied repertoire and made presentation a priority. Thanks to Pam, Angelica's upgraded the dialogue about vegan cuisine.

Peter Berley was Angelica's executive chef for seven years, ending his tenure in summer 1999. He attended the New York Restaurant School, fell in love with Mediterranean cuisine, and eventually moved to Maine to become chef, co-owner, and sommelier of the Firepond Restaurant in Blue Hill from 1986 to 1990.

"When I came back to New York," Peter recalls, "I was much more of a gourmet. My focus had changed from Oriental philosophy and healing to European style and celebration." I contacted Peter in 1992 when he was freelancing as a caterer and instructor. He was attracted by my insistence on organic foods and my commitment to sustainable agriculture and small family farms. "For me, starting at Angelica Kitchen was a little like going back in time. Most chefs would have been hard-pressed to give up all non-plant products and wine for cooking. Because of my background, though, it seemed an interesting challenge."

One of the first things Peter did was eliminate all pre-ground herbs and spices in favor of fresh herbs and freshly ground spices. And what a difference that makes! He also broadened the ingredient list, continued to lighten up the menu, and created sandwich recipes. Peter has been a true talent in the kitchen, developing recipes, working side by side with the cooks, and helping them develop their repertoire.

"For the first year or so at Angelica's, I was shy about telling people where I worked. Soon, my enthusiasm started to grow and I began to sell the place more. And that's the way I feel to this day—proud of our accomplishments in demonstrating the full and glorious potential of vegan food."

In a recent issue of *Vegetarian Times* magazine, I spotted an article with a cover headline about top chefs. I opened the magazine and was surprised we weren't included. On closer reading, I realized it was about how top practitioners of "haute cuisine" across America are adopting more vegan recipes. This caused me to reflect on how far we've come in the past two decades—from a scarcity of plant-based menu items made with ecologically sound ingredients to the point where these foods are part of the mainstream.

Cafe Royal—A Step Back in Time

The current site of Angelica Kitchen used to be the back room of the Cafe Royal, where in the 1920s and 1930s patrons played klabyash (a two-card Rumanian game), pinochle, and hearts day and night. Back in the days when Second Avenue was the Yiddish Broadway, Cafe Royal, at the corner of Twelfth Street, was its Sardi's. The Royal was a twenty-four-hour club for a rich theatrical culture. In 1937, the New Yorker proclaimed, "Everybody who is anybody in the creative Jewish world turns up at the Cafe Royal at least one night a week."

By day, the Royal was a sedate New York version of a Viennese cafe, with a black-and-white-tile floor and dark, wood-paneled walls. But around midnight, when shows at the Eden and other theaters let out, the place would start jumping—Die Meshuggeneh Shtunde ("The Crazy Hour") began in earnest.

The Royal's original owner was a Hungarian gentleman who, legend has it, lost the place in a card game to his head waiter and compatriot Oscar Szathmary. After Oscar passed away, his wife Mary ran the place. Its specialty back then was palatschinken, a Hungarian crepe, much like a cheese blintz. This was generally accompanied by a cup of coffee or, in warm weather, an iced coffee with thick cream. The Royal's star-studded list of patrons included Charlie Chaplin, Oscar Hammerstein II, George Gershwin, George Burns, the Marx Brothers, Moss Hart, Elmer Rice, Sergei Rachmaninoff, Boris Thomashefsky, Eddie Cantor, Jack Benny, Sarah Adler, Mayor Fiorello LaGuardia, Al Smith (before he became governor), and gangsters Louis Lepke, Lefty Buchalter, Bugsy Siegel, and Charlie Garah. Even Albert Einstein is said to have stopped by for a che cafe and palatschinken.

The Royal's most famous employee was waiter Herman Tanzer, who worked hard for his nickel tips over a period of more than three decades. The cafe only accepted cash, so Herman ran a check-cashing service on the side. He also helped out valued customers with his famous phony phone call announcements to alert impresarios and producers to the presence of unemployed actors in their midst. With all of these stories of bygone times to entertain us, waiting for a table at Angelica's becomes an amusing pastime, no?

Philosophy & Principles

*It may be observed that the natural life and the
supernatural life have a conformity to each other
which neither has with the mechanistic life.*
—*T. S. Eliot*

The phrase "living the mindful life" perfectly expresses the ideas of living according to one's principles and making responsible choices. The first step is to acknowledge our place in the natural world. We are a part of Earth's ecosystem, not its masters. When we lose our awareness of our interconnectedness with the natural world, it is easy to become accomplices to global industrialization and the destruction of the environment. The now familiar words of Chief Seattle (Dwamish) continue to serve as a model and an inspiration for me:

> *This we know,*
> *all things are connected,*
> *like the blood*
> *which unites one family.*
> *All things are connected.*
> *Whatever befalls the Earth,*
> *befalls the sons of the Earth.*
> *Man did not weave the web of life;*
> *he is merely a strand in it.*
> *Whatever he does to the web,*
> *he does to himself.*

We have the power to avoid infatuation with objects and technology for technology's sake. As consumers, we drive the market and need to stay awake at the wheel. We can question the media-driven message that this new gadget will not only improve our efficiency but also fulfill us in some deeper way. When we think about it, we know this is not true. We are being programmed for greater and greater consumption. Meanwhile we're abandoning life's traditional rituals—sitting down to a family meal, cultivating a backyard garden, buying from the local produce store or farm stand—in favor of technological advances and so-called convenience. When we reflect on it, we see that the activities we've given up to "save time" are the very things that give meaning to our lives.

A mindful, questioning approach to what we buy and how we live involves a commitment of time and effort. Is this food healthy for me and the environment? Am I using the most efficient transportation? How does my choice of laundry detergent/household cleaner/pet food/toilet paper/cooking oil/shampoo/diapers, and so forth affect me, my family, the larger society, the environment? Sorting our needs from our wants and applying fundamental questions to daily choices is not easy nor is it always cheaper or faster, but the freedom of spirit we gain when we release ourselves from the emotional and financial chains of consumerism is priceless. I urge you to take that extra step.

Discipline Is Remembering What You Want

Being aware of your choices and of the power those choices have to help you achieve a desired goal is what I call living with intent. If your wish is to live a life that does as little harm as possible to the environment, for example, you must first become aware of all the ways your lifestyle has an impact on the Earth—and make choices and changes based on what you learn. However, intentions, no matter how worthy, are meaningless if they are not backed by appropriate action. Building a system of integrity and honor, where each action matters, reflects living with intent. Taking just any road won't do.

One day, not so long ago, a woman approached me on the street to say that she had just started eating regularly at Angelica Kitchen again and was just delighted. She loved the background music and the decor, she found the staff attentive but not hovering, and the food was perfect. Her praise was a sweet reward, particularly satisfying because what pleased her was the cumulative result of many deliberate choices we've made over the years. Careful attention given on a daily basis to innumerable details has made Angelica a special destination for our patrons.

Running a Socially Conscious Business

One of the finest rewards of running Angelica Kitchen is the ability to take a stand about specific issues. It has given me the opportunity to vote with the restaurant's dollars for the kinds of political, social, and economic changes the staff and I believe are important. Keeping the business strong and healthy by maintaining high standards increases our economic power and our voice in the community.

If you don't believe in worker exploitation, then you don't do it in your business. If you believe in recycling, then you do it in your business. It's that simple, but relentlessly complicated in its application. For example, in order to provide take-out and delivery service, we supply disposable containers—horrendously at cross-purposes with our ecological concerns. While we do offer a 10 percent discount to customers who bring their own containers, very few people have taken advantage of it. The restaurant is a massive consumer of gas, water, and electricity, which is another concern. We do what we can today and are prepared to make more changes as alternatives become available.

To minimize the restaurant's impact on the web of life in every possible way is extremely important. For instance, did you know that virgin rainforests in Indonesia are being clear-cut to make disposable chopsticks? Since Angelica Kitchen uses these for take-out orders and for those customers who prefer them over reusable ones, I make sure our supply comes from a highly renewable resource—bamboo. In another example, the restaurant had been working with a recycling center to haul away plastic and glass years before New York City enacted its recycling laws. After the laws were in place, recycling became the responsibility of private sanitation companies, which, unfortunately, were notoriously lax and controlled by organized crime. It thus became necessary to take a stand against their opportunistic price increases and blatant disregard for regulations.

Playing Robin Hood on menu pricing is another way of fulfilling our goal of nourishing the whole community. We always offer a dish called the Dragon Bowl—rice, beans, tofu, vegetables, and sea vegetables—priced very close to cost. Anyone can come in and enjoy a wholesome, filling meal for $5.00 (the Wee Dragon). Labor-intensive and more expensive items such as daily soups, specials, and desserts subsidize the Dragon Bowl and other basics. All that said, meals at the restaurant are priced according to what they cost to produce, not what I think we can get away with charging. The point is to set an ethical standard and charge what's fair. If I find income isn't meeting expenses, we work to eliminate inefficiency and waste before raising prices. Angelica Kitchen is a nutrition-based restaurant, which, to me, means taking responsibility for both the vitality of the food and the message it's sending. Gouging customers—charging higher prices just because I can—is not part of this message.

Another one of our important tenets is to actively support the community. In order to contribute to the local economy, the restaurant must continue to function as a responsible, thriving business. As with all endeavors, this involves making choices. Recently, for example, a well-known filmmaker wanted to negotiate a deal to shut the restaurant down for a couple of weeks to use it as a film set. Impossible, I said. Shutting down to pocket extra dollars is not what Angelica Kitchen is about.

Part of the restaurant's commitment to community service is donating food. Our daily leftovers are always given away to the hungry. Whereas we used to give handouts directly at closing time, now leftovers are picked up by an organization called City Harvest, which redistributes them. Food is regularly donated for fund-raisers and benefits for organizations such as the Whole Foods Project, Just Foods, and Green Guerrillas (which creates gardens and offers school programs in the New York City area), and to Northeast Organic Farmers Association–New York for their farmer conferences. Sharing what we have in support of local causes is one way of giving back to the community that supports us.

Mark Dunau and Lisa Wujnovich, Farmers in the Dell

In just thirteen short years Mark Dunau and Lisa Wujnovich, who run Mountain Dell Farm, have created a small, diversified family farm that produces gorgeous vegetables and embodies many of the values we at Angelica Kitchen hold dear. I feel like Mark, Lisa, and I are co-conspirators, doing our part to bring respect for nature back into the food production system. I love handing the money over to Mark to pay for Angelica's purchases. You can't say that about everybody!

Mountain Dell, located near Hancock in Delaware County, New York, is a real working farm complete with swimming pond. The whole family—Mark and Lisa and their two kids, Bera and Shane—get their hands in the dirt. Seven acres are under cultivation, where they grow about sixty different crops, including "anything that goes in a salad": at least twelve types of lettuce along with radicchio, beets, fennel, squashes, bok choy, and basil.

The atmosphere of the farm is relaxed and friendly. Neighbors drop by to chew the fat, and friends from the city come up to help with the planting. The discussion around the table always centers on politics and food and the politics of food. The whole place is infused with a strong creative spirit.

During the 1980s, Mark, a playwright, and Lisa, an actress, writer, and chef, lived in the East Village of Manhattan. They decided to move to the country to farm, write, and have babies, and in 1988, with no training or background in farming, they bought the Mountain Dell property. "Until I came up here I never put a seed in the ground my whole life," Mark told me. "Being new at farming is sometimes a good thing, because you can do things differently. You don't know any better."

One secret to the farm's success is floating row covers, a polyethylene mesh that protects crops from pests and extends the growing season. Lisa read about them and bugged Mark to try them until he finally relented. Now he's hooked. The covers afford a six-month growing season for salad ingredients, and the brassicas (cabbage, cauliflower, broccoli, kale, collards, bok choy, and tatsoi) grow 50 percent faster, with no insect problems.

Mark and Lisa are both actively involved in their community as well. Lisa founded a writers' group in Hancock, and Mark, who loves to get on his soapbox, ran for Congress in New York's Twenty-sixth District on the Rural Party ticket, which he founded. In July 1998, he became the first candidate to complete a 190-mile walk across his district from Ithaca to Kingston. In 2000 Mark was also the Green Party of New York nominee for U.S. Senate and received 41,000 votes.

Mountain Dell Farm is just a couple of miles away from Cannonsville Reservoir, a lovely spot that provides much of New York City's water supply. Gazing across the landscape toward the reservoir, Mark reflects on the state of farming: "New York City is crazed about protecting its water supply, but not about protecting its farmers. Those farmers are going out of business big time due to the supply-and-demand myth. In the short run it may be smart to buy from California. But if you have any notion of the history of civilization, you know you have to protect your food source. To let farmers go out of business is ridiculous. It's madness. We've been sold the notion that all food is the same, it's the price that counts. But if it isn't the guy next door you're counting on, it's the guy from California who's counting on water from the Colorado River. If that doesn't work out, you're going to wish the guy next door was still there. It's very shortsighted to let local farmers go."

In the greenhouse,
I pluck baby lettuce seedlings,
move fetal upstarts to new environments,
playing goddess,
pulling extras.
I say a vow to each I withdraw,
to uproot what isn't needed from my life,
anger, oh always too much anger, and
things that don't belong inside of me,
things I collect,
like a pack rat at a yard sale.

I step outside and feel earth,
a sponge giving under my feet.
Open buds quiver on the mountain side,
a dreamy maroon beige cherry sexy color,
smelling up the air,
shaking up our tails,
big, little, invisible tails,
like mine and yours,
buried in the bottom of our butts,
vibrating like a bee's backside,
this clear spring afternoon.

From "Root Chakra Poem"
by Lisa Wujnovich, 4/10/98

Setting Standards: Everybody Speak Up!

"No cutting corners" is a phrase that Angelica Kitchen customers have learned to rely upon. Always striving for higher standards, I expect customers to demand this from Angelica as well as from other establishments. Speak up! Let us know if you think we're living up to our standards.

When you go to a restaurant and the water tastes like chemicals, ask, "Have you ever thought about filtering your water? It tastes mighty disagreeable." When you order steamed greens and they come to the table flat and lifeless, you have a right to demand a higher standard. If you accept an inferior or mediocre product, you are co-conspiring to lower standards everywhere.

Eliminating the Middleman: Let's Get Reconnected!

Angelica Kitchen is committed to eliminating the middleman. We prefer to deal directly with our farmers, tofu makers, and sea vegetable harvesters. Direct connections, proven through years of experience, assure the quality, vitality, and freshness of the food. When a middleman or wholesaler is introduced into the equation, I begin to question the freshness of the food. How long has it been stored in a warehouse? Has it been repackaged and relabeled before being shipped? Was it rolled up and down chutes, trundled and bundled and thrown around? In other words, has the food been treated with respect?

Treat your food right—I might even add with love and care and respect—and it will treat you right. Rather than throwing the food on the chute that goes into Angelica's inventory area, the growers place the crates of veggies carefully on the chute and gently ease them on down. The person who planted, tended, and harvested the food will handle it with care, guaranteed. Another benefit of buying direct is that the farmers and producers receive more money for their goods while the restaurant pays less than if we had ordered through a middleman. This is another part of the Angelica strategy for keeping menu prices as low as possible.

We have a cheerful little note on the menu saying, "We happily accept only cash." Not accepting credit cards is another way of eliminating the middleman and of maintaining a more direct relationship with your dining experience. We hand you the food, you hand us the money. This policy isn't always convenient, nor does it please everyone, we realize, but hopefully after hearing the reasons behind it, objections will fade.

Here's the message we circulate to our customers regarding credit cards:

> Credit card companies do not grow our ingredients, prepare our dishes, or bring your selections to your table. In other words, they do not make any essential contribution to this business.
>
> I feel that involving these companies in the experience you have at Angelica Kitchen would be untrue not only to the spirit of the restaurant but also to your expectations when you come here. When you walk through the door, you have a right to anticipate delicious fresh dishes prepared with the best ingredients and served to you in a friendly way. You certainly do not anticipate having to support lending corporations whose policies may be dubious, if not out-and-out perverse.
>
> On a more practical note, Angelica Kitchen is dedicated to charging you only what it costs us to produce the food. Shoving a credit card company between your plate and our kitchen would drive up our prices. Who needs that?
>
> So while we apologize for any inconvenience our cash-only policy may cause, we know that you'll understand. This is one restaurant you can come to where nothing will be plastic.

Supporting Our Growers and Producers

When I came to New York twenty-one years ago, Windfall Farms, from upper New York State, was the only local organic farm delivering to the restaurant. At that time the farmers markets were just getting started, and I'd scout around seeking additional sources of organically grown produce. I joined with others who were also in the market for organics, and together we worked to develop a network of growers and suppliers. The restaurant provides a stable economic base for local growers, cottage industries (tofu, maple syrup, cider, etc.), and artisans who operate their businesses in a conscientious manner, because Angelica is a thriving business that depends on fresh ingredients direct from the farm. For example, each year we use approximately 10,000 pounds of apples and an equal amount of beets, over 16,000 pounds of cabbage, 35,000 pounds of tofu, 10,000 bunches of kale, 4,000 gallons of cider, and 900 gallons of maple syrup.

Buying local is important to me even when goods appear to cost more. Keeping the double bottom line in mind, buying cheaper produce shipped from California when you live on the East Coast ignores the hidden costs of long-distance transportation such as nonrenewable fossil fuels (both their production and effluent pollution). Another hidden cost is loss of nutrients as time and storage conditions rob the produce of vitality. Of course there are times when we do have to go out of the region, in the winter especially. But when we look to procure the 94,000 pounds of organically grown carrots we typically use each year, for example, we do make an effort to stay on the East Coast when we can't find them all locally.

Buying local also makes it possible for Angelica Kitchen to maintain close working relationships with its suppliers, trading basic information and educating each other. I wanted to know whether the soybeans for the tofu we use were hybrid or non-hybrid. I asked that question of Gary Abramowitz, the tofu maker in Pennsylvania. Not only were the soybeans non-hybridized, they were also New York State grown. We also discovered that the tempeh makers used the same local soybeans.

It has been gratifying to support so many different suppliers over the years, many of whom are featured throughout the pages of this book. They represent the kinds of producers and cottage industries that are essential for the long-term health of ourselves, our soil, and our culture.

ANGELICA KITCHEN YEARLY SUPPLIES

Here is a sampling of the quantities of certain ingredients we use annually—all ecologically grown.

Apple cider	4,032 gallons	Fresh pressed N.Y. State non-pasteurized
Apples	10,264 each	
Tofu	34,608 lbs.	17,750 lbs., or approximately 9 tons of non-hybridized N.Y. State organically grown soybeans
Tempeh	10,000 lbs.	Approximately 7,150 lbs. of non-hybridized N.Y. State organically grown soybeans
Hard (winter) squashes	9,125 lbs.	Red Kuri, Delicata, Butternut, Buttercup, Sweet Dumpling, etc.
Soft (summer) squashes	10,190 lbs.	
Spinach	2,160 lbs. (not bunches)	
Yams	7,680 lbs.	
Yukon Gold potatoes	12,600 lbs.	
Maple syrup	900 gallons	36,000 gallons of Vermont sap; 40 gallons of sap make 1 gallon of syrup
Kale and collards combined	16,128 bunches	
Parsley	3,942 bunches	
Daikon	4,800 lbs.	
Basil	2,400 bunches	
Cilantro	4,320 bunches	

GUY JONES, BLOOMING HILL ORGANIC FARM

I haven't raised my prices in ten years but they haven't asked me the
prices in ten years either. That's just not their policy.
—Guy Jones, Blooming Hill Organic Farm

Blooming Hill, a beautiful, aptly named spread located in Blooming Grove, Orange County, New York, is Guy Jones's small, diversified farm. Guy is a concerned, conscientious, fun, and nitty-gritty guy who used to practice civil rights law until he became disillusioned in the early 1980s and decided to become an organic farmer. Blooming Hill grows over 150 different types of plants on fifteen acres: salad greens, herbs, squashes, peppers, tomatoes, tomatillos, flowers, flowers, flowers, and so much more.

Unlike many farmers who try to undercut each other's prices in a desperate attempt to stay ahead of the competition, Guy welcomes others into the market. "The rising tide carries all ships," he states philosophically. "We're all going to sink or swim in this thing together."

As part of a cadre of individuals who laid down their pens and took up their shovels, Guy speaks from experience about one of the greatest problems America faces: our fundamental lack of respect for the farmers who grow our food. "Earl Butz, the secretary of agriculture, said, 'We've been able to free 95 percent of the people from the drudgery of farming.' When you've got the secretary of agriculture calling farming drudgery, it's like the secretary of labor saying nobody has to work! Is that how people want to look at farming?"

Guy feels strongly about the importance of acknowledging both how valuable our farmers are and the harsh economic realities they face: "We're interviewed a lot for newspaper stories and they ask us, 'What is the biggest problem facing an organic farmer?' They expect me to say the bugs, but my biggest problem is paying my workers a living wage. People don't want to pay fair value for the food they eat. They're willing to pay fair value for other things—the car they drive, for example. There isn't an auto worker in this country who works harder than a farm worker. It's always the next wave of immigrants who are expected to do the farm work. For some reason people think it's okay to pay them nothing. The fact is, we're eating too cheap. The whole economy is built on the backs of a million guys working out in the fields for nothing. But if they stopped doing it, everything would come to a grinding halt. A dialogue needs to be started that leads to an attitude that farming is a good and essential occupation that needs to be fairly compensated."

Guy has three young sons, Travis, Austin, and Skyler. Maybe someday they'll take over Blooming Hill and continue their father's legacy. "We need to show that farming can be as intellectually and spiritually rewarding as any other occupation. I'm trying to show my sons and their friends that farming isn't some kind of novel, romantic notion. There was a time when this county had six farming programs in six different schools. Now there are none." He notes that even at Cornell University, his alma mater, the agricultural school is strong on theory but has essentially no practical farming program.

Pioneers like Guy are demonstrating that it is possible to succeed at sensible farming. Now that agribusiness is moving into the organic niche, will the likes of Guy Jones be able to survive? Time will tell. "The organic foods industry is not a lifestyle anymore. Guys like me are lifestyle organic farmers. We're living with our kids, growing our hair long. The Doles and the Minute Maids have seen the niche and are going organic. But while agribusinesses can survive on 1 percent profit, we need to make 25 percent to survive." If we want to continue to enjoy the beautiful produce lifestyle farmers like Guy grow, we had better heed his call and not take our food supply for granted. We need to speak out and support our local small diversified family farms—now!

Love, Respect, Humor, and Other Important Ingredients

How does all this talk about values relate to soup? you might ask. The quality of the care, attention, and respect food is given during its preparation is as important as the quality of the ingredients.

At Angelica Kitchen, we've discovered another element that is essential to the well-being of our operation: humor. Ours is a very labor-intensive business. We cook twenty-four hours a day, preparing food—breads and some of the appetizers and desserts—all night long for the next day. A shift starts at midnight, another begins at 5:30 A.M. Working together in such an intense environment can at times be difficult and hectic. But a steady current of humor keeps everyone going, in the form of endless banter and the sudden appearances of alter-personas invented by the staff. We've had spontaneous visitations from opera singers, transvestites, priests, rap singers, to give you an idea.

Humor appears on the menu as well. We all participate in the daily ritual of naming the specials: Edith Pilaf, Edna St. Vincent Millet, Ciao Down, Hot to Trotsky, Mounds over Matter, To Bean or Not to Bean, Pâté Hearst, and Don't Make a Pesto Yourself are but a mere suggestion of our indulgence. In addition to puns—some clever, many corny—we rely on topical humor and inside jokes.

When people try to define what it is they love about our restaurant, it always seems to come back to—love.

We must see that it is foolish, sinful, and suicidal to destroy the health of nature for the sake of an economy that is really not an economy at all but merely a financial system—one that is unnatural, undemocratic, sacrilegious, and ephemeral.

—Wendell Berry

If You Don't Chew
Your Food, Who Will?

The Healing Properties of Food

If we wish to sustain health and well-being, the food we choose must provide our bodies with adequate nutrients—vitamins, minerals, fiber, micronutrients, and so forth. However, nutrition is often way down on the list of considerations when it comes to deciding what to eat. How we feel about our bodies, what's going on in our lives, how we were raised, the food we ate as youngsters, the culture we live in, and our finances all play important roles in determining how we regard food, feeding ourselves, and the quality of our diets.

The food choices you make have ramifications for your health. Every time you put something in your mouth, you are making a choice; it's important to become conscious of that choice and decide if it's one you really want to be making. I'm here to tell you it is possible to obtain vital nutrition, avoid chemicals, additives, and harmful levels of saturated fats, and still eat satisfying, great-tasting dishes. The key is to educate yourself about basic sources of nutrients, eat a variety of fresh, local, whole foods, and not worry so much.

As the tempo of present-day society escalates at warp speed, it's a major challenge to slow down and enjoy a more balanced pace of life, especially at mealtimes. Too often we rush through our meals so fast we don't even remember the taste of what we've eaten. When we eat on the run, we risk indigestion, and our bodies can't receive optimum benefit from our food choices. Digestion begins with chewing, which breaks the food into small pieces and mixes it with saliva, which contains enzymes that begin the digestion of starches. If this stage is skipped, you're asking your pancreas and its enzymes to do a job they're not designed to do. Take advantage of your food's available nutrition by chewing it—if you don't do it, nobody else will.

Through balanced, appropriate eating, the body's systems are kept strong and vital, ready to combat any destructive invaders. The cost of maintaining good health is far less than the cost of treating disease. What I'm referring to is the concept of "food as preventive medicine." Our bodies are designed to maintain health naturally. By choosing to eat well we support our bodies' wisdom. Further, certain foods have specific effects on health. Broccoli, brown rice, millet, apples, and daikon, for example, have a gentle cleansing effect on the liver. Incorporating these foods in the diet is a good idea, since the liver is especially hard hit by the various toxic chemicals in our food and environment. By teaching ourselves about the effects certain foods and herbs have on our health and putting what we learn into practice in our daily lives, we can begin to take responsibility for our own health. There are many excellent teachers, workshops, and books available to help you begin this process. Annemarie Colbin's *Food and Healing* and Paul Pitchford's *Healing with Whole Foods: Oriental Traditions and Modern Nutrition* are excellent places to start. (See Suggested Reading at the end of this book for more suggestions.)

Now, Industrial Agriculture

Pesticides It's no secret that most of the food found in supermarkets today has been treated to a witch's brew of toxic chemicals. Herbicides, pesticides, and fungicides are regularly sprayed on crops to kill weeds, pests, and fungi, respectively. These poisons are ultimately absorbed into the food and no amount of washing or peeling can remove every trace. Many of the agricultural chemicals used on our food today were developed by chemical companies during World War II. After the war ended, in order to protect the chemical companies from heavy losses the government helped find private markets for many of them, deliberately integrating toxic chemicals into agriculture (and other areas such as forestry). They were also exported as the linchpin in the so-called green revolution, which was supposed to provide food for all. But instead, hunger and starvation, expanded deserts, rain-forest destruction, depleted and poisoned water supplies, displaced peasant and tribal societies, violence over access to land—and massive profits for chemical companies—have been the result. Today people are less food self-reliant than ever as control over land and food systems has been wrenched from families and communities and given over to multinational corporations and the global supermarket.

The use of pesticides is increasing. Close to three billion pounds of pesticides are used every year in the United States alone, and pesticide use is rising in other countries as well. Manufacturers have facilities in many Third World countries, and these factories often produce older and more hazardous chemicals for which patents have expired, as well as those that have been restricted or banned for use in the United States. Eventually these chemicals make it back here, a cycle known as the "circle of poison." Despite the increase in pesticide use, losses of crops to pests have nearly doubled as pests have developed genetic resistance to one chemical after another. Today, virtually all major insect pests will show some form of genetic resistance.

Pesticides pose a wide range of risks from cancer to birth defects, from neurological damage to immune deficiencies. Recent studies also support a link between pesticide exposure and an increased tendency toward violent behavior. Globally, millions of cases of severe pesticide poisoning are reported each year, thousands of them fatal. At greatest risk are field workers and their families, because they are exposed to the chemicals in greater concentrations. It's not unusual, for example, for families to store water in empty pesticide containers. But even small doses of these poisons can make us sick or cause birth defects. The elderly, people with compromised immune systems, and children are most at risk.

Here are some rather frightening pesticide facts obtained from the Environmental Research Foundation's *Rachel's Environment & Health Weekly*, no. 660, July 22, 1999: In April 1999, researchers in Switzerland announced that much of the rain falling on Europe contains such high levels of pesticides that it would be illegal if it were supplied as drinking water. Also in 1999, for the first time pesticides were found in the amniotic fluid of 30 percent of pregnant women tested in Los Angeles, California. According to Consumer's Union, many fruits and vegetables sold in the United States have pesticide residues that exceed the limits the Environmental Protection Agency considers safe for children: "Even one serving of some fruits and vegetables can exceed safe daily limits for young children."

Environmentally, pesticides are a nightmare. Farmers apply more and more of the toxins to their fields as pests build resistance. Chemical-laced runoff pollutes rivers, streams, lakes, and ground-water. The common practice of aerial spraying results in what is called pesticide drift—not all the pesticide goes where it's supposed to. In fact, as much as 50 percent of what's sprayed from the air never makes it to the target area. But even pesticides applied from the ground often end up where they shouldn't. What happens to the birds, animals, and fish whose habitat is contaminated by pesticide applications? Deformities, tumors, and low fertility—the same things that happen to people. In the Pacific Northwest, pesticides are a major threat to the habitat of salmon, many native species of which are already in danger of extinction. Wartime or peacetime, pesticides are still a weapon of destruction.

Biotechnology Genetic engineering, also called biotechnology or genetic modification, is the latest corporate ploy to increase profits at the expense of human and ecological health. Genes from plants, bacteria, viruses, and animals (including humans) are spliced into the embryonic cells of another plant or organism. Biotech is one of the fastest-growing industries, with 1,300 companies in the United States alone. Monsanto, one of the largest biotech companies, has also given us polychlorinated biphenyl (PCB), dioxin, Agent Orange, and Roundup, the world's biggest-selling herbicide.

Since 1990 thousands of varieties of genetically engineered plants, animals, and bacteria have been developed and field-tested in the United States in virtually every state. Examples include the controversial rBGH (bovine growth hormone), which increases milk production in dairy cows by 10 to 25 percent; the FlavrSavr Tomato, designed for greater shelf life, a flop because it is virtually tasteless; frost-resistant strawberries; a genetically engineered bacteria used as a substitute for natural rennet in a number of vegetarian cheeses; numerous genetically enginered crops including cotton, canola, soy, corn, and tobacco; and human growth hormone in pigs, for pigs that grow bigger, faster.

At the time of this writing, genetically engineered cotton varieties account for upwards of 50 percent of the United States cotton crop. Keep in mind that not only do we wear cotton but also cotton seed oil is often used in processed baked goods and in some restaurants for frying. Genetically engineered soy, canola, and corn are so common the only way to positively avoid them is to know the producer, who knows the seed source—again, all based on trusted relationships. The real issue is that labeling of genetically engineered products is not required, therefore the consumer cannot make that "informed choice."

The most prevalent biotech products available today are seeds. Roundup-Ready soy and cotton are the most common, with corn and even beets soon to follow. As the name indicates, these crops are designed to withstand repeated sprayings of Monsanto's weed-killing Roundup without being adversely affected themselves. Over time weeds will become resistant to the chemical, requiring more and more of it—a boon for Monsanto, but what about the air, water, and soil? How do you feel? Do you want more Roundup in the environment?

Bt corn and cotton incorporate genes from *Bacillus thuringiensis* (Bt), a bacterium toxic to many varieties of crop-damaging caterpillars. While the natural form of Bt's toxin is only activated under special circumstances, which makes it safe for use by organic growers, the toxin released by engineered plants is already killing a wide variety of beneficial insects, including butterflies and bees. Furthermore, the Environmental Protection Agency projects that widespread use of Bt crops will result in many of the target pests becoming Bt resistant in three to five years, making it useless for organic production.

As if all this weren't enough, Monsanto is developing what is called Terminator Technology to prevent farmers, mainly in Africa, Asia, and Latin America, from saving seeds from year to year. Terminator Technology is a broadly framed patent for the "control of plant gene expression," meaning that the seed will have a genetically engineered suicide mechanism. As a result the seeds of the next generation will self-destruct. This technology directly contradicts Monsanto's claim that biotech will feed the world's hungry, since it threatens to undermine the very basis of traditional agriculture—seed saving.

Some would argue that genetic engineering is really not very different from the various crop-breeding techniques used by farmers for generations, but this is simply not true. Farmers do not insert genes from, say, fish into corn, or from humans into pigs. With the advent of biotech, we now have the ability to direct the evolution of life itself to suit our economic, political, and social desires and preferences. With *Homo sapiens's* track record so far, I don't feel or think we are ready for that responsibility. We must remember, we are a part of nature, not its master.

Impact on Land and Culture As corporate agriculture is exported to other countries, it destroys intact, sustainable, self-reliant communities and traditional cultures. And it's just as detrimental in the United States. In 1950, more than 2,000 counties listed agriculture as their main source of income. Today less than 20 counties nationwide can make that claim. Farm failures lead to dropping land values, tax delinquencies multiply, and the spiral of economic decline spins out of control. The toll on rural families is high, as people who have farmed the land for generations are forced into bankruptcy, forced to let go of everything they have ever known. As farmers are replaced by factories and farmland is converted to parking lots and shopping malls, we lose our collective connection to the land. The world over, people are losing the wisdom traditionally passed down through generations about soil, seeds, wildlife, the seasons and rhythms of nature, and the knowledge of how to work with natural systems.

Food Irradiation The industrialization and corporate control of our food system have meant the increasing contamination of food with dangerous pathogens like *E. coli* and salmonella. Until recently, meat was most at risk for contamination due to filthy conditions at slaughterhouses and meat packing plants. But in the past few years, *E. coli* has been found on nonmeat foods as well. Rather than clean up their act, industry's solution is to zap food with large doses of ionizing radiation to kill pathogenic bacteria.

Despite claims to the contrary, irradiation does not ensure uncontaminated food. It kills most bacteria but doesn't remove toxins created in the early stages of contamination, plus it kills bacteria that produce smells that indicate spoilage. In addition, it is likely that irradiation will have a mutagenic effect on bacteria and viruses and that some of these mutants will be radiation resistant; such strains of salmonella have already been developed under laboratory conditions.

Although irradiated food is not rendered radioactive, it is zapped with the equivalent of tens of millions of chest X rays, enough to break down the molecular structure of the food, destroy essential vitamins and minerals, and create chemical substances called radiolytic products. These include formaldehyde, benzene, formic acid, and quinones, which are harmful to human health. Benzene, for example, is a known carcinogen. In addition, unique radiolytic products are also created—completely new chemicals that have not yet been identified, let alone tested for toxicity.

The word *radiation* covers a wide spectrum of energy. On the low end are emissions from power lines and visual display units; on the high end are X rays and gamma rays from radioactive material. Radio waves, microwaves, and the infrared, visual, and ultraviolet light spectrums fall in the middle. Radiation at the high end of the spectrum has sufficient energy to break the molecular structure of the material being radiated, leaving positively and negatively charged particles called ions and free radicals, hence the term "ionizing radiation." Two radioactive materials have been identified as suitable for food irradiation: cobalt 60 and cesium 137. Food can also be irradiated with high-energy electron beams, euphemistically called electronic pasteurization.

The same problems associated with nuclear power plants are associated with irradiation facilities, and numerous accidents have already occurred. If we were to irradiate a large portion of our food supply, hundreds more facilities would be needed. Currently, the radiation source for most irradiators is cobalt 60, but it is in limited supply. The only isotope available in sufficient quantities for large-scale irradiation is cesium 137, which is one of the deadliest. Cesium 137 remains dangerous for nearly 600 years. Cobalt 60 has a half-life of 5 years.

The Department of Energy (DOE) was one of the first developers and promoters of food irradiation. Its Byproducts Utilization Program was created in the 1970s to promote the use of nuclear byproducts, which the DOE claimed "have a wide range of applications in food technology, agriculture, energy, public health, medicine, and industrial technology." DOE's reason for promoting nuclear by-products was made clear at hearings held in 1983 before the House Armed Services Committee: "[T]he utilization of these radioactive materials simply reduces our waste handling problem . . . we get some of these very hot elements like cesium and strontium out of the waste."

Today virtually our whole food supply—fruits, vegetables, spices, poultry, and meat—has been approved for irradiation. However, the solution to widespread contamination is not irradiation, it is ecologically sustainable agriculture. The nation's food supply is contaminated because the scale of operations, whether in the meat industry or in the growing and processing of fruits and vegetables, is simply out of control. Moreover, as fewer and fewer corporations, including government agencies, control more and more of our food system, there is little accountability. The fact is, growing food for profit is hazardous to our health.

No Place for Synthetics

Synthetic chemicals and genetically altered foods have no place in the food chain. Period. Amen. Customers at the restaurant often ask me, teasingly, what it is we put in our food that makes it taste so good. I reply, "It's what's not in it that does the trick."

Let's put the information in the previous section in context by taking a look at a typical breakfast item: a mass-produced blueberry muffin. We can assume this muffin was made from flour ground from grain altered through genetic engineering. Not only is it missing the inherent intelligence of nature, but it was also sprayed with various chemicals in the field and even in storage, to keep bugs out. The flour was mixed with aluminum-based baking powder and chemically processed sugar, then treated with a preservative for longer shelf life. The blueberries are often relatively clean, or they may have been sprayed. The point is, you don't know. The muffin also contains oil that you can be sure is barely food grade and extracted from genetically altered seeds (see *Fats That Heal, Fats That Kill* by Udo Erasmus). Yummy, huh?

Perhaps your breakfast also included coffee, eggs, or juice. Most likely the eggs are the product of large-scale, commercial practices in which hens are raised in filthy, confined conditions, their beaks clipped, and fed a diet laced with antibiotics, hormones, steroids, and who knows what else. Coffee was traditionally grown in the shade of the rain-forest canopy, but now, thanks to industrial agriculture, it is grown in cleared rain forest using chemicals, often ones restricted or banned in this country. The impacts on the environment and local cultures of clearing rain forest for agriculture are devastating. When we lose the rain forest we lose not only species of plants, animals, and insects, many of which haven't yet been identified, at least by nonindigenous peoples, but also an incredible diversity of human culture that knows how to live in balance with these delicate systems. The drive for more at a cheaper price reflects the ultimate in ignorance.

The oranges squeezed into your "morning dose of vitamin C" have their own story. Citrus orchards are notoriously heavy users of pesticides. Imagine the skin on the orange absorbing these chemicals. Then imagine those chemicals being squeezed out along with the juice, and you get the picture. If the orange comes from a tropical country like Brazil, and many do, you have no way of knowing exactly what chemicals were used. Just like the coffee, the pesticides may have been those restricted or banned for use in this country, but they come right back in—it's that circle of poison at your breakfast table. Like the coffee, if the oranges were imported from a tropical country, they may be responsible for more rain-forest destruction. Growing food for export on large plantations displaces local people, forcing them into the rain forest, where they practice slash-and-burn agriculture in a desperate attempt to feed their families. All the key ingredients in your healthy meal have been tampered with directly or indirectly. And we haven't gotten past breakfast! Day in and day out, what is your body going to do with all these chemicals? As discouraging as this sounds, you do have a choice.

Organic farming is nothing new; we built a nation on it.
—Guy Jones

PAUL BRENEMAN (1917–2001), CLEAR SPRING ORGANIC FARMS

Paul Breneman was my dream farmer, full of the spirit and integrity upon which this country was built. Humble, hardworking, practical, plainspoken, and smart as a whip, Paul farmed his entire life. His family is large, with four daughters and four sons, one of whom worked with him full-time, helping manage the farm. Several grandsons also helped as school schedules permitted. Even into his early 80s Paul never showed signs of slowing. His kids would often ask him when he planned to take it easy, but Paul would simply shrug and say, "I really like what I'm doing."

Clear Spring Organic Farms was comprised of about eighteen acres in the Lancaster Valley of southeastern Pennsylvania, eight at the Breneman's home site, the rest on land leased by Paul. The farm provided about thirty different fruits and vegetables including cantaloupes, watermelons, potatoes, sweet corn, zucchini, winter squash, cucumbers, tomatoes, cabbage, cauliflower, broccoli, beets, radishes, peppers, white and purple eggplant, kale, turnips, pumpkins and gourds, and some herbs. Paul also made and sold sauerkraut and horseradish.

Back in the 1940s, as Paul told it, he was introduced to DDT by a farm extension agent who extolled its virtues as a great farm aid. Paul decided to give it a try. He used it once. By the end of a day spent broadcasting it on his plants, he had a terrible taste in the back of his throat. It told him something wasn't right and he never used it again, relying instead on natural methods. There aren't many farmers who can honestly say, as Paul could, that they've farmed organically for nearly half a century. "I think it's the right way, the best way, the natural way. When I tell my neighbors, who still use chemicals, what my yield is, they say, 'I'd like to raise organic crops too.' But they don't believe you can farm without chemicals. People think if everybody raised organic food we'd starve, that there wouldn't be enough to eat. But I get better crops than my neighbors."

The day some friends and I spent with Paul at Clear Spring, we walked the fields digging potatoes and picking hot peppers and melons to take home. Paul was brimming with pride as he showed us his collection of vintage John Deere tractors. We had such a good time we didn't want to leave. On the way home we stopped at a picnic spot and cut into one of the melons Paul had given us. He was right. They were delicious, the best we had ever tasted.

Saddened by Paul's passing, I was pleased to learn that a friend of his daughter, Marsha Baron, submitted *The Angelica Home Kitchen* to two public libraries in his honor. Knowing of my fond regard for Paul and inclusion of his story in the book, it was her wish to memorialize our dear friend on the shelves of the Ephrata and Lititz, Pennsylvania, local public libraries.

Organic, Biodynamic, and Sustainable Agriculture

When food is ecologically grown in healthy soil, it maintains its essential nutrients. It does not need to be artificially fortified with vitamins or minerals that were destroyed by chemical inputs. The inherent vitality of the plant is simply maintained. But for something to be truly sustainable it must take more into account than soil inputs and outputs. It must include the whole community—air, water, soil, people, plants, forests, animals, insects, birds, fish. Life is the essence that holds it all together.

Organic is as old as agriculture. Using chemicals is new. The concept of organic foods would not exist were it not for industrial farm practices that feature chemicals and additives. Here is the definition of organic food as it is understood at Angelica Kitchen:

> Organic foods are grown and harvested with no synthetic chemicals, no herbicides, pesticides, fertilizers, or fungicides. They are never irradiated or genetically engineered. Organic farmers are committed to renewing and replenishing the soil and maintaining a beneficial impact on the ecosystem through the use of crop rotations, legumes, animal and green manures, cover crops, and biological pest controls, to maintain and build soil productivity and tilth, to supply plant nutrients, and to control weeds, insects, and other pests.

Biodynamic farming sees the farm as an organism, a living entity with parts that function together for the life of the whole, much as our bodies are organisms with a heart, lungs, a digestive system, and so forth, which all work together to keep us alive and healthy. Each part is essential to the health of the whole. The Biodynamic Farming and Gardening Association defines biodynamics as "a science of life-forces, a recognition of the basic principles at work in nature, and an approach to agriculture that takes these principles into account to bring about balance and healing." It is based on a series of lectures given by Austrian philosopher Rudolph Steiner in 1924, but since it is "an ongoing path of knowledge," based on keen observation of nature, it is not static. There is a definite spiritual foundation to biodynamics that acknowledges the inherent life and spirit present in plants and the soil. The more vital the life force in our food, the better it is for us, nutritionally and spiritually. Biodynamic farms make use of special preparations called medicines, recipes that combine plant and animal materials, prepared during specific times of the year and applied to compost or directly to the soil. Demeter is an association that certifies biodynamic farms worldwide. It is a "higher level" of certification, which has requirements above and beyond those of normal organic certification. Demeter certifies not only the complete absence of chemical use on a farm (fertilizers, insecticides, or herbicides) but also that the farm has become so self-contained in regards to its sources for fertility and seed stock that it has become an "individually unique ecosystem" or, in biodynamic terms, "a farm organism."

Sustainable or ecological agriculture describes practices that improve and regenerate the entire ecosystem. Organic farming generally fits this definition, but not always. In other words, sustainable agriculture includes organic farming, but not all organic farming methods promote sustainable agriculture. For example, there are large organic operations that practice monoculture farming. These farms often import essential elements like manure, which may

well come from industrial-style animal farms. It is difficult for huge farms, organic or not, to be sustainable. Reducing the scale of production increases the likelihood of sustainability.

Wendell Berry sums it up brilliantly; his definition is simple, elegant, and succinct: "A sustainable agriculture does not deplete soils or people." Terry Gips, cofounder of the International Alliance for Sustainable Agriculture, writes, "A sustainable agriculture is ecologically sound, economically viable, socially just, and humane." He goes on to say that these four values can be applied to farming and production as well as to marketing, processing, and consumption. The goal of his and other similar organizations is not to dictate methods but to establish standards. He states that sustainable agriculture is "neither a return to the past nor an idolatry of the new. Rather, it seems to take the best aspects of both traditional wisdom and the latest scientific advances. This results in integrated, nature-based agro-ecosystems designed to be self-reliant, resource-conserving, and productive both in the short and long terms."

Some Basic Definitions

Establishing standards and living and working by our principles are crucial to building the foundation for a healthy diet. Therefore, it's important to agree on some basic terms.

Health food or natural food: Whenever you see "health food" or "natural food," think twice. These terms are generic and nonspecific and can be misleading. In other words, they may mean nothing at all. It's very easy for food conglomerates such as General Mills or Quaker Oats to slap a label on a product that says "all natural." Even if the ingredient list reveals no chemicals, which is unlikely, you can be sure that synthetic chemicals have been used to grow these "natural" foods. Kraft or Skippy can easily dress up one of their peanut butter products with "natural" labeling and presentation. Educate yourself about the quality of the raw ingredients and the process used to make the product; don't be fooled by opportunistic marketing. The peanut butter may look like the genuine article right down to the way the oil separates from the solids in the jar, but it is a far cry from the real thing.

Hybrid produce/heirloom produce: The process of hybridization is not new. Nature does it when bees fertilize one variety of corn with pollen from another variety. Since the advent of agriculture, farmers have taken pollen from one organism and cross-fertilized it with another organism of the same biotype to increase yields or produce a strain that is drought resistant or more tasty or has better storage qualities. It was often a hit-and-miss process, and seed from successes was saved and planted the following year. The result was crops suited to a specific locale and a greater diversity of varieties.

Over the years the process became more exact, and with the advent of modern technology it became even more so. Today hybridization is the domain of large corporations that develop fruits and vegetables with specific traits suited to the requirements of industrial agriculture. For example, fruits and vegetables are bred to withstand being transported hundreds or thousands of miles from farm to market. They need to arrive appearing fresh. In addition, consumers expect produce to be blemish-free and of a certain size and shape or they won't buy it. The unfortunate result is that farmers the world over grow pretty much the same varieties of vegetables, resulting in a frightening lack of diversity in our food supply. We are losing the rich biological diversity that is natural to the Earth in favor of human-created varieties that can't even reproduce themselves. If you plant a seed from a hybrid plant, what you get will be a crapshoot.

Like the term *organic,* the concept of heirloom seeds has arisen to counter the homogenization of modern agricultural practices. Heirloom varieties are open-pollinated, unhybridized versions of fruits and vegetables that when sown retain their authentic size, shape, color, taste, and nutrients. And the taste of heirloom varieties is beyond compare. Taste a home or locally grown heirloom variety of tomato, then a mass-produced variety sold at the supermarket. Which do you prefer? Corn is another vegetable that has been changed dramatically. Heirloom corn is nothing like the supersweet varieties most of us are familiar with. Its kernels are often multicolored and chewy with a delicious, nutty taste and creamy texture. It tastes like—corn! Eating the original is a revelatory moment of rediscovery.

Whole: The term *whole* refers to food that is in its original form, for example whole grains that have their bran, germ, and endosperm intact. Products that are processed or refined ("less whole") lose some or most of their beneficial vitamins, minerals, and fiber. The more a food is processed, the more nutritionally depleted it becomes.

THE BURKHOLDER FAMILY FARM

Aaron Burkholder is a Mennonite farmer with one foot in the eighteenth century and the other in the twenty-first. His Swiss ancestors came to this country in 1754 and settled in the Groffdale Valley, Lancaster County, Pennsylvania. In 1946, Aaron's grandfather bought several farms in Berks County, including the one near Kutztown where Aaron farms today.

The Burkholder spread is a small, diversified family operation, on forty-four tillable acres, that has been farmed organically since the early 1990s. It supplies Angelica Kitchen with kale and collards as well as squash and pumpkins. In a typical season, the Burkholders grow about twelve acres of corn, twelve of hay, and several smaller plots of various vegetables and fruits. In addition, the family, which includes ten children, has geese, ducks, guinea hens, chickens, cows, pigs, and a horse. They also breed Lhasa apsos and Yorkshire terriers. It's a funky, dynamic place with lots going on.

Although the family lives a simple life and follows Mennonite traditions, they are also connected to the modern world in many ways. Aaron is a sophisticated thinker who readily integrates generations of farming experience with the latest information on different farming techniques obtained from an agronomist at the University of Michigan. When I visited the farm, for example, he was using a refractometer to measure the sugar content of his corn. He also has a penchant for tinkering, which is reflected in the many jury-rigged contraptions and inventions scattered about the yard, such as plows constructed from recycled bicycle parts.

Aaron feels strongly that consumers have a major role to play in making organic produce more readily available in the marketplace. "The buyers at auction are middlemen," he explains. "They don't care if something is organic or not." But they would respond to consumer demand. "Once the middleman had that pressure, he would be looking for organic produce."

Like many sensible farmers, Aaron laments the bigger-is-better mentality that pervades America these days, especially when it comes to produce. His cantaloupes, for example, are smaller than those that bring top dollar at produce auctions, but they're tastier and even have a longer shelf life. "I asked one of the buyers at the auction if he didn't have older people who would buy smaller cantaloupes. 'Sure,' he told me. 'But we just buy the big ones, cut them in half, and put plastic over them.'"

American consumers, Aaron feels, have been brainwashed with regard to fresh produce. They have come to believe that a perfect vegetable is always large and unblemished, like the plastic ones used in centerpieces—an ideal of perfection that gives industrial-style agriculture a real advantage over organics in the marketplace.

The Complexities of "Organic"

While organic agriculture has been around for millennia, the labeling of organic food is a new phenomenon—a consumer demand in response to what has been the recent domination of our food supply by "conventional," nonorganic foods. As consumers, we want to know what we are eating, and we have certain expectations of what organic means. However, uniform labeling implies that some one is in control, and in the United States, in 2002, it is the U.S. government that has taken control of the organic label. As we begin to see what that actually means, in terms of crops, livestock, and processed foods, it is important to understand who is defining organic, and what the implications of that definition are.

In 1990, the United States Congress passed The Federal Organic Foods Production Act (OFPA), as part of the 1990 Omnibus Farm Bill legislation of the U.S. Department of Agriculture (USDA). This legislation enabled the National Organic Program (NOP) and the National Organic Standards Board (NOSB) to: "1) establish national standards governing the marketing of certain agricultural products as organically produced products; 2) to assure consumers that organically produced products meet a consistent standard; and 3) to facilitate interstate commerce in fresh and processed food that is organically produced" [OFPA 1990 Sec. 6501 Purposes].

This law, regulating the production, manufacture, and handling of organic foods, required national standards be established in order to "protect consumers from fraud and misrepresentation." It took until 2002 for OFPA to be fully enacted, and it has inspired at least as many questions as it answers as to who and what makes up this standardized definition.

According to the NOSB definition (April 1995), "Organic agriculture is an ecological production management system that promotes and enhances biodiversity, biological cycles and soil biological activity.... Organic food handlers, processors and retailers adhere to standards that maintain the integrity of organic agricultural products. The primary goal of organic agriculture is to optimize the health and productivity of interdependent communities of soil life, plants, animals and people." While this definition is largely seen as acceptable for the National Organic Program by the organic community, worldwide definitions of organic nearly always include a social/cultural component. The International Federation of Organic Agricultural Movements (IFOAM)—a network of 750 groups from over 100 countries—adds in their definition, "Organic agriculture adheres to globally accepted principles, which are implemented within local social-economic, climatic and cultural settings."

The process of deciding what practices will and will not be allowed under the law has been a dozen-year-long tug-of-war between, on the one side, the family farmers, private certifiers, and their supporters who created the organic farming movement in this country, and on the other side, the corporate agribusinesses and government agencies who see organic as a trendy and profitable way of doing more business as usual.

In December 1997, the USDA released for public comment its first proposed National Organic Standards, a 600-plus-page document detailing specific standards for organic agriculture. The document was so dense and technical as to be unintelligible to the average person; and as the standards began to be understood, it became apparent that they would undermine the entire philosophy and integrity of the organic community. Many of the proposals made in the previous five years of work by the National Organic Standards Board, the advisory committee in charge of making recommendations, were ignored. According to the USDA proposal, biotechnology, sewage sludge, and irradiation were "organic." The huge public outcry against the USDA's proposal—an unprecedented response of over 275,000 letters written to the USDA by consumers as well as farmers—sent the document back to the drawing board. A revised proposal was released for public comment in March 2000, and no longer included biotechnology, sewage sludge, or irradiation, but had other, more subtle problems.

Actually, there have been standards for organic for decades: IFOAM wrote its guidelines over thirty years ago, and these have served as the template for standard writing all over the world. Over half the states and numerous private organizations have worked since the 1970s to establish and refine legal criteria for organic farming methods and third-party-verified certification programs with standards for growing, processing, storing, and transporting goods. Farmers are constantly trying out new and better methods of growing in harmony with nature while building healthy soil, and their successes have been codified in accepted standards, which are verified on the farm by independent inspectors. This system has worked well until the major economic/industrial growth of organic in recent years.

Organic is no longer relegated to the counterculture; it is big business (sales have been growing at 20 percent annually and are expected to reach $20 billion by 2005)* and global corporations are getting into the act. Your favorite Kellogg and General Mills breakfast cereals are available as organic, and Dole offers its many salad mixes as conventional or organic. Suddenly, differing regional standards have become a barrier to international trade as well as to manufacturing standardized processed products, and ever higher standards are too challenging on the industrial

* $20 b. by 2005: cooperative study by OFRF and National Marketing Institute

41

scale. A consumer- and industry-driven demand for national standards has meant that standards-setting is no longer a case of upwards innovation initiated by farmers on a local/regional level and implemented by certifiers; rather it is a race to the bottom to determine what minimum standards are needed to "grow the industry" while maintaining the illusion of consumer confidence.

In fact, the standards-setting arena has been governmental, and has been subject to the same pressures of the entire U.S. federal agriculture policy debate—encouraging the growth of the industrial model at the expense of the family farmers.

What the National Organic Program doesn't take into consideration with its national standards is that organic agriculture is more than a formula for growing food without toxic chemicals. Certainly there are huge, monoculture farms that produce food labeled organic because no toxic chemicals are used. However, the organic movement has been built over the years by committed farmers and their customers who support not only food grown without chemicals but the social and cultural aspects of local agriculture. Alan LaPage, an organic market grower in Vermont, stated in the winter 1997 *Food & Water Journal,* "My reason for being involved in farming is that I want to bring the culture back into agriculture. That means people should know the farmers they buy from and they should be part of the community. That means keeping it local."

The issue is not easy. The NOFA-NY 2001 Organic Food Guide notes that "federal government involvement in the regulation of organic agriculture, requiring certification to federal standards is both a simplifying and complicating factor in the organic community. For some farmers, many of whom have been leaders in setting voluntary standards, the new federal standards are not good enough. In addition, the federal rule has some problematic provisions that have no practical basis (e.g., specification of one way and one way only to make compost). Other farmers find the involvement of the federal government inappropriate and especially object to the provision that [according to the USDA] no one can use the term *organic* unless they are certified organic. Some farmers believe that the establishment of uniform organic standards will allow the industry to expand more easily. Small and large farmers may both favor expansion, yet there continues to be an inherent conflict between corporate 'organic' agriculture and family farms on which production is carefully tuned and appropriately limited by the farm's land base."

"The problems with the new national standards and the federal implementation of OFPA mean that constant vigilance is required if the integrity of organic standards is to be maintained. Additionally, the looming threat of corporate takeover of organic as it becomes more profitable is of grave concern. Corporate control of organic could mean the end of small-scale organic farming and a serious eroding of the standards themselves. . . . Our challenge is to develop practical strategies for promoting and preserving organic integrity." Notes Michael Sligh, in his chapter in *Fatal Harvest.*

We need to fight regulations that allow conglomerate producers, who compromise organic integrity, to put small, diversified family farmers out of business. Our nation was founded on the strength of the family farm. This aspect of our rural culture is endangered—we should list family farmers alongside the panda as an endangered species. We must mobilize and focus on what each of us can do to feed a true sustainable/organic system, just as it feeds us. You can do this by supporting small, diversified farmers and the stores and restaurants that sell or use their products—and be vocal about it. Let people know what you're doing and why by writing letters to local, state, and national representatives and to the editor of your local paper. You can join a campaign like the National Campaign for Sustainable Agriculture (see Resources). For an eloquent and concise view of this issue, read the foreword to Wendell Berry's *The Gift of Good Land.* Then, I am sure, you will want to read the entire book.

In response to the current organic trend, some in the industry are shying away from "the O word" in favor of other terms such as *ecological,* which is what I prefer. As Mark Dunau at Mountain Dell Farm says, "It's almost better that we don't have a catchword for it because it becomes bastardized and taken advantage of by industry." As the owner of Angelica Kitchen, I make it my business to know who the true organic farmer is. Knowing Guy Jones of

Blooming Hill Farm, for example, I trust him. I know his practices, and if he doesn't have federal certification, it doesn't stop me from supporting him. Stacy Burnstein, in the winter 1997 issue of *Food & Water Journal*, got it right when she wrote, "Substantive and progressive change in organic agriculture will not come from laws meant to standardize a type of agriculture that thrives off of unique local geographies, cultures, and markets."

In the end, we can share the basic principles of organic with whatever other word(s) work best to describe individual situations, but we come back to describe a system of agriculture that means, according to farmer Elizabeth Henderson, "working in harmony with nature to produce food and fiber in ways that are environmentally sound and socially just."

THOUGHTS FROM FOUR FARMERS ABOUT THE NEW NATIONAL ORGANIC PROGRAM

Elizabeth Henderson
Peacework Organic Farm
Newark, New York

"My partners and I gave a lot of thought to discontinuing certification because of our disagreements with the National Organic Program, particularly its mandatory nature, the extremely cumbersome and politicized process required for any revision of the standards, and its total failure to acknowledge the social agenda of organic agriculture. Our farm sells everything we produce within a fifty mile radius of the farm, and we know most of our customers personally so certification is not a necessity. Finally, though, we decided to continue with certification. Since the mid-80s, we have contributed countless hours to the development of the NOFA (Northeast Organic Farming Association of New York) certification programs. NOFA's process has been and continues to be democratic and decentralized, and we would like to help keep it that way. USDA bureaucrats and agribusiness cannot steal the word organic: they can exploit it, as they do any resources, human and natural, that come within their grasp. But the people who eat our food recognize the difference between food that is handcrafted and fresh, and industrially produced food shipped thousands of miles. They assume that certified organic means both ecologically produced and socially just, and they vote with their food dollars for a more sustainable future. We should rejoice at the increase in organic acres and continue to push certification to encompass the full meaning of organic agriculture."

Lou Johns and Robin Ostfeld
Blue Heron Farm
Lodi, New York

"To associate USDA with organic is a stretch of the imagination. Organic farming has always been a political statement, a challenge to the norms of the day, a lifestyle choice. For years, the USDA has promoted and force-fed farmers and consumers toxic chemical based farming. This system is based on strict capitalistic economics, and often used for world trade domination. The USDA is now the gatekeeper of an industry that grew up on small diverse farms all over this country and that is growing in annual sales by 20 percent a year. Who do you think wants in? Big conventional style

(continued)

(continued)

farm operators and corporate food giants. Who's now in a position to let them in? The USDA. This winter at Blue Heron Farm, we will be talking about our options concerning the USDA certification. And, as always, we will talk about organic farming."

Lisa Wujnovich and Mark Dunau
Mountain Dell Farm
Hancock, New York

"While it is entirely proper for the USDA to create and protect 'USDA Organic,' it is outrageous for it to declare illegal commercial use of the word "organic" outside of its auspices. According to the Final Rule, beginning in October 2002, only farmers certified by an accredited USDA certifier may use the word "organic" in commercial speech (with the exception of farmers whose gross sales are under $5,000). As there has never been a federal organic certification program, and up to 50 percent of organic farmers were not certified organic in 2001, this is radical implementation. Equally radical is the edict that organic farmers and organic certifiers have to comply with the USDA's definition of 'organic,' or give up the word, even though the USDA only defines 'organic as a production and marketing standard, not as a safety standard.'"

John and Sue Gorzynski
Gorzynski [used to be Organic] Ornery Farm
Cochecton Center, New York

"In 1976 I was seduced by Organic. She answered many questions about my future. Here was a way of life itself. In the years that have passed, my wife and three children have been tolerant of my mistress, Organic. Organic has helped us make a comfortable living and has given us incredible sustenance. Organic, it turns out, has been mistress to many; she has fulfilled the needs of many.

The USDA has decided that organic must be more to even more people. In order for this to happen, the USDA concluded that materials such as streptomycin, tetracycline, and ethylene, must be included within the newly defined organic for crop production. For animal production they will allow twenty-five synthetics, such as calcium hypochlorite, phosphoric acid, and synthetic inert ingredients. For processed food production synthetic materials, such as ethylene, and mono- and diglycerides are allowed.

Unfortunately this set of regulations redefining our Organic are also not acceptable to the rest of the world. So, in order for U.S. citizens or businesses to export, they would have to be double certified. This is a short list of a few of the problems associated with the USDA definition of organic.

I hate to part ways with an old friend and provider, but if this is what she must become, I must leave our old friend who existed long before these synthetics.

As a certified organic grower of twenty-plus years I will continue to grow as I always have."

Putting It All into Practice

Planning a Healthy, Whole Diet

Planning your everyday diet is a positive effort; any such effort constitutes progress. Being overly focused on calorie counts and grams of fat makes eating seem like a chore when it should be a pleasurable experience. I recommend educating yourself about sources of important nutrients and then simply eating a varied and complete diet of whole foods. Start by reading *Food and Healing*, by Annemarie Colbin, the founder of the Natural Gourmet Cookery School.

Healthy eating is as much about what you don't eat as what you do. Take stock of the refined foods in your diet, which include processed oils and refined flour and sugar, and moderate or eliminate them. Replace these highly processed foods with healthier alternatives such as cold-pressed oils, whole-grain flours, and unrefined sweeteners. Your body will thank you.

Once you've decided what to moderate, then you can think about what to include. The key is to follow a few basic guidelines and listen to your body. Annemarie Colbin proposes the following seven criteria for healthful food selection:

1) Choose whole foods whenever possible.

Whole foods are those that have most or all of their edible parts intact: whole-grain flours, fresh vegetables, fruits, nuts and seeds, and legumes (beans). Whole wheat, for example, has bran, germ, and starch, whereas refined white flour has had the bran and germ removed, leaving only starch. Whole foods contain all the nutrients nature intended in the correct proportions. Eating large amounts of refined foods, or fragmented foods high in single nutrients such as vitamin supplements, can create an imbalance that may ultimately result in nutritional deficiency. Eventually our bodies let us know something is out of whack. We may experience extreme cravings, go on eating binges, or get sick.

2) Choose foods that are fresh, natural, and organically grown or raised.

Our bodies were not meant to eat extensively processed, chemically treated, irradiated, or artificially flavored and colored food with preservatives added to ensure a long shelf life. In addition, imitation foods, such as margarine, artificial sweeteners, and fake fats, have been shown to have a detrimental effect on health. Many food additives (as well as commercial fertilizers and pesticides) are made from petrochemicals. Saccharin, for example, is derived from coal tar.

Keep in mind that canned and frozen foods may lose from 10 to 80 percent of their nutrients. I can't stress enough the value and importance of choosing fresh vegetables whenever possible— and I mean really fresh, not vegetables harvested a month ago 3,000 miles away, then sold in the fresh vegetable section of the supermarket.

3) Choose seasonal foods.

Eating according to the season puts us in harmony with our environment: For example, summer fruits, salad greens, and summer squashes are cooling and therefore appropriate to consume in warm weather. Winter squashes, root vegetables, and dried beans are warming and heavier, and appropriate for the cold of winter. As creatures of the Earth, our bodies thrive on a varied diet that shifts with the seasons. Seasonal foods are tastier and higher in nutrients as well. A fresh-picked pear is superior to a pear grown hundreds of miles away in a warmer climate and then shipped north. That pear may look fresh, but is it? Similarly, salad greens shipped from California or Mexico in February can't compare with greens picked fresh from the garden in June.

4) Choose local foods.

Locally grown foods are packed with more nutrition and taste better because they are fresher and picked riper. They may cost less, too. And local foods require less energy to transport from grower to consumer, making them kinder to the environment.

5) Choose foods that are in harmony with tradition.

Beware of foods labeled "new and improved." They may be genetically engineered, and even if they aren't they have not been truly tested in the laboratory of life. Pay special attention to what your ancestors ate a few hundred years back and incorporate these foods into your diet. For example, oats and barley in the British Isles; rye and wheat in northern Europe; wheat and barley in southern Europe; kasha and buckwheat in eastern Europe and Russia; wheat in various forms (couscous, bulghur) around the Mediterranean and the Near East; teff, sorghum, and millet in Africa; millet and rice all over Asia; and corn, quinoa, and amaranth in the Americas.

6) Balance your meals.

Eat a variety of foods to ensure the consumption of a proper variety of nutrients. For example, protein can be obtained from legumes, as well as from organically raised animal products (free-range poultry and meat), fresh fish, and organic eggs. Whole grains, starchy vegetables, and legumes provide complex carbohydrates and B vitamins. Fresh vegetables and fruits supply important vitamins, including A and C, and minerals such as calcium, iron, magnesium, and potassium. Organically raised produce will ensure better flavor and a higher nutrient content.

7) Your food should be delicious!

No matter how healthy your food may be, if it doesn't taste good, eating won't be much fun. Our taste buds give us information about the food we are about to swallow. Listen to them when they protest. The exception is if you're used to commercially processed foods. Highly refined foods often become bitter and unpleasant. To improve the taste, fats, sugars, and artificial flavorings are added. If your diet contains an inordinate amount of these foods, it may, unfortunately, take a while to recondition your taste buds with natural foods.

How foods are combined in your diet is as important as the individual foods you eat. In *Healing with Whole Foods,* Paul Pitchford gives an excellent explanation of how to combine foods for maximum benefit. "When a grain- and vegetable-based diet is followed without good results," he writes, "it is usually due to improper food combining." He suggests a few basic guidelines: Don't overindulge or eat lots of complex foods or a complex combination of foods, as it confuses and overtaxes the digestive system; eat high-protein foods first, because they are harder to digest; salty foods are best eaten at the beginning and the end of the meal, since they stimulate the production of digestive enzymes, which assimilate other foods. "Proteins, fats, and starches combine best with green and non-starchy vegetables." Sweet foods should be eaten alone or at the end of the meal.

Nutritional Background

What follows is a basic guide to the most important nutrients. If you're interested in learning more, consult the Suggested Reading.

Amino acids are the building blocks of protein that are necessary for building such essential bodily substances as the immune system's antibodies, hemoglobin in red blood cells, most hormones, and all enzymes. Of the twenty-two known amino acids, fourteen are synthesized by the body and are classified as "nonessential." The eight that aren't produced by the body are called "essential" and must be obtained each day from the food we eat. (Foods containing all eight are considered sources of "complete protein.") Unrefined vegetable foods contain all the amino acids, so if you eat a diet that consists of a variety of whole foods with ample protein, you should not need to take amino acid supplements.

Carbohydrates are converted into glucose, the body's primary fuel. There are two types: complex (polysaccharides) and simple (mono- and disaccharides), which can be refined or unrefined. Unrefined complex carbohydrates are found in all whole grains, legumes, vegetables, and tubers. Refined complex carbohydrates, such as white flour, white rice, and degermed cornmeal, have been stripped of their fiber and most nutrients. ("Fortified" foods have artificial vitamins and minerals added after the real ones have been removed.) Cane sugar, white as well as brown and raw, is a refined simple carbohydrate. Research has implicated sugar as a contributor to heart disease, diabetes, and hyperactivity.

Protein is contained in all foods to a greater or lesser extent and is essential for building muscle and tissue. In the Angelica Kitchen diet, protein is derived from a variety of vegetable foods: grains, beans, nuts, and soy products such as tempeh, tofu, and miso. Some grains are higher in protein than others. Wheat, for instance, has more protein than rice; teff and quinoa have remarkable amounts of protein. So does miso. Plant-based protein is widely available and relatively easy for the body to digest and metabolize.

ON EATING ANIMAL PRODUCTS

For many people, grains and beans (as well as other vegetarian protein sources) combine to adequately fulfill their total protein requirement. Others, however, find their metabolism just doesn't work well without some animal protein. For years I had hoped that I was getting enough protein from the grain-and-bean combination, yet I felt run-down and depleted. A blood test revealed that my protein level was alarmingly low. I learned that my body needs some animal protein to provide me with sufficient energy to live my life fully. Other people I know do just fine without it.

Different body types and different phases of life demand different amounts of protein. Children, for example, need more because their bodies are growing. Similarly, some vegetarian women find that they crave meat when they become pregnant. Some body and blood types are true vegetarians and others are not. A reliable way to discover your type is to do without animal protein for a time and see how you feel. Then gradually introduce small amounts into your diet—an organic egg or some fish every so often—and see what happens. Listen to your body, gauge your energy. Are you sluggish or upbeat? If your body doesn't want the animal protein, digesting it will tire you out; if it does, you will be energized.

If you're using animal products, take the time to learn where this food came from and how it was raised and slaughtered. Unless it's clearly labeled otherwise, meat obtained from supermarkets comes from animals raised under inhumane conditions and fed artificial diets full of antibiotics and hormones. The slaughterhouses and packing houses are often filthy, making microbial contamination likely. However, there are many smaller-scale farmers practicing responsible animal husbandry. If you eat meat, seek these people out. I highly recommend checking at your local farmers market or natural food store. The meat may well be more expensive, and that is a small price to pay for chemical-free meat from animals raised with respect and treated with care and integrity.

Personally, I'm not ethically opposed to eating animal protein. However, I believe in using it prudently and with respect. Acknowledging the source of any food before it's consumed, animal or not, is an important part of my philosophy. I often find myself imagining where the food came from while I am eating. I can see the fields under the hot sun of a midsummer afternoon, or during a pounding thunderstorm, or while it's calm and quiet in the starlight. By paying attention to the source of my food, I feel connected to it and appreciate it all the more.

Experience has shown me there is no one diet that is best for everyone. I would not presume to say what anyone should or should not eat. One thing I do know for sure, by experimenting, by education, by empirical evidence, my best way is constantly evolving.

Cholesterol is a crystalline fatty alcohol produced by the liver. It is essential for the production of estrogen, testosterone, brain and nerve cells, and bile, which digests fat. It is found in all animal products but not in any vegetable foods. Too much cholesterol contributes to hardening of the arteries and heart disease.

Fats and oils Just as proteins are composed of amino acids, fats are made up of fatty acids. They provide essential calories for the body to burn and convert into energy and are necessary for the assimilation of fat-soluble vitamins. There are two main types of fat molecules: saturated and unsaturated. The former is more stable and less likely to oxidize than the latter. Saturated fats are solid at room temperature, whereas unsaturated fats are liquid.

Unsaturated fats are divided into two categories: polyunsaturated and monounsaturated. Oils contain different percentages of each. Those higher in monounsaturated fats reduce cholesterol and are healthier. Olive oil is an excellent example. The less beneficial polyunsaturated oils include safflower, corn, soy, sunflower, and sesame. Hydrogenated vegetable oils have had extra hydrogen atoms forced into them, making them solid at room temperature. They are then made into products like margarine and shortening. Like saturated fats, they are believed to increase the risk of cancer and heart disease. (See Fat and Oil, *The New Whole Foods Encyclopedia*; Suggested Reading.)

Unrefined vegetable oils normally have a taste reminiscent of their source, which can sometimes be rather strong. This is why oils are often refined by heating, filtering, and bleaching to remove all traces of their original flavor and color. Refined polyunsaturated oils oxidize easily and become rancid—their shelf life is limited. They also have a lower smoke point, meaning that they smoke and burn at lower temperatures. Heating oils to the smoking point releases free radicals, which are unstable, reactive, roaming groups of atoms believed to encourage cancers, chronic diseases, and aging. Unrefined oils such as extra virgin olive oil and sesame oil are more stable, have a higher smoke point, and can handle heat better. Keep in mind that all fats and unrefined oils have distinct flavors and consistencies that can completely alter the character of an ingredient.

With Angelica-style cuisine, fats generally have to be added, since plant-based foods have no cholesterol and a minimum of saturated fats. Many vegetable foods do, however, contain some natural fat—avocados, seeds, nuts, whole grains, and beans and grain or bean products such as tofu and tempeh, for example. Still, the main sources of fat in the Angelica Kitchen diet are the oils used in preparing the dishes. These are selected carefully, stored in a cool, dry environment, and used sparingly.

While it's important not to eat too much fat, it isn't wise to eliminate it completely from your diet. Like any fine-tuned engine, our bodies need lubrication and fats do an excellent job. Fats and cholesterol aren't bad per se; pay attention rather to how much of which kinds you include in your diet. Buy organic, buy quality, and store it carefully away from heat and light. For more information, I highly recommend *Fats That Heal, Fats That Kill* by Udo Erasmus.

CANOLA OIL

Canola oil is an economical, all-purpose oil with little or no taste. It has the lowest percentage of saturated fat of all cooking oils (about 6 percent) and is more than 50 percent monounsaturated fat (only olive oil is higher), which acts to reduce the amount of cholesterol in the bloodstream. Canola oil used to be known as rapeseed oil, after the plant it comes from, but was renamed for marketing purposes by the government of Canada, the leading producer.

A controversy erupted around canola oil when it was found to cause damaging buildup of fatty deposits on the heart, kidneys, and other internal organs in tests on rats. However, later tests indicated that rats don't metabolize fats the same way humans do, and canola oil thus came back into favor. Companies with integrity produced it and Angelica Kitchen used a lot of it.

Then I got word that canola oil was no longer in use at the Natural Gourmet Cookery School and that Sally Fallon, author of *Nourishing Traditions,* considered canola oil suspect. Clearly this merited further research. I learned that even the natural companies bleach and deodorize the oil (using clay) and that the rapeseed plants used for the oil have been selectively bred for low acids. This was enough to give me pause.

At this time, the official Angelica Kitchen position on canola oil is that we have completely removed it from our inventory.

Fiber is the indigestible portion of plant foods, particularly the bran of whole grains and the outer skins of legumes, vegetables, and fruits. It facilitates the passage of waste through the intestines and reduces the risk of cancer and heart disease. Eating a diet high in fiber obtained from whole foods is an excellent example of using food intentionally as preventive medicine.

Vitamins are organic compounds that work in combination with enzymes to metabolize proteins, carbohydrates, and fats. (Enzymes are complex organic molecules that are catalysts for a number of chemical reactions necessary to life including metabolism, the body's process of breaking down and assimilating nutrients.) Fat-soluble vitamins (A, D, E, K) are stored in the body, but water-soluble ones (B-complex and C) must be consumed regularly. Vitamin A is obtained from animal foods such as butter and liver, but the body can convert it from beta carotene found in orange and deep green foods (carrots, yams, squashes, collards, kale, mustard greens). The body produces vitamin D under the influence of sunlight and it is also found in cold-water fish oils and in shiitake mushrooms. Vitamin E is commonly found in the germ of whole grains, and vitamin K is plentiful in leafy green vegetables. Whole grains, beans, and meat contain B-complex, and vitamin C is abundant all throughout the vegetable kingdom, especially in leafy greens and citrus fruits.

VITAMIN B$_{12}$ IN VEGAN DIETS

"This vitamin is made by bacteria and certain microscopic blue-green algae (not sea vegetables, which are plants). Well stored, bacterially fermented foods contain B$_{12}$, but the amounts in miso and tempeh vary and these are not always reliable sources. Any source of animal protein is a source of B$_{12}$—fish, eggs, milk, etc. Serious deficiencies of B$_{12}$ are rare, even among vegans, but strict vegans need to ensure that they obtain adequate amounts of this vitamin to avoid anemia (reversible) and neurological problems (irreversible). Aging affects absorption of B$_{12}$ as well, so make extra sure to keep up your levels after age fifty-five."

—Marion Nestle, Ph.D., M.P.H., friend, professor, and chair of the
Department of Nutrition and Food Studies at New York University

Minerals are inorganic compounds that are important building blocks for the bones, tissues, and glandular systems. Trace elements such as copper, zinc, and fluorine are believed to be important as well. The minerals calcium, magnesium, sodium, iron, and iodine are found in small amounts in vegetables, beans, and nuts. Sea vegetables are especially rich in minerals and are a valuable addition to your diet.

Sea Vegetables

Sea vegetables are among the most nutritious foods you can eat. Relatively new to our diet in this country, they have been a part of the human diet since ancient times, particularly in places like Japan and Ireland, where people have always looked to the sea for sustenance. Sea vegetables provide all the minerals essential for human health, including calcium, iodine, phosphorus, sodium, and iron. In addition, they are one of the few sources of complete vegetable protein and are a better than average source of vitamins.

Sea vegetables have important medicinal qualities as well. They help reduce blood cholesterol, prevent goiter (enlargement of the thyroid gland), and have antibiotic properties found to be effective against penicillin-resistant bacteria. According to Asian traditions, sea vegetables counteract obesity and strengthen bones, teeth, nerves, and digestion. They also contribute to healthy skin and hair and apparently can have anti-aging properties.

Studies at the Gastrointestinal Research Laboratory of McGill University indicate that the alginic acid found in sea vegetables binds with certain metallic ions and toxic metals and carries them out of the body. Alginic acid is impervious to digestion and renders heavy metals insoluble, meaning they can't be absorbed into body tissues. Alginates can even remove radioactive materials, such as strontium 90, that have already been absorbed into the tissues.

On the Rocks with Maine Coast Sea Vegetables

Two of our most basic goals at Angelica Kitchen are to spread the word about noteworthy nutriments, encouraging people to include more of them in their everyday diets, and to strengthen that all-important connection to Mother Nature. Both of these aspirations are resoundingly

echoed in the work of Maine Coast Sea Vegetables. There aren't many foods in the United States less well-known than seaweed, and work doesn't get much more hands-on than harvesting these nutritious plants from exposed rocks in pounding surf.

Maine Coast Sea Vegetables, our sea veggie connection, is the industry pioneer and still its undisputed leader. The company story begins in 1971 when Shep Erhart and his wife, Linnette, had a picnic at Schoodic Point on the rocky shores of Frenchman's Bay. They spotted some seaweed that looked like alaria, took it home, dried it, and put it in their miso soup. It turned out to be delicious.

After that, Shep started harvesting seaweed regularly, selling it first to friends and acquaintances, then to an ever-widening circle of customers. He built a business through good old-fashioned diligence, relying on word of mouth to do his marketing. Based in the town of Franklin, the company now accounts for roughly 50,000 (dry) pounds of sea vegetables per year and sells to a list of around thirty distributors and fifty manufacturers. (They even sell to Stouffers!) MCSV employs about fifteen people, including Shep and his general manager, Carl Karush, and relies on some thirty-five independent harvesters. The edible seaweeds they sell are found clinging to rocks between the high- and low-water marks throughout the thousands of miles of estuaries in the region.

I remember first meeting Shep and Carl at a whole foods trade show in the late 1980s. It was one of those instantaneous connections—personally and professionally. Both are really salt of the earth—or should I say the sea? I think I sensed right away they would become key suppliers. Clearly, we could trust them to deliver the goods—clean, reliable, and brimming with all their natural vitamins and minerals. To this day, we feel connected and that's the way we want it. We've grown our businesses together and relied on each other's careful handling of nature's bounty. I feel if more of us could connect with the real gathering of food this way, the natural respect that is Earth's due would transform any theoretical environmental movement into real action.

When we went Down East to take part in a harvest, we could really feel the connection. Shep had us put on our waders and we went out in his boat with the tide. He dropped anchor; I took up my position on a rock and, using an old lawn tool, started to pull in kelp fronds. I promptly slipped off, filling my waders with water. It felt like some sort of christening. Nothing can take the place of rolling up your sleeves and experiencing, firsthand, this type of food gathering.

In the early 1990s, Shep was instrumental in creating some commonsense organic standards for sea vegetables, namely that they can't be harvested in polluted waters and that they must be handled, transported, dried, stored, and packed in clean, additive- and pollutant-free environments. More recently, he began working with the state of Maine to survey and define the growing areas and to create harvest limits. In Maine, anybody with a little seaweed savvy and fifteen dollars to spend on a license is permitted to join the harvest. Private property extends down to the high-water mark; access to the shoreline is open to anyone approaching from the sea. Thus far, commercial harvesters have respected each other's territories, and demand has not exceeded Nature's supply. Clearly, though, the time will come for limits—indiscriminate harvesting won't allow the beds to restore themselves—and Shep and other responsible industry leaders want to be ready for that eventuality.

There are actually thousands of kinds of seaweeds, some inedible, even poisonous, some totally inaccessible. To emphasize their nutritional value, Shep & Co. have always called the edible ones "sea vegetables." Certain types, such as alaria, grow amply in the most turbulent waters on windswept headlands. This propensity allows the plants to absorb a wide variety of nutrients from the passing sea water. It also renders the harvest a tricky and perilous occupation. Kelp grows in calm bay settings as well as in rougher waters; dulse grows closer to the low-tide mark far out on the rocks. Most of the sea vegetables are dried in the sun—a good six- to eight-hour day in the sunshine will do the trick—although some are hung up indoors. Once the moisture content drops to between 10 and 15 percent, the seaweed can be stored for about two years. At any given moment, the MCSV warehouse contains up to 10,000 pounds each of several different types of seaweeds.

MCSV offers ground sea vegetables in shakers, plain or blended with sesame, cayenne, ginger, garlic, and other spices; sea chips, which

(continued)

(continued)

are organic corn chips flavored with dulse, kelp, garlic, and onion; kelp crunch, which is kelp blended with barley malt, sesame seeds, maple syrup, and vanilla; and sea pickles, which is kelp pickled in a brine of shoyu, rice vinegar, and garlic cloves. They also sell ground sea vegetables in bulk to restaurants and manufacturers.

At Angelica Kitchen, those wonderfully salty, garlicky kelp pickles go directly onto our pickle plate. Sea vegetables are the key ingredient in many other Angelica dishes, including Hijiki-Cucumber Salsa, Marinated Sea Vegetable Topping for sandwiches and salads, Dragon Bowls, and even desserts such as Kanten and Tofu Whip, which make use of agar. We use kombu, arame, and wakame in beans, bouillon, dashi, miso soup, and in various salads, for example the Sea Caesar Salad, which calls for dulse and nori, and specials.

Next time you take a bite of the kelp pickles (also available in small jars in natural food stores), close your eyes; imagine fifteen-foot fronds of kelp being swept with the tidal waters, the wildness, and the harmony you are ingesting. Hallelujah! Glory be.

A Word about Balance

Until recently, the United States Department of Agriculture's food pyramid was considered to be a graphic representation of a balanced diet. It was heavy on the meat due to lobbying efforts of the meat industry, particularly pork producers. Then Oldways Preservation came out with a pyramid closer to the Mediterranean Diet recommended for years by health care practitioners. This diet includes animal products but recommends they be eaten more as garnishes or side dishes than as the main component of a meal.

Whether you eat a vegan or vegetarian diet or include some animal protein, the important thing to keep in mind when planning your meals is balance. Eat a wide variety of natural, whole foods. Cut back on or eliminate refined foods and pay attention to where your food comes from and how it is processed and prepared. Once you start doing these things on a regular basis, eating a healthy diet becomes second nature. Your taste buds will adjust to the new foods and come to prefer them over their refined, "fortified" counterparts. And if you cook some of the dishes in this book, I guarantee you'll eat your veggies (both land and sea) and love them!

Fats, oils and sweets

Milk, yogurt and cheese

Meat, poultry, fish, dry beans, eggs and nuts

American Diet

Vegetables

Fruits

Bread, cereal, rice and pasta

The U.S. Department of Agriculture's Food Guide Pyramid

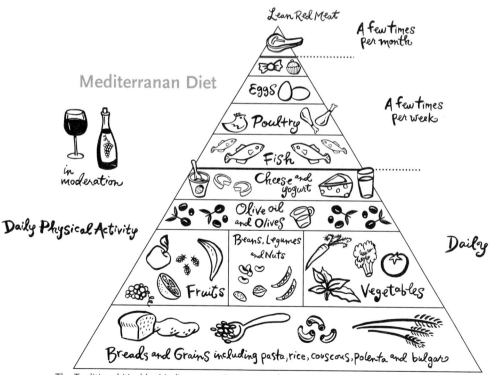

Lean Red Meat

A few times per month

Mediterranan Diet

Eggs

Poultry

A few times per week

Fish

in moderation

Cheese and yogurt

Olive oil and Olives

Daily Physical Activity

Beans, Legumes and Nuts

Daily

Fruits

Vegetables

Breads and Grains including pasta, rice, couscous, polenta and bulgar

The Traditional Healthy Mediterranean Diet Pyramid © 2000 Oldways Preservation & Exchange Trust

Implements: Equipping Your Home Kitchen

My kitchen at home has many family implements handed down from previous generations—a rolling pin, a cheese board, a hand mixer, the egg beater that belonged to my grandmother. I always reach for the hot chocolate cups I remember from my childhood or the pot holder my nephew Austin made for me. When I pick up one of these objects, it has meaning to me. I love knowing that my grandmothers used them, that they were familiar, comforting objects to my mom and dad as they were growing up. Part of what I consider the principle of connectedness is continuity and respect for tradition. The newest store-bought device may be attractive and shiny, but nothing can replace my grandmother's egg beater. Every time I use it she's right there in the kitchen with me.

Some basic guidelines regarding kitchenware: Buy good quality. Use glass whenever possible instead of plastic. Avoid aluminum (see the following box). Don't overstock your kitchen. It's a good idea to think in terms of versatility and practicality. Better to have a few items that are used regularly than a plethora of gadgets that languish on the shelf. A cast-iron pan or pot is an excellent example of a useful, versatile, durable implement. You can sauté in it, dry-cook herbs, or bake in it. And it will literally last a lifetime with proper care. Stocking your kitchen with basic, quality cookware makes cooking a pleasure.

Just as important as what you use is where you place things. It's no fun to go searching for something when your hands are covered with flour. Keep often-used utensils like stirring spoons, knives, and pot holders at arm's length. Once you develop a sense of ease in the kitchen, you'll be on your way to becoming a skilled, inventive, and spontaneous chef.

Aside from the usual complement of mixing bowls, measuring cups, wooden spoons, saucepans, sauté pans, and casseroles, I recommend the following implements for producing Angelica Kitchen cuisine at home:

> ❖ *Baking pans, including an ovenproof glass lasagna dish, cookie sheets, a couple of 9-inch springform pans, a muffin tin, and a 9^1/$_2$-inch fluted quiche pan with removable bottom.*
>
> ❖ *3- or 4-quart pressure cooker.*

- Steaming equipment: an 8- to 10-quart stockpot with steam basket and lid, or a bamboo steamer to fit an 8- to 10-inch sauté pan.
- A fine strainer (7 inches), box grater (9 inches), 10-inch tongs, 12-inch wire whisk.
- Electric food processor or old-fashioned food mill, electric blender, or handheld mixer.
- A mandoline (a versatile slicing tool), lemon peeler and/or zester, salad spinner.
- Spice grinder. (Note: keep a small electric coffee grinder to use for spices only. To clean one that's been used for coffee, use a small, natural-bristle paint brush or a round pastry brush.) To grind your spices the old-fashioned way, use a mortar and pestle.
- A suribachi. This is a Japanese mixing bowl with a serrated interior good for grinding seeds—but don't pound too hard or it could break.

ALUMINUM AND OTHER TOXIC METALS

Living in an industrial society as we do, it's hard to avoid absorbing toxic metals like lead, arsenic, cadmium, mercury, and especially aluminum. These metals are in the air we breathe, the water we drink, and the food we eat. Many municipal water supplies are filtered with aluminum sulfate, and traces remain in the drinking water. Other possible sources of aluminum include cookware, baking powder, antacid tablets, and antiperspirants. To limit exposure when cooking, buy aluminum-free baking powder and avoid using aluminum cookware; if the latter is impossible, make sure to use wooden utensils with it to avoid scraping minuscule bits into the food.

Note: Angelica Kitchen uses aluminum containers for take-out orders because of their recyclability. However, we always recommend that customers transfer the food to glass or ceramic containers. Don't reheat food in them and don't use them for food storage.

Shopping Tips: Sourcing

It's important to establish a foundation of ingredients and sources. If you live in a community where you don't have easy access to good organically grown food, you're going to have to put some planning and effort into sourcing the ingredients. Fifteen years ago, finding healthy fresh ingredients seemed nearly impossible; now, we have some choices.

By understanding that the market—what's available—is driven by consumer demand (or apathy), we can choose to ask for the best, to demand integrity. The market will respond. Otherwise, shopkeepers, grocers, and their suppliers will understandably offer the low-end ingredients that stay on the shelf longer.

Successful food sourcing is about sensitizing yourself to what's good and what's not. In the modern era of shrink-wrapped packaging and convenience shopping, we've lost some of that discernment. Like anything else connected with food and cooking, selecting your produce is a sensual experience—you've got to use your senses of sight, smell, and touch to assess what you're buying.

> People won't buy a small tomato. If American consumers wouldn't be so piggy, so stingy, so selfish or whatever, the chemical industry wouldn't have nearly the advantage it does to push chemicals. I've watched people at a store. They pick up a tomato, squeeze it, turn it around. They look for a perfect tomato. They won't eat the others. That gives the chemical people a big advantage. They can kill every insect, keep all the fungus controls on so the vegetables appear perfect. They pump them with water and nitrates to make them big. The look is nice and the consumer falls in love with it but doesn't really know what he's demanding. Consumers complain about the chemicals but they're actually asking for them. I don't mind if there's a scar on a tomato. It doesn't hurt you. Same with an ear of corn. If there's a little worm at the edge you just take that off and the rest of the ear is good.
> —Aaron Burkholder, Mennonite organic farmer

Community-Supported Agriculture

Community-Supported Agriculture (CSA) is a movement that's about eighteen years old. It grew out of the concept of a neighborhood garden, a small plot of land that could feed a lot of people.

Robin Van Eyn and friends launched the concept in 1986 at Indian Line Farm in western Massachusetts. When you join a local branch of CSA, you pay an annual membership fee in exchange for an allotment of produce that you go and pick or collect in season. The farmer is paid out of the membership fees.

There are hundreds of CSAs in the United States now. Joining one is an excellent way to reestablish our diminished connection with the land. Ask most kids in this country today where a potato comes from and they'll probably answer "McDonalds" or "the supermarket." If you join a CSA, your kids will learn the right answer: "It grows underground on a farm." Urban CSA members don't actually go to the farm; the food is delivered. But what could be better than fresh organically grown produce delivered right to your door once a week for a minimal annual fee? It just makes too much sense not to do it.

With the demise of the small diversified family farm, groups like CSAs can fill in the gap in educating future generations. Farming lore and technique that were passed from generation to generation may be disappearing, but these organizations are in the process of reviving them by providing apprenticeships for young people who are interested in farming as a vocation. That does my heart good.

To find a CSA in your area, and obtain further information, contact:

Alternative Farming Systems Information Center
10301 Baltimore Avenue, Room 132
Beltsville, Maryland 20705-2351
Telephone: 301-504-6559
Facsimile: 301-504-6409
http://www.nal.usda.gov/afsic/
Email: afsic@nal.usda.gov

For a truly sound and practical view of CSA, Elizabeth Henderson has written *Sharing the Harvest: A Guide to Community-Supported Agriculture,* published by Chelsea Green Publishing Company, 1999. This book puts into perspective many of the issues regarding the future of our food supply. A wonderful book!

Cooking Principles

Because we are subject to the fluctuations of what is fresh and available at any given time, we at Angelica Kitchen change a large percentage of our menu daily; we have, of necessity, become flexible and resourceful. We practice what we call "intuitive cooking," improvising recipes from a range of seasonal ingredients and injecting our own energy, inspiration, and enthusiasm. The goal of

this book is to provide readers with the foundation they need for creating their own wonderful vegan dishes at home—through recipes as well as helpful hints and suggestions.

Among the cooking principles for your home kitchen, probably the first one is to be flexible, not formulaic. It's crucial to taste and adjust, stay connected, be aware of the process. The key in approaching any recipe is to understand that it's merely a set of guidelines (except with baking, which is more prescriptive). Consider it a springboard for experimentation. The

people who don't do well in the kitchen are the ones who think they can follow a recipe exactly, carry out the steps in an orderly, mechanical fashion, and be guaranteed a successful dish. It ain't necessarily so. Cooking is a process. You've got to smell, taste, observe, and adjust. You must be willing to experiment, to learn from successes and failures. Likewise, don't hesitate to improvise or substitute. Once you've tried a recipe in a standard way, try following a few creative impulses.

Another important principle is to be economical, both in terms of time and space. Consolidate your steps. For example, when you're roasting mushrooms and vegetables for sandwiches, roast them all on the same tray. Likewise, make sure you overlap steps: While your vegetables are roasting, you can carry out other steps of a multistep recipe and/or start assembling an accompanying dish. Put the oven and two or three burners on the stove to work for you, then start making the salad. Whether shopping for, preparing, or cooking ingredients, always look for efficiencies. Any step that increases your cooking efficiency saves the world energy—yours and everyone else's.

Be sure to plan ahead so there are no unpleasant surprises. Read a recipe carefully, decide exactly how you'll carry it out, then rehearse the procedure in your mind step-by-step before you start prepping and cooking. Run through a mental checklist of equipment and ingredients in advance, and know where everything is and when you'll use it. Scrambling for a missing ingredient or a misplaced utensil while you're in the middle of carrying out a recipe takes away from the enjoyment. A little preventive energy helps because you know there will be some kind of interruption no matter what—the phone, the doorbell, the kids . . .

Be resourceful. Think of all the things you can do with leftover mashed potatoes, for example: Form them into patties, sauté them, then serve as an appetizer with dipping sauce.

Presentation

A lot of effort is put into presentation at Angelica Kitchen. That final product, the meal placed in front of the diner, represents everybody who's been involved in producing the food, from the grower to the buyer to the chef. We want it to look great. By arranging it beautifully, to showcase nature's wonderful palate of colors, we honor the food. Eating should be a healthy experience; it should also be an aesthetically pleasing one. Being "wowed" by the plate of food enhances the whole experience.

Ingredients

Angelica Kitchen stocks over 350 ingredients at a given time and guarantees that a minimum of 95 percent of them are organically grown. Much of Angelica cuisine is based on ingredients that may not be familiar to many of you, since they are of multi ethnic origins. While you can cook successfully from this book with purchases from just about any store that sells fresh produce and other quality ingredients, we feel it's absolutely crucial that you find the best organic products (preferably local).

That way, you can achieve the potential of these recipes and give your body the best possible nutrition. This list is meant as a handy reference to ingredients in our cuisine with some background information on provenance, history, nutrition, and criteria for selection.

For a more comprehensive guide to these, and many more healthy ingredients, see *The New Whole Foods Encyclopedia,* listed in Suggested Reading.

> **aduki beans** (alternate spellings **adzuki** or **azuki**): A small, dark red traditional Japanese bean with a mealy texture, it has a light nutty flavor, which enhances both savory and sweet dishes. The aduki is easier to assimilate than other legumes and does not need pre-soaking.
>
> **agar:** A dried form of a marine algae from the red seaweed family, it is tasteless and is used as a settling or gelling agent (like gelatin). It comes in bars, flakes, or powder. The bar form of agar is called *kanten,* which is also the name of the gelled fruit juice dessert at Angelica Kitchen. The most convenient form is flaked, which is widely available at health food stores and natural foods markets. Recommended brands: Mitoku and Eden.
>
> **alaria:** Delicate to taste, and dangerous to harvest, these sea plants love rocky, windswept peninsulas where they curl and crash with every breaking wave. This algae makes calcium-rich soup and goes well in pots of grains or stews.
>
> **amaranth:** A tiny golden seed with the crunch and appearance of blond caviar, amaranth has the aroma of fresh corn and was a major crop of the Aztecs. This spunky-tasting grain is higher in protein (16 percent) than cereal grains and is a good source of calories and fiber.
>
> **anasazi beans:** A mottled maroon and white bean, similar to the pinto bean in size and shape, it is sweet with a slightly mealy texture and is excellent in Mexican dishes. The anasazi is a traditional Native American food, and its name means "ancient one" in Navajo.
>
> **apple cider:** Cider is made by pressing fresh apples in a cider press. Apple juice differs from cider in that it is made from cooked fruit juice, meaning it has been pasteurized, and is sweeter but less flavorful than cider. Always look for fresh, locally pressed brands without preservatives.

arame: A thin, threadlike dark brown sea vegetable with flat strands and a mild, sweet taste, arame is rich in iron, calcium, and iodine. It is an excellent source of protein and contains starch, sugar, unsaturated fat, and vitamins A and B complex. See pages 95–96, 124.

arrowroot: Arrowroot is a thickening agent that comes from the tropical arrowroot plant. Its root is ground, sun-dried, then powdered. Arrowroot is dissolved in cold water prior to use. It is easily digestible and superior to highly refined cornstarch.

baking powder (aluminum-free): A combination of baking soda and an acid, such as cream of tartar, along with another powder that absorbs liquid, such as cornstarch, baking powder is used as a leavening agent to make baked goods rise. Make sure you purchase aluminum-free baking powder. At Angelica Kitchen, we use the Rumford brand.

balsamic vinegar: If you want to splurge, buy the authentic, aged balsamic vinegar from Modena, Italy; otherwise, there are many good reasonably priced varieties; we like the Gaeta brand. Dark red with a pungent sweetness, aged for years in wooden barrels, this is an exquisite vinegar.

barley, hulled: A large, plump, dark grain, barley has a very chewy texture. Possibly the oldest cultivated cereal, it was used as money by the Sumerians around 4000 B.C. Barley has two inedible hulls and a bran layer covering the central white pearl. Hulled barley is a staple at Angelica Kitchen. It is readily available at natural food stores.

barley malt: A thick, dark brown sweetener made from sprouted, roasted barley, it tastes like a cross between *molasses* and honey; similar to *rice syrup* but darker, richer-flavored, and not as sweet. Available at specialty shops and natural food stores.

basmati rice: Long-grain rice with a nutty aroma and a chewy, light, fluffy texture, basmati rice is available in brown or white. Authentic basmati only comes from its original source, the area of India in the shadow of the Himalayas. Its name translates as "queen of fragrance."

brown rice vinegar: This vinegar is mild and delicate in flavor with relatively low acidity—about 4–5 percent as opposed to 6–7 percent for other vinegars such as apple cider and wine vinegar.

buckwheat: Often grouped with cereal grains because of its similar culinary use and nutritional value, this fruit is actually a relative of rhubarb. Buckwheat originated in Siberia and Manchuria and is still a staple of those regions. Heart-shaped and deep amber in color, buckwheat has a complex, assertive flavor and aroma and is considered a good blood-building food.

bulgur: Wheat berries with hull and bran removed are steamed, dried, and crushed to create light brown, gritlike pieces. Medium and coarse bulgur are light and fluffy, resembling couscous.

burdock: A long, dark brown root with grayish white fibrous flesh, burdock has the rich, heady aroma of freshly dug earth. Slightly sweet, burdock root is delicious in soups, stews, and sea vegetable dishes, or sautéed with carrots. Known as *gobo* in Japan, it is a hearty plant that grows wild throughout many parts of the world, including the United States. It has more protein, calcium, and phosphorus than carrots and is an excellent source of potassium. It is considered a blood purifier. Two tips about purchasing burdock: It needs to be firm, not limp; it shouldn't be too fat. Older burdock that's more than an inch in diameter tends to be spongy and tough. Available at Oriental markets, health food stores, and farmers markets.

chickpea flour: High-protein flour made from ground uncooked chickpeas, it lends a sweet, rich chickpea flavor to baked goods.

chickpeas (a.k.a. **garbanzos**): These are round, mini-hazelnut shaped, creamy beige legumes with a nutty flavor. One of the most nutritious legumes, chickpeas have a subtly sweet taste and firm, creamy texture. They are historically popular in Middle Eastern and Indian dishes.

chiles or **chile peppers** (a.k.a. **chili peppers**): These peppers, often very hot and spicy, comprise the capsicum family of pod vegetables that are natives of the Americas. They are classified as nightshades. Among the various types of chile peppers are jalapeño (chipotle is the smoked version), ancho, habanero (Scotch Bonnet), Thai, serrano, and hot cherry.

cider vinegar: Cider vinegar is made from hard cider, transformed by a complex of bacteria known as "mother of vinegar," which converts alcohol into acetic acid. Choose organic brands such as Spectrum, Eden, and Omega Nutrition.

cilantro (a.k.a. **Chinese parsley** and **coriander**): Similar to parsley but with a distinctive spicy flavor, the green leaves are used in many Asian dishes. The dried seeds are also ground and used as a key ingredient in curry powder.

corn grits: Field (dent) corn is ground into a much coarser grind than for meal. "Grits" refers to any broken cereal grain.

cornmeal: Dried field (dent) corn is ground into a coarse flour that is used for bread or polenta.

daikon: A long, cylindrical white Japanese radish, daikon can grow up to fourteen inches in length. Buy it with the tops on; the leaves are great for adding to soups or for steaming. Daikon should be firm with shiny skin and a clear white color. More pungent than the small red radish, this crisp, juicy root has remarkable medicinal qualities. See pages 118, 165, 175.

dulse: This is a rich, reddish purple sea vegetable with a soft, chewy texture, perfect for soups and salads or dry as a snack. It's salty but not particularly fishy tasting and is often an immediate favorite of those first tasting seaweed. Unique to the North Atlantic and Pacific Northwest, dulse is the best source of iron of any food.

flours: All cereal grains can be ground into flour or meal. The type of mill that grinds the grain has a surprising effect on a flour's performance, flavor, and nutrition. The best flour comes from stone-ground mills, where layers are flaked off the grains. This milling process does not overheat the flour, which allows it to retain its nutrients. The types of flour we use at Angelica Kitchen include whole wheat bread flour, whole wheat pastry flour, unbleached white flour, cornmeal, spelt flour, and brown rice flour. As needed, we grind certain grains or legumes to make our own specialty flours. The white flour we use is not as refined as commercial white flour; it still has its germ but not its bran. Flours should be bought as fresh as possible; patronize a store with high turnover that refrigerates bulk flour.

French (DuPuy) lentils: A tiny, slightly sweet variety of lentil, these petite gray beans cook very quickly, hold their shape well, and are excellent in a salad, in soups, or as a side dish.

ginger: This knobby tuber, with its sharp, fresh, palate-cleansing bite, is a favorite seasoning in Asian cuisines and one that we use frequently at Angelica Kitchen. Ginger is generally used sliced or diced in cooking but can also be pickled, candied, juiced, dried, and ground. It should be firm, plump, and shiny without signs of shriveling. Refrigerate fresh ginger unwrapped. Use promptly.

hijiki (alternate spelling, **hiziki**): A very dark brown sea vegetable with stringlike strands, it has a nutty aroma. Hijiki is the most mineral rich of all foods and is particularly high in calcium and iron. It has a strong flavor of the sea—stronger than *arame*—and the Japanese consider it "esteemed beauty food."

hominy: Corn treated with an alkaline substance, such as wood ash or limestone, to remove the hull and germ is called hominy. This ancient practice makes the corn more nutritious because it makes more niacin available. Hominy is widely used in stews and for fritters. It comes dried and is white or yellow. Broken or coarsely ground dried hominy is known as *samp*. Hominy grits, a finer grind, are a traditional side dish in the southern United States.

kale: A strong-tasting, green, curly-leafed member of the cabbage family, kale is a superior source of calcium, iron, and vitamin A. It's simple to grow your own!

kamut: An ancient grain, kamut is plump, golden, chewy, and high in protein and minerals. It is about three times the size of wheat berries and is unhybridized, which makes it easier to digest, particularly for people who are allergic to wheat.

kanten: This is a soothing, light, satisfying all-natural gelled fruit dessert made with agar as the gelling agent. See pages 223–24.

kelp: The world's largest vegetable, kelp is capable of growing up to 180 feet long. *Kombu, wakame,* and *arame* are all types of kelp, which grows in cold water. It contains a compound called glutamic acid, a natural flavor enhancer that, when refined, becomes monosodium glutamate (MSG). Kelp cooks quickly, dissolving readily in beans, soups, and stews. An outstanding nutritional supplement in powder form, it also contains calcium, iodine, starch, sugar, and various vitamins including A, B_6, C, D, and K.

koji: Koji is the catalyst that ferments *miso, shoyu,* and *sake.* To make it, cooked grain (or beans) is inoculated with spores of the mold *Aspergillus oryzae,* held at specific temperatures and humidity for three days, and then dried.

kombu: A sea vegetable that grows in wide green strips, kombu is very high in sugar, potassium, iodine, calcium, and vitamins A and C and contains other minerals as well. It improves the digestibility of beans and grains when added while they are cooking. Glutamic acid, a main ingredient of monosodium glutamate (MSG), was originally synthesized from kombu. Glutamic acid has a stimulating effect on the taste buds and therefore enhances the flavors of many foods; it is also a tenderizer. Synthetically produced MSG is unhealthy, unlike naturally occurring glutamic acid found in kombu. See also *kelp* and page 138.

kosher salt: This is a salt that is mined from the Earth. While not a great source of minerals, it contains no additives and has a very pure taste. A good all-purpose salt that doesn't clump, it is especially suited for sprinkling on top of vegetables or salads or for seasoning the water for blanching vegetables or cooking pasta. Kosher salt is also excellent for pickling vegetables or making Ruby Kraut (page 122). See also *sea salt*.

kuzu (alternate spelling, **kudzu**): A starch used for thickening sauces, soups, and so on, it is made from the root of the wild kudzu vine and has been an important ingredient in Japanese and Chinese cuisine for thousands of years. It is white and powdery and lends a subtle sweetness and smooth texture to sauces and desserts. As a home remedy, it provides relief for digestive disorders, headaches, and hangovers when combined with *umeboshi, shoyu,* and *ginger.* Kuzu is available at natural food stores in white chalky chunks. It keeps indefinitely in a dry place.

maple sugar: Twice as sweet as *maple syrup,* it is the result of boiling maple sap until nearly all of the water has been evaporated to form crystals. Maple sugar was the principal confection for eastern woodland Native Americans, who also tapped birch, hickory, and black walnut trees.

maple syrup: This natural sweetener is made by a simple refining process: The sap from maple trees is boiled down to remove water. Because maple sap contains only 3 percent sucrose, it takes 40 gallons to make 1 gallon of syrup. The sucrose content of maple syrup is 65 percent, as compared with 100 percent in refined white sugar. At Angelica's, we use grade B, or medium amber, which is a good all-purpose product suitable for baking. Lighter-colored grades are more expensive and better for serving on your pancakes.

millet: A small yellow whole grain with a relatively bland nutty flavor, millet is a staple in Asian countries and goes well with many types of sauces. Due to its high alkaline content, it is the easiest grain to digest; millet is the only grain that can be cooked without salt and still remain alkaline rather than acidic. It is also gluten-free.

mirin: This sweet Japanese cooking wine is naturally brewed and fermented from rice, *koji,* and water, often with *sea salt* as an added ingredient. It has an alcohol content of about 6.5 percent and imparts a mild sweetness that can round out the flavor of many dishes. Recommended brands: Eden and Mitoku.

miso: Miso is a protein-rich fermented paste made from *soybeans, sea salt,* and a grain, usually rice or barley. It is an important ingredient in Japanese cuisine that is added to hot foods after cooking. There are many kinds of miso, the lighter-colored being milder and sweeter, the darker-colored having a richer, deeper taste. Miso is extremely nutritious, high in protein, low in fat, and contains all eight essential amino acids. It also neutralizes environmental pollutants. Always look for unpasteurized miso. We use traditional barley miso for our soup. Lighter, sweeter varieties, such as chickpea miso or sweet white miso, tend to be better for salad dressings, sauces, and marinades. There are many good brands, including Miso Master and South River.

molasses: A dark, sweet, sticky by-product of the sugar-refining process, molasses is a sweetener with a powerful taste; it should be used in moderation because it can easily overwhelm other flavors in a dish.

mung beans: Small, round, and olive-green, mung beans can be used either whole or sprouted. They are easy to digest and rich in vitamins A and B (five times more so when sprouted). They do not need presoaking.

mustard: We use mustard in three forms: powdered, for dressings and dips, and as a seasoning; whole seeds, toasted and used in Indian cooking and curry dishes; and prepared mustard—almost exclusively Eden English-style grainy mustard, which has more texture and is spicier than Dijon.

nori (a.k.a. **laver**): Thin black or dark purple sheets of dried sea vegetable, nori is used for the outer layer of cylindrical rolls of seasoned rice and vegetables or fish known as *maki,* a very popular Japanese dish. Nori has a mild sea flavor. Remarkably, it contains more vitamin A than carrots. And it is 35.6 percent protein, which is higher than the percentage of protein in soybeans, milk, meat, fish, or poultry. It is also high in vitamins and trace elements. Dry-roasted nori has a salty, nutty flavor and can be crumbled over popcorn, soups, or grains as a garnish. See pages 146–47.

pickles: A time-honored way of preserving the harvest, pickles stimulate the appetite and promote digestion. The classic pickle is made with cucumber, but just about any vegetable can be pickled by curing it in either vinegar or brine (salt water), often with the addition of aromatics and/or herbs. At Angelica Kitchen, we generally make our own pickles. Naturally fermented, unpasteurized, low-salt pickles are a quality fermented food.

porcini mushrooms: The Italians call them porcini, the French cepes, and they are one of the most sought-after and delicious varieties of wild edible fungus. Very tasty and very expensive. It is important to soak dried porcini and let the dirt drop to the bottom of the container. If they are fresh, simply brush them off.

quinoa (pronounced "KEEN-wah"): Light, fluffy, and transparent, quinoa is a grain the size of a sesame seed, with a small outer filament (sprout). It has a mild flavor, which has been compared to that of couscous, and is easily digested. It cooks faster than rice and is equally versatile. Native to the high valleys of the Andes, quinoa was a staple of the Incas, who called it the Mother Grain. It's been available in the United States since 1984. Quinoa has a very high protein content of 16 percent.

rice flour: Gluten-free flour from ground rice, it adds a crunchy texture to baked goods.

rice syrup (a.k.a. **yinnie syrup**): A thick, sweet syrup made from brown rice and barley, it is frequently used in dessert recipes. Rice syrup is nutritionally preferable to simple sugars such as honey, maple syrup, and molasses. Because it is metabolized more slowly, entering the bloodstream steadily over a two-hour period, it does not cause the problematic rapid fluctuations in blood sugar levels attributed to the more quickly metabolized sweeteners.

sea salt: Sea salt is obtained from evaporated seawater, whereas rock salt is mined from inland beds. Sea salt is either sun-baked or kiln-baked. It has good flavor, is high in trace minerals, and contains no sugar or chemical additives. Fleur de Sol from Brittany, France, is the crème de la crème of salts. It comes strictly from the material that floats on the surface of the water. It is a table salt, not a cooking salt, and is very expensive (more than $24 per pound). Regular sea salt is grayer and is used for cooking. French gray sea salt costs about $5 per pound. See also *kosher salt*.

sea vegetables: Among the dried sea vegetables we use at Angelica Kitchen are the various types of *kombu, hijiki, dulse, nori, arame, sea palm, smoked dulse,* and *agar*. Most of the sea vegetables mentioned in the recipes are dried, except for fresh ones used in salads. Recommended (dry) brands: Eden, Ocean Harvest, Gold Mine, Maine Coast Sea Vegetables, Mitoku.

seitan: Succulent, hearty, and wholesome, seitan is wheat gluten made from whole wheat flour. A traditional food in China, Japan, and the Middle East, it is also known as *kofu*. Gluten is the protein component of wheat; thus seitan is concentrated wheat protein. We make our own fresh seitan at Angelica's.

shoyu: See *soy sauce*.

soba: Traditional Japanese noodles made from *buckwheat* flour alone, or in combination with sifted wheat flour, soba noodles are available at health food stores and Asian groceries. Recommended brands: Eden, Mitoku.

soybeans: These bland-tasting beans are an ancient source of human nutrition. There are more than 1,000 types of soybeans, and they are used to produce many different food products including soybean oil, *soy sauce, soy milk,* soy flour, *miso, tamari, tofu, tempeh,* and sprouts. One of the most nutritious plant foods, they are relatively inexpensive, high in protein, and low in carbohydrates. Soybeans provide more protein per acre of land than does the raising of cattle for beef.

soy milk: This is the liquid strained from *soybeans* after they have been soaked in water, ground to a puree, cooked, and pressed dry. This milk substitute has the same amount of protein as cow's milk, approximately one third the fat, fewer calories, no cholesterol, many essential B vitamins, and fifteen times the iron. Because it is lower on the food chain, it also contains one-tenth of the chemical residues. Fresh soy milk, manufactured by small regional soy dairies, is preferable to packed. Always buy organic from unhybridized soybeans.

soy sauce: Made from boiled, fermented soybeans and roasted wheat or barley, it is dark in color, salty, and used frequently in Asian and vegan cuisines. Soy sauce is known by three different names: *shoyu, tamari,* and *soy sauce.* Tamari and shoyu are naturally fermented seasonings that enhance the flavor of food because they contain glutamic acid and sodium. (See also *tamari.*) Recommended brands: Johsen, Eden, Mitoku, Ohsawa—all naturally brewed, no additives. Look for organic; top brands market both organic and nonorganic sauces. Commercial soy sauce is another story. It is commonly made by reacting hydrolyzed vegetable protein with hydrochloric acid. After twenty-four hours, during which time the acid has broken down the soybeans and has been removed, the remaining soy substance is mixed with caramel coloring, *sea salt,* corn syrup, and water. A preservative is usually added. Its flavor is harsh, abrasively salty, sweet, and bitter and leaves a metallic aftertaste.

spelt: An ancestor of contemporary strains of wheat, spelt is native to southern Europe. It has a mellow, nutty flavor and a slightly higher protein content than wheat. People with sensitivities to wheat often have better tolerance for spelt because it contains a unique form of gluten that is easier to digest. The grain itself can be prepared in the same manner as rice.

spices: Always buy organic; otherwise, they could be irradiated. Buy whole spices in small quantities (their shelf life is limited) and grind as needed.

sun-dried tomatoes: A traditional, convenient way to preserve the tomato harvest, sun-dried tomatoes can be reconstituted before cooking. At Angelica Kitchen, we like to use the Timber Crest brand from California. They have no added salt, unlike the Italian ones, and no sulphur dioxide as a preservative, yet their color is rich and beautiful.

tahini: This is a smooth, creamy paste made from hulled sesame seeds. Tahini may or may not include salt (check the label). If made from roasted seeds, it tastes nuttier; from raw seeds, it is sweeter. Tahini has the same nutrient content as hulled sesame seeds. We use Dispasa, a mechanically hulled and stone-ground brand. Arrowhead Mills, Joyva, and Sahadi are also recommended.

tamari: A wheat-free *shoyu,* tamari is a darker, thicker, richer, more flavorful form of *soy sauce* originally made in Japan. It contains only soy, salt, and water. Tamari is high in amino acids and glutamic acid.

teff: A staple cereal in Ethiopia, teff was originally foraged as a wild grass and later cultivated. Teff seeds dating back to 3359 B.C. have been found in a brick of the Dassur Pyramid in Egypt. We now cultivate teff in Idaho. Highly nutritious, it provides plenty of calcium and iron and is rich in protein (12 percent). Grains of teff are so tiny—smaller than a poppy seed—they are too small to hull; therefore, teff is always consumed as a whole food with its nutrients intact. See page 194.

tempeh: A traditional Indonesian fermented soy food, high in protein, tempeh is made from soybeans, water, and a special culture and formed into cakes. It is the richest known source of vitamin B_{12} in the realm of vegetables and provides many other vitamins and minerals, including copper, niacin, folic acid, iron, calcium, magnesium, and zinc. Look for firm-textured tempeh with no signs of mushiness. It should have white or black mold; avoid tempeh with any green or orange spots. Our favorite brand: Cricklewood.

tofu: Soybean curd made from soy milk pressed into blocks, tofu is a cholesterol- free, easily digested, high-protein food that is low in saturated fats. It is an excellent source of calcium as well as a good source of other minerals such as iron, phosphorus, potassium, sodium, B vitamins, choline, and fat-soluble vitamin E. Tofu comes in different consistencies: soft for creamy foods such as Russian Dressing, harder or denser for boiling or roasting. At Angelica Kitchen, our favorite brand is Fresh Tofu (see pages 101–2). Silken tofu is made by a different process and is creamy, which makes it suitable for dressings and desserts.

udon: These are flat Japanese-style noodles made from wheat, whole wheat, or whole wheat with unbleached white flour. Udon have a lighter flavor than soba noodles and can be used in the same ways.

umeboshi (a.k.a. ume or salt plum): Salty, refreshingly sour pickled plums, which stimulate the appetite, enhance digestion, and alkalize the blood, umeboshi can be used whole or in the form of a paste. Shiso (or beefsteak) plant leaves impart the characteristic pink color and act as a natural preservative. (Shiso is a purple-red herb popular in Japanese cooking.) Recommended brands: Eden, Mitoku, and Ohsawa.

umeboshi vinegar: A pink liquid with a fruity sour flavor, it is drawn out of the fermenting *umeboshi* by means of salt. Technically, it is not a vinegar since it contains salt. Umeboshi vinegar imparts a light, refreshing citrus flavor, which especially enhances salad dressing and steamed vegetables. It's a good substitute for vinegar and salt in any recipe.

vinegars: The word comes from the French term *vin aigre,* which means sour wine. Vinegar is made when certain bacteria act on fermented liquids such as wine or cider, creating acetic acid. Among the many types of vinegars we use at Angelica Kitchen are *balsamic, apple cider, brown rice, umeboshi,* red wine, white wine, raspberry, cranberry, and elderberry. Always buy organic or make your own!

wakame: A long, thin green sea vegetable, wakame is a variety of *kombu.* High in protein, iron, calcium, and magnesium, wakame contains numerous trace minerals, and vitamins A and C. It also contains alginic acid, which helps eliminate heavy metals from the body. Wakame has a sweet taste and delicate texture and is especially good in *miso* soup. See also *kelp* and pages 138, 143–44.

wheat flour: There are two major kinds of wheat: hard winter wheat, which has lots of gluten and is therefore suitable for all bread-type products; and soft spring wheat, low in gluten, very light in texture and flavor, and therefore suitable for pastry, quick breads, and crusts. Other members of the whole-wheat family of grains (e.g., *kamut, spelt*) are also low in gluten and seem to be better tolerated by people who have difficulty digesting wheat.

Food Storage Tips

Food is best stored in a container with a minimum of air and moisture. This provides the least friendly environment for bacteria to grow. Always put food in the smallest possible container and make sure the container is very clean. Glass is best because it gets the cleanest, but when freezing use food-grade plastic containers since glass can shatter when the contents expand. When freezing food underfill the container a bit to take the expansion into account; if you're just refrigerating the food, fill the container to capacity. Store flours, powders, meals, grains, and beans in clean, dry, well-sealed containers away from direct sunlight and heat.

apple cider: During apple season, cider is delivered fresh-pressed to Angelica Kitchen. Unlike juice, which has a long shelf life if unopened, cider is unpasteurized and will spoil if not refrigerated. Even so it only keeps for about a week. In spring, summer, and winter, our cider is delivered to us frozen, which is the next best thing after fresh. If cider is allowed to ferment it becomes lightly alcoholic and is known as "hard cider."

apples: Apples ripen ten times faster in a dry, warm atmosphere than when they are in cold storage. Warm temperatures can cause a mealy texture and loss of flavor, so after removing any with bruises (use immediately), store them in your refrigerator.

berries: Use berries immediately. Avoid sealing berries in plastic, which promotes the growth of mold. Unused portions can be frozen.

bread: Bread freezes well; wrapped tightly, it will keep for up to three months. It can also be stored in a paper bag at room temperature—it will dry out somewhat but it won't mold. If you wrap or seal it in plastic, the humidity of the bread will cause it to mold.

cabbage: Store refrigerated. Once cut, cover cabbage to prevent it from drying out or oxidizing.

carrots: These are best stored in a paper or plastic bag in the refrigerator.

cauliflower: Cover and refrigerate unused portions to prevent drying.

dried fruits: Dried fruits (dates, currants, apricots, figs, raisins, etc.) have an amazingly long shelf life. But they keep best when refrigerated in a well-sealed container. It's possible for them to ferment if kept too warm for too long.

flour: Whole-grain flours should be kept refrigerated in a well-sealed container. They can also be frozen.

fresh vegetables: Store all of the following vegetables in paper or cloth sacks in the refrigerator or root cellar. Some stay fresher when kept dry: cucumbers, jalapeño peppers, mushrooms, bell peppers, root vegetables, zucchini, leeks. Others keep better wrapped in plastic or sealed in a plastic bag: green leafy vegetables, cabbages, herbs, scallions, sprouts, parsley, fennel, lettuce.

garlic: Use garlic fresh, don't buy too much at one time. Store at room temperature in a ventilated container because humidity encourages sprouting.

ginger: Ginger will mold if you keep it in a plastic bag in the fridge. It's best kept in a cool, dry place unwrapped, or refrigerated unwrapped. Use promptly.

herbs: There are a number of excellent methods of preserving herbs. To store fresh herbs, put them upright in a glass of water covered with a plastic bag or wrap them in a damp paper towel, then refrigerate. They will keep for up to one week. You can dry herbs by hanging them upside down in a bundle or laying them on a straw mat to ensure air circulation. Then strip the leaves off the stalks and put them away in an airtight jar. They will keep their flavor for about a month. You can make herb vinegar with various fresh herbs. We make batches when we close the restaurant in August for our annual summer holiday and refurbishing. Simply put the herb(s) in a pot with enough vinegar to cover and bring the contents to a simmer. Turn the heat off and let the pot sit overnight. Strain into a decorative jar, put a sprig of the fresh herb inside, and seal the jar. This will keep one year. The vinegar captures and preserves the essence of the herbs beautifully. This works with any type of vinegar except balsamic, because it's already dark and has complex flavors.

maple syrup: This sweetener must be kept in a cool, dark place. Otherwise, it will ferment or develop mold. In either case, however, it can be rescued. Strain it through a sieve into a pan and bring it slowly to a boil (careful it doesn't boil over). Allow it to cool and pour it into a clean container. Refrigerated, it can keep up to a year.

miso: Always buy unpasteurized miso. (If the container is completely sealed with no room for the naturally generated gases to release, the miso is pasteurized.) Store tightly covered in the refrigerator, where it can last for four to five months.

mushrooms: Keep them dry by storing them in paper, not plastic, and keep them cool. Use within three days.

nuts: Store nuts refrigerated and tightly sealed.

oils: Keep them in a dark place, tightly covered. When buying oils, look for bottles that have been nitrogen flushed (the oxygen has been replaced by inert nitrogen) and are made out of dark glass, which helps avoid spoilage from the light. It's a good idea to buy in small quantities—only what you're going to use within a relatively short period of time. If held for more than a few weeks, oils should be refrigerated (with the exception of olive oil).

onions: These are best stored unrefrigerated in a well-ventilated area.

peppers (bell or sweet peppers and hot ones, such as jalapeño): Store peppers refrigerated in a paper or cloth bag. Dried peppers should be stored on the shelf in airtight containers.

phyllo: Store phyllo tightly wrapped first in paper and then in plastic. Frozen, it will keep up to a couple of months; in the fridge, it will keep for several days.

root vegetables: These can be stored in a cool, dark place or refrigerated. Keep them in paper or cloth bags away from moisture to avoid sprouting.

sea vegetables: Dried sea vegetables will keep indefinitely at room temperature in a dry place. Fresh sea vegetables come packed in sea salt. Refrigerated in a sealed container in their salt, they can keep for several months.

seitan: Seitan will keep in the refrigerator for three to five days submerged in its stock or drained and tightly wrapped in plastic. It can be frozen for up to three months.

spices: We highly recommend that you grind your own spices fresh each time they're needed for a recipe. Whole spices, as well as freshly ground spices, should be kept in a tightly covered container away from light. They will retain their pronounced flavor for up to a month; after that they begin to fade.

squash: Winter squash should be stored at room temperature in a cool, dry place because moisture promotes rot. Summer squash must be stored in the refrigerator.

sun-dried tomatoes: Buy dried tomatoes, not those packed in oil, and store them in a sealed container in a cool, dark place. After several months, they eventually turn dark and somewhat bitter.

tahini: Since it is made from sesame seeds, tahini, like any seed or nut, is perishable due to its high oil content. It should be bought as fresh as possible and kept refrigerated.

tempeh: This soy product can be kept in the refrigerator for about a week, where it will retain its characteristic yeasty, mild, aromatic flavor. It also freezes well, tightly wrapped in plastic. Those brands that come frozen (Cricklewood, for example) should be kept frozen; defrost the tempeh overnight in the fridge before using it.

tofu: Bulk tofu should be stored in fresh, pure water and refrigerated. Change the water regularly. Gary Abramowitz of Fresh Tofu, Inc., recommends doing it every other day and making sure that the water stays cold. Properly stored tofu will last ten days to two weeks. When it starts to get old, it will take on a sour taste. Fresh Tofu's vacuum-packed, one-pound package has a refrigerator life of three weeks. Once you've opened a sealed package, treat it like bulk tofu.

tomatoes: Store tomatoes in a paper bag at room temperature, never refrigerated. Contrary to popular belief, it is not a good idea to put them on the windowsill in direct sunlight to ripen.

umeboshi paste or plums: This ingredient keeps almost indefinitely, unrefrigerated. Both plums and paste need to be well covered, otherwise they dry and form crystals due to the high salt content.

vinegar: Store covered at room temperature.

A Thursday on the Farm,
by Keith Stewart

6:30 A.M. The alarm goes off. I get up and make my way a little stiffly to the bathroom. Check the weather forecast. Eat a bowl of oatmeal. Stretch for fifteen minutes. Prepare a pick list for the Friday market, looking back at sales figures from the last couple of Fridays.

Turn off the electric fence. Check on the cows. Untie the dogs from their posts in the field (both the fence and the dogs are meant to deter hungry deer during the night, but sometimes they don't).

8:00 A.M. Meet with the crew (Matt, Laura, Graham, Ione, Jessie, Sandra). Exchange a few words of greeting, then a quick preview of what we need to accomplish in the day ahead. Each apprentice receives his or her pick list for the morning. Friday is our smallest market so the pick is relatively light. We hose out the number of lugs and crates that we'll need, load them onto the old Dodge pickup, sharpen our knives and head for the field, each to his or her assigned task.

For an hour or two we work quietly, filling lugs with kale, collards, swiss chard, lettuces, mizuna, tatsoi, carrots, squash, zucchini, dandelion, mustard greens, potatoes, onions . . . whatever is ready for harvest and looking good.

10:15 A.M. Jessie hears a faint bleating sound in the pasture behind Field 05. Matt and I climb over the barb wire fence and after a few minutes stumble upon a calf hiding in a thicket. It is lying down, not much more than skin and bones, and certainly too weak to walk. We carry it back to the barn and give it water. It drinks and drinks and drinks as we stand and watch, touched by its gentle, frightened eyes and tenuous hold on life.

I call Ronnie Odell, the dairy farmer who rents our pasture, and he comes right over to claim the little foundling. Its mother is back at his place. He had taken her in a trailer a week earlier expecting that she would have her calf in the safety of his own barn, only to find out that she had given birth prematurely. Ronnie had spent some hours searching our pasture but hadn't found the calf and had given it up for dead. Now here it is. After seven days alone and unnourished in the world, its new life is a gift.

(continued)

(continued)

Back to the vegetables. We spray everything we've just picked with cold water and then load the lugs into an air-conditioned cooler, where they will sit for the rest of the day. As we work we munch on a few freshly dug carrots and maybe a Japanese turnip or two. Graham peels a clove of garlic and chomps it down raw.

11:00 A.M. Time to get the mesclun. We head up the driveway with fifteen or twenty plastic tubs and set about cutting an assortment of baby greens in Field 08. A couple of turkey vultures are circling overhead. The sun is getting hotter and some of us are beginning to feel a little mid-morning fatigue. But we keep going and an hour later the mesclun is all cut and each of us is ready for a break from bending.

Thank God for the mesclun washing. We do it in big white laundry tubs in the old milk room, which is pleasantly cool. The radio is on or maybe a Bob Dylan tape. We chat, relax a little, and engage in a little light banter.

1:00 P.M. Lunchtime. And we're ready for it. I eat a sandwich and several cookies and jot down a few "must-dos" for the afternoon. Then, something I've been looking forward to for the last hour or so: a few minutes of reading followed by a nap—a sweet, undisturbed twenty-minute-long nap. Boy, does that feel good.

Around **2:15 P.M.** I get a call from Jim Elsasser at Angelica Kitchen. I tell him what vegetables and herbs we have and which are at their peak of quality and flavor. He considers his menu for the next couple of days and places an order that usually includes plenty of greens, maybe some sungold cherry tomatoes, carrots, parsley, garlic, rosemary, and thyme.

After lunch, two or three of us continue washing mesclun while the rest set about filling the Angelica order. Perhaps we'll move the irrigation sprinklers or connect drip lines to the basil. And often I'll try to fit in a little tractor work or planting. The afternoon moves fast. There's lots to do and not quite enough time in which to do it.

4:00 P.M. We still need to get tomatoes, peppers, and eggplant. We need to cut parsley and other herbs for Friday and we need to mix the mesclun, which by now should be dried and free of any stray leaves of pigweed or offending blades of grass. And the Angelica order needs to be weighed and carefully packed and labeled.

If we're lucky, by **7:00 P.M.** we're ready to hose out the milk room and start packing for market. Now the sun is low in the sky and the temperature is just right. A dozen barn swallows, most of them born on the farm this season, are lined up on the electric line that feeds the barn, and the pigeons that roost in the silo are coming in for the night. We laugh and joke as we load the truck, feeling good about the work we have done, looking forward to the rest that the night will provide. And maybe there's still time for a quick dip in the pond.

Tomorrow Laura and Ione will head out at **4:30 A.M.** for the market at Union Square in Manhattan. The forecast is good so they should have a decent day. The rest of us will stay back at the farm and pick for Saturday, a much bigger market. It's a full life.

Keith Stewart, a New Zealander by birth, gave up site consulting in New York City in 1986 to begin farming upstate in Orange County. He grows the best garlic I've ever eaten.

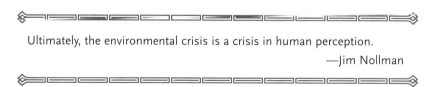

Ultimately, the environmental crisis is a crisis in human perception.

—Jim Nollman

PART II

Recipes

A Few Words about Olive Oil

In the recipe section, olive oil is recommended throughout. We use extra virgin olive oil and olive oil (commonly referred to as pure or light olive oil) by Gaeta Imports (see profile on page 127). As owner John Fusco explains, his extra virgin olive oil is top quality first cold press from olives grown in his ancestors' orchards. The second pressing, which makes the ingredient we refer to as "olive oil" is distinguished from commercial producers by an alternative system that uses no heat or solvents in extraction.

I open the recipe section with the components of our famous Dragon Bowl—rice, beans, tofu, sea vegetables, steamed vegetables, and salad garnish piled high and served with choices of dressing or gravy. Familiarity with the fundamentals of preparing these ingredients is advantageous on its own and indispensable when preparing more complicated dishes.

Many ingredients listed in the following recipes are from diverse cultural backgrounds. I assure you they are readily available from natural food stores; now even many supermarkets stock these items. I encourage you to welcome these new acquaintances into your pantry—get to know them as they are lively, fun, and beneficial to your well-being. Mail-order catalogs, full of useful information, are available from companies listed in Resources at the back of the book.

Note: For any ingredient listed in the recipes with which you may be unfamiliar, refer to Ingredients on pages 68–79 for definitions.

The Dragon Bowl and Other Basics

basic beans

YIELD: 4 to 6 servings   COOKING TIME: 1¹/2 hours

At Angelica Kitchen, cleaning, soaking, and cooking beans are a daily ritual. We use up to twenty-five different kinds of beans, from yellow eye to snowcap, scarlet runner to rattlesnake. Some of the more "exotic" varieties come and go in terms of availability, but there should always be a number of interesting choices at your local market.

Conventional wisdom says to soak beans in water overnight. More recently, it's been shown that the hot-soak method, as called for in this recipe, works much better. It's quicker, more convenient, and more effective in breaking down the oligosaccharides, which are complex sugars that cannot be digested by our stomach enzymes. (Beans cause their famous flatulence because these sugars proceed, undigested, from the stomach into the intestine, where resident bacteria eat them and produce gas.)

Cooking times for beans vary, which is why it's important to test them in the pot as they cook. The older and drier the beans, the longer the cooking time.

If you decide to stick to the old cold-soak method, simply sort out any dirt, rocks, or broken beans, rinse the beans in a strainer, and put them in a bowl or pot with enough cold water to cover by two inches. Leave them in the refrigerator for at least eight hours or overnight, then drain and they're ready to cook.

> 1 cup dried black beans (kidney, pinto, or Great Northern
>   also work well)
> 1 quart plus 5 cups cold water
> 1 (3-inch) piece of dried kombu
> sea salt

❖ Sort through the beans and discard any broken ones or pebbles.

❖ Rinse the beans in a strainer under cold running water.

❖ Place the beans in a 1¹/2- to 3-quart heavy-bottomed saucepan with 1 quart of the water, bring to a boil, and cook for 2 minutes.

❖ Remove from heat and allow the beans to swell for 1 hour.

(continued)

A Tip about Beans

Richard Corichi, owner of Community Mill & Bean, Savannah, N.Y., rejoices in the beautiful and multifarious coloring of beans. He doesn't like to see that coloring lost in the cooking. The important thing to remember is that when you presoak the beans, they swell up and absorb some of their soaking water. As part of the exchange, the water also turns grayish and the beans lose some of their color. Always discard that soaking water, cook your beans in fresh, clear water, and they will retain their natural, vibrant colors.

(continued)

❖ Drain and rinse the beans; place them in a pot with the kombu and the 5 cups of cold water.

❖ Bring to a boil, cover the pot, lower the flame, and simmer gently for 50 minutes, or until the beans and kombu are tender.

❖ Add sea salt to taste and simmer uncovered for 5 more minutes.

❖ At this point the beans are ready to eat or use in another recipe. Just remember to save the cooking liquid (or "liquor," as it is known). It can be used in a soup or stew, but more importantly, it is the best medium in which to store any unused beans.

gomasio

YIELD: 1 cup   COOKING TIME: 30 minutes

Gomasio is a staple of the macrobiotic diet and a traditional Japanese condiment that you'll find on every table at Angelica Kitchen. In Japanese, *goma* means sesame and *shio* means salt. Gomasio brings out the flavor in whole grains and is highly recommended for salads. You can also make it with black sesame seeds. If you want to give it an extra kick, add some cayenne pepper.

The proportion that follows will yield a medium-strength gomasio. For a milder version, use 3/4 tablespoon of salt or omit the salt entirely and use sea vegetable powder, a mildly salty substance that is available at natural food stores. Stored in a tightly sealed container, gomasio will keep up to two weeks.

> *1 cup brown unhulled sesame seeds*
> *1 tablespoon unrefined sea salt*

❖ Preheat the oven to 350°F.

❖ Rinse the sesame seeds in a fine sieve under cold running water. Drain well.

❖ Spread the seeds on a cookie sheet and toast in the oven at 350°F for about 25 minutes. To test if the seeds are done, place several of them between your pinkie and thumb. If they crush easily, they're done.

❖ Allow the sesame seeds to cool to room temperature.

❖ Combine them with the salt in a suribachi, food processor, or mortar and pestle and grind until almost half of the sesame seeds have been crushed. The final product should be coarse in texture with whole sesame seeds still visible in the mixture.

The Dragon Bowl & Other Basics

mashed potatoes with garlic and rosemary

YIELD: 4 to 6 servings   COOKING TIME: 45 minutes

We recommend Yukon Gold potatoes for this recipe because they come out smoother and richer than russet potatoes, the ones commonly thought of as "regular baking potatoes." Yukon Golds have a great flavor when combined with olive oil. If you're used to having your potatoes with butter, you won't miss it at all in this recipe. Customers rave about these potatoes. We prefer not to peel them—a more rustic texture is created and, more important, the vitamins and minerals contained in their skins are retained.

Another key to the recipe is the long simmering of whole garlic cloves. Peel the cloves carefully by hand without smashing them, which will lead to a mellower garlic flavor, not so sharp and pungent, that melds perfectly with the flavor of the potatoes.

Try this: Let the leftover potatoes firm up overnight in the fridge, form them into patties, pan-fry them in olive oil, and serve as a side dish.

> 2 pounds Yukon Gold or Yellow Finn potatoes
> 1/3 cup peeled garlic cloves
> 1 teaspoon minced fresh rosemary leaves
> 1 teaspoon sea salt
> 6 tablespoons extra virgin olive oil
> Sea salt and freshly ground black pepper

* Wash the potatoes.
* Peel half of them and cut all of them into 1-inch cubes.
* Place the potatoes, garlic, rosemary, and salt in a 3- to 4-quart saucepan with water to cover by 1 inch.
* Bring to a boil over high heat.
* Lower the heat, cover, and simmer for 30 to 40 minutes, or until the potatoes crush easily with the back of a spoon against the side of the pan.
* Drain the potatoes, reserving the cooking water.
* Add the oil to the potatoes, and beat with a wire whisk, wooden spoon, or potato masher.
* Add the reserved cooking water to the potatoes in small increments, adding more only after each addition has been absorbed, to create the desired creaminess.
* If the potatoes are too wet, you can put the entire pan, assuming it is oven safe, into a 350°F oven for 10 minutes or so, until the potatoes dry out.
* Season with salt and pepper to taste, mix well, and serve hot.

Garlic

How to Get the Right Amount of Flavor
To impart the most potent garlic flavor to your dishes, crush or press the cloves. Garlic is somewhat less potent when chopped or minced, milder if sliced. It is milder still if left whole, while the most subtle flavor comes from leaving the cloves in their skin.

How to Get the Smell off Your Hands
Mix a spoonful of baking soda in a cup with water to form a paste. Rub it over your hands for a minute, then rinse.

millet, angelica style

YIELD: 3 to 4 servings   COOKING TIME: 1 hour

One of the most frequent compliments from our customers is that a certain dish tastes so much better at Angelica Kitchen than at other places they've had it. We are convinced that it is because our ingredients are fresh and organic. We'd also like to think that we've devised some clever flavor-enhancing twists, such as preparing our millet with carrot juice.

Originally from Africa, millet is a grain that requires a fair amount of seasoning—more than rice, for example. It can certainly benefit from a little fat, which in this recipe comes in the form of olive oil. Toasting the millet before simmering it enhances its flavor, giving it a nice nutty fragrance.

Try this: Instead of using carrot juice, use water with a sprig of thyme or rosemary or several whole sage leaves. Omit the cinnamon stick and be sure to remove the herb sprig before serving.

> 1 cup whole-grain millet
> 1/2 cup freshly pressed carrot juice
> 1/2 cup finely diced onion
> 1 tablespoon olive oil
> 1 bay leaf
> 1/2 stick cinnamon
> 1 teaspoon sea salt
> 1 cup water

* Preheat the oven to 350°F.
* Rinse the millet in several changes of cold water and set aside in a strainer to drain.
* Make the carrot juice.
* Spread the drained millet on a cookie sheet and toast in the oven for 15 minutes.
* Combine the oil, onion, bay leaf, cinnamon, and salt in a 2-quart, oven-proof saucepan with a tight-fitting lid. Cook over a medium flame until onions soften, 5 to 8 minutes. Regulate the heat to prevent the onions from browning.
* Remove the millet from the oven and stir it into the onion mixture. Keep the oven heated to 350°F.
* Add the carrot juice and water.
* Raise the heat to high and bring the mixture to a boil.
* Remove from the heat, cover, and return to the oven to bake for 25 to 30 minutes, or until all liquid has been absorbed.
* Remove from the oven. Discard the cinnamon stick and the bay leaf, fluff with a fork, and serve.

The Dragon Bowl & Other Basics

polenta

YIELD: 6 to 8 servings   COOKING TIME: 45 minutes

Corn was brought over to Europe from the Americas as an inexpensive way to feed the peasants and, in the form of polenta, has become a staple of northern Italian cuisine. Polenta is incredibly versatile. It can be eaten as a hot cereal for breakfast topped with maple syrup, cinnamon, and toasted pecans or in a soft mound right out of the pot with gravy on top for lunch or dinner. It can be cooled, allowed to harden, cut into squares or triangles, and baked, panfried, or grilled and then topped with any number of sauces.

We like to cut it into rounds, spread it with tapenade, and sprinkle it with julienned vegetables. Two toppings that go particularly well with polenta are Ragout of White Beans with Gremolata and Spicy Sun-Dried Tomato Sauce (page 208, page 210). We also like to chop up one of the following and mix it in with the polenta to create an interesting flavor accent: leeks or ramps (in season), hijiki, chopped sun-dried tomatoes, roasted garlic, or fresh rosemary.

> 1 cup yellow cornmeal
> 1 cup yellow corn grits
> 1 teaspoon sea salt
> 6 cups water
> 2 tablespoons olive oil

❖ Whisk the cornmeal, grits, and salt together in a small bowl.

❖ Bring the water to a boil in a heavy 3-quart saucepan with lid (cast iron is best).

❖ Add the oil, then whisk the cornmeal mixture into the boiling water a little at a time. To avoid lumping, continue whisking until smooth. If the polenta is sputtering, lower the flame to avoid catching a bit of bubbling polenta on your hand.

❖ Reduce the heat to low, cover, and simmer for 30 to 45 minutes.

❖ Stir every 5 minutes to prevent sticking. The polenta is done when you can pull it away from the sides of the pan with a wooden spoon.

❖ Serve immediately as a soft gruel topped with the sauce of your choice.

Optional:

❖ Lightly oil an 8 x 8-inch ovenproof glass dish and pour the polenta into it.

❖ Let the polenta cool until firm, about 30 minutes in the fridge or 1 to 1¹/2 hours at room temperature.

(continued)

Ramps

Ramps, or wild leeks, are in season from April through late May or early June. The whole plant is edible. The whites make an excellent addition to the quick pickle recipe (page 118). The green tops can be steamed and added to spinach or other greens. Ramps can also be served sautéed or finely chopped raw as a garnish in place of scallions. Guy Jones of Blooming Hill Farm organized a ramp festival at the Union Square Green Market in New York City in 1996 and many of our city's greatest chefs contributed their ramps recipes. It was one of Peter's most memorable cooking experiences. He made a crepe of grilled ramps with shiitake mushrooms and asparagus, spread with herb tofu "cheese"—it was a big hit.

(continued)

❖ Once the polenta has set, preheat the oven to 350°F. Cut the polenta into desired shapes and arrange the pieces on a lightly oiled cookie sheet.

❖ Brush the tops with oil and bake for 20 minutes.

basic brown rice

YIELD: 3 cups   COOKING TIME: 40 to 45 minutes

The key to cooking rice properly is to use a heavy-bottomed pot with a tight-fitting lid. Once the rice comes to a boil, do not disturb it until all the water is absorbed. When a chopstick is poked down through the rice and you feel the grains sticking to the bottom of the pan a little, you know it's ready.

> *1 cup organic short-grain brown rice*
> *¹/₄ teaspoon sea salt*
> *2¹/₂ cups water*

❖ Place the rice in a strainer, rinse under cold running water, and drain well.

❖ Bring the water to a boil over high heat in a 1-quart saucepan with lid.

❖ Add the salt and rice.

❖ When the water returns to a boil, reduce the flame to low.

❖ Cover and simmer for 40 to 45 minutes, or until the water is absorbed and the grains are tender.

❖ Remove the pan from the heat and allow the rice to rest for a few minutes before serving.

pressure-cooked brown rice

YIELD: 6 cups   COOKING TIME: 40 to 45 minutes

Pressure cooking yields a stickier, more dense pot of rice. We use it for making nori rolls; the consistency is just right. Try sprinkling the rice with a little gomasio for a satisfying side dish or base for a main course.

> *2 cups organic short-grain brown rice*
> *3 cups water*
> *¹/₂ teaspoon salt*

❖ Place the rice in a strainer, rinse under cold running water, and drain well.

❖ Pour rice into a 2- to 3-quart pressure cooker.

The Dragon Bowl & Other Basics

- Add the water and salt, secure the lid, and bring to full pressure over high heat.
- Lower the flame and slip a flame tamer under the pot.
- Simmer under pressure for 40 minutes.
- Remove the cooker from the heat and run cold water onto it to relieve its pressure.
- Allow the rice to rest for 5 minutes covered before serving.

baked rice

YIELD: 3 cups   COOKING TIME: 1 hour

At the restaurant, we bake many of our grains, including rice. It saves burner space and they cook in about the same amount of time. It's virtually impossible to burn them because they aren't subjected to direct heat, and the grains come out tender and fluffy.

> 1 cup organic short-grain brown rice
> 2$^1/_2$ cups water
> $^1/_4$ teaspoon sea salt

- Preheat oven to 350°F.
- Place rice in a strainer, rinse under cold running water, and drain well.
- Bring the rice to a boil in 2$^1/_2$ cups salted water in an ovenproof pot on top of the stove.
- Cover, place in the oven, and bake for 40 to 45 minutes, or until all of the water is absorbed.

sea vegetables

YIELD: 3 to 4 servings   COOKING TIME: 25 to 30 minutes

This simple, straightforward way of preparing sea vegetables has been a staple of the Angelica Kitchen menu for a long time. Arame and hijiki are our basic sea vegetables. (You can substitute sea palm or alaria.) Arame is delicate and mild. Hijiki has a chewier texture and stronger sea flavor. While they both cook up as strands, arame is cut to that shape whereas hijiki grows that way.

> $^1/_2$ ounce hijiki, approximately $^1/_3$ cup
> $^1/_2$ ounce arame, approximately $^1/_2$ cup
> 1 quart water
> $^1/_3$ cup onion, sliced into thin crescents

(continued)

(continued)

> *¹/₃ cup carrots, scrubbed and julienned*
> *2 tablespoons shoyu or tamari*

* Place the sea vegetables in a strainer and rinse under cold running water.
* Drain and place the sea vegetables in a bowl with the water. Set aside to swell for 30 minutes.
* Place the sea vegetables along with their soaking liquid, the onions, carrots, and shoyu in a 2- to 3-quart saucepan.
* Bring to a boil, lower the flame, and simmer uncovered for 25 minutes.
* Allow mixture to rest for 5 minutes and serve.

seitan

YIELD: 6 to 8 main course servings   COOKING TIME: 3 hours

Along with soy products, seitan is one of the most important protein bases in our vegan cuisine. It was invented by vegetarian Buddhist monks in China. We make it fresh at Angelica Kitchen every week. It's a true staple that we use as the basis for all kinds of wonderful recipes, including lasagnas, enchiladas, and chilis.

The seitan-making process begins with a flour dough, which is kneaded under running water until all the starch and bran are washed out and only the gluten remains. The gluten is then cooked in water flavored with tamari, kombu, and herbs, which firms up the protein and provides a delicate taste. Seitan has a very satisfying chewy texture and takes on the flavor of other ingredients with which it is cooked.

For the flour dough:
2 pounds organic unbleached white flour
2 pounds organic whole wheat bread flour
6 cups cold water

For the stock:
1 pound onions, quartered
3 carrots, halved lengthwise
2 stalks celery (including leaves), halved lengthwise
4 cloves garlic, halved
8 pieces (quarter-size slices) ginger
2 sprigs thyme
2 bay leaves
12 peppercorns
1 cup shoyu or tamari
1 gallon of water

The Dragon Bowl
& Other Basics

- Combine the flour with the water in a 5-quart mixing bowl and form into a ball.
- Place dough on a counter and knead for 150 strokes until it is smooth and elastic and has the feel of a firm ball of bread dough. This can be done in an electric mixer with the dough hook attached.
- Return the dough to the mixing bowl and cover with warm water.
- Allow the dough to rest for 30 minutes while you assemble the ingredients for the stock.

To make the gluten:

- Place the dough in a colander and put colander inside the mixing bowl.
- Put the mixing bowl into the sink and fill with cold water.
- Keep in mind that the final product, the gluten, will be approximately one-fifth the size of the original dough. So do not worry that you are washing too much down the sink, you are supposed to!
- Knead the dough for 5 minutes, then drain all the water out. Repeat this procedure two more times.
- Fill the bowl with hot water and pull and knead the dough until the water becomes almost clear, about another 5 minutes.
- Finally, rinse the dough in cold water for an additional 5 minutes.

NOTE: What you are left with is the glutinous part of the wheat—the protein, all of the starch and 90 percent of the bran having been washed away.

- Divide the gluten into two equal-sized balls. Place in an 8- to 10-quart stockpot with the stock ingredients and the water. Bring to a boil, then lower heat, and simmer for 3 hours.
- Add water from time to time as necessary to keep the gluten submerged.
- Strain the stock and use for soup or sauce.
- The seitan is now ready to use. Slice it into bite-size pieces or slabs for sandwiches, braisings, etc.

STORAGE: Seitan will keep in the refrigerator for three to five days submerged in the stock or drained and tightly wrapped in plastic. It also freezes beautifully for up to three months.

three-bean chili with seitan

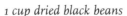

YIELD: 4 to 6 servings   COOKING TIME: 2 hours

This is one of the most popular items on our menu—we sell about fifty gallons of it per week—and probably the spiciest. It is your basic middle-of-the-road chili in terms of heat, not enough to peel the roof off your mouth. If you want to crank up the heat, add an extra chipotle pepper. To cool it down, put in just half a chipotle or leave it out entirely.

1 cup dried black beans
1 cup dried kidney beans
½ cup dried green lentils
1 3-inch piece of dried kombu
1 dried ancho chile
2 dried chipotle chilis (any hot, smokey-flavored chili can be substituted)
½ cup sun-dried tomatoes
2 tablespoons olive oil
2 cups chopped onions
4 cloves garlic, minced
2 teaspoons ground cumin
1 teaspoon oregano
½ pound seitan
1 carrot, diced
2 stalks celery, diced
1½ tablespoons mirin
1 tablespoon freshly squeezed lemon juice, strained
2 teaspoons sea salt
½ cup tofu sour cream (optional)

* Sort through the beans and lentils and discard any broken ones or stones. Rinse them in a strainer and pour into a 3-quart pot. Cover with cold water by 2 inches, bring to a boil over high heat, and boil for 2 minutes.

* Remove from heat and allow to soak for 1 hour.

* Drain and rinse the beans and lentils.

* Wash the soaking pot and return the drained beans and lentils to it. Add cold water to the pot to cover them by 1 inch. Bring to a boil over high heat. Skim away any foam that may form and add the kombu. Lower heat and simmer covered for 45 minutes, or until the beans and lentils are tender.

* While the beans and lentils cook, remove the stems and seeds from the chilis. Place the chilis and sun-dried tomatoes in a small saucepan with 2 cups of water and bring to a boil.

*The Dragon Bowl
& Other Basics*

- Remove from heat and let stand for 5 minutes, or until the chilis and tomatoes are softened. Puree the chilis and tomatoes in a food processor with enough soaking liquid to form a paste.
- Place the olive oil and onions in a heavy 4-quart casserole over medium heat and sauté for 5 minutes.
- Add the garlic, cumin, and oregano and sauté for 5 more minutes. Add the chili-tomato paste.
- Grind the seitan in a food processor until it resembles coarse soil. Stir the seitan into the onion mixture and continue to cook for 5 more minutes.
- Pour the beans and enough of their cooking juice into the vegetable-seitan mixture to form a thick soupy chili.
- Add the carrot, celery, and mirin and cook for 20 to 30 minutes, uncovered, or until all the vegetables are tender and the chili has thickened to desired consistency.
- Add lemon juice and sea salt to taste.
- Continue to cook 5 minutes longer.
- Serve topped with Tofu Sour Cream (page 128), garnished with chopped scallion or cilantro, and with a big wedge of our Southern-Style Cornbread (page 158) on the side.

steamed greens

YIELD: 2 to 3 servings   COOKING TIME: 4 to 5 minutes

Steamed fresh organic greens are a beautiful emerald color glowing with vitality. Not only do they help cleanse your system of toxins, they are also treasure troves of vitamins and minerals, including calcium and iron. Among the greens we feature in our Dragon Bowls are collard greens, mustard greens, Swiss chard, bok choy, kale, and radish tops (daikon leaves). Go to your grocer or farm stand and buy plenty of whatever's in season. They're great as leftovers, reheated, or served cold.

Some of the stronger-tasting greens, such as dandelion and mustard, are best blanched in boiling water for a minute or two before cooking.

Try this: After you've steamed and drained the greens, place 1 tablespoon of olive oil in a pan over medium heat and sauté one smashed garlic clove until sizzling, about two minutes. Add the greens to the pan and cook two minutes longer. Season to taste with sea salt and freshly ground black pepper serve with balsamic vinegar or lemon juice.

Serving suggestions: Garnish with chopped herbs of choice such as parsley, dill, or cilantro. Dress with any of the dressings on pages 148–50.

(continued)

(continued)

> *1 bunch greens of choice, approximately 10 ounces*

❖ Strip the leaves of any tough stems and coarsely chop. You should have approximately 6 to 8 cups.
❖ Submerge the greens in a large bowl or basin of cold water.
❖ Wash the greens and place them in a colander to drain.
❖ Bring 1 inch of water to a boil in a pot with a steamer basket and put the greens in the basket (you may have to do this in batches).
❖ Cover tightly and steam 4 to 5 minutes, or until tender.

root vegetables, squash, and other seasonal vegetables

YIELD: 3 to 4 servings   COOKING TIME: 10 to 15 minutes

Here is a quick and efficient way to render vegetables such as carrots, turnips, parsnips, potatoes, winter squash, red onions, rutabaga, zucchini, summer squash, and string beans eminently edible.

> *1 quart seasonal vegetables, washed and cut into bite-size pieces*

❖ Bring 1 inch of water to a boil in a pot equipped with a steamer basket and a tight-fitting lid.
❖ Add the vegetables, cover, and steam over high heat 7 to 12 minutes, or until fork tender.

basic herb tempeh

YIELD: 3 to 4 servings   COOKING TIME: 30 to 40 minutes

Heartier than tofu with a satisfying texture, tempeh is particularly good with assertive seasonings and sweet-and-sour flavors. It holds its shape beautifully and is wonderfully versatile, a great vehicle for all sorts of marinades. We slice it into batons, triangles, and cubes. Unlike tofu, tempeh can tolerate a relatively large amount of oil in cooking.

This is a simple, light treatment for tempeh, delicately seasoned with no fat whatsoever. This is the "house" version available à la carte on the menu or as a substitution in the Dragon Bowl.

> *1 pound tempeh*
> *1 quart water*
> *3 cloves garlic*
> *2 bay leaves*

The Dragon Bowl & Other Basics

*1 tablespoon fresh herbs such as thyme, rosemary, or sage, carefully
   stemmed and minced*

3 tablespoons shoyu or tamari

❖ Slice the tempeh into 1-inch cubes.

❖ Combine with the remaining ingredients in a 2-quart saucepan and bring to a boil.

❖ Lower the flame, cover the pan, and allow tempeh to simmer for 30 minutes.

GARY ABRAMOWITZ, FRESH TOFU INC.

Each year Angelica Kitchen uses 35,000 pounds of tofu. It's served baked, boiled, steamed, braised, marinated, herbed, sweetened, put into casseroles, soufflés, cakes—even made into sour cream. Thank heavens for Gary Abramowitz of Fresh Tofu, Inc., in Allentown, Pennsylvania, who works hard to maintain the highest possible standard—fresh and organic. The company's logo says it all—a block of tofu with wings, flying out of the factory straight to your table, where it will most definitely land fresh.

Gary's first culinary venture was a vegetarian food truck at Rutgers University called Wok'n Roll—an alternative to the ever present "grease trucks" that foist fries, burgers, subs, and pizza on college students. It was a resounding success. Later he became a chef at the vegetarian High Street Café in Morristown, New Jersey. There he met Jeff Connerton, who had started a tofu shop in Easton. They joined forces in 1984. "In those days," Gary recalls, "people were still getting a good chuckle when you said the word *tofu*."

Fresh Tofu has certainly benefited from the boom in the natural foods industry, but the extent of its tremendous growth is strictly due to word of mouth from satisfied

(continued)

(continued)

customers. The company does no advertising, instead Gary builds customer loyalty through regular personal contact. Angelica's is one of those customers. "Angelica Kitchen is a very good barometer for us because they use so much tofu and they have very high standards," Gary explains. "When they're happy with our product I know we're doing well. For example, when they said our tofu wasn't firm enough we were able to go back and see what was wrong and get back on track."

Nothing goes into tofu except soybeans, water, and a coagulant, so it's crucial for the manufacturer to stay close to their sources. All the soybeans Fresh Tofu uses come from non-hybridized plants that are organically grown in upstate New York. Unlike larger manufacturers who rely on brokers for their beans, Gary buys directly from growers, developing long-term relationships based on trust.

Fresh Tofu sells about 20,000 pounds a week, primarily in bulk to health food stores, restaurants, and manufacturers of other tofu products in New York, New Jersey, and Pennsylvania. That's a lot of beans—about 44,000 pounds each month. (One pound of dry beans yields about 1.95 pounds of tofu.)

baked tempeh with soy-mustard marinade

YIELD: 4 to 6 servings   COOKING TIME: 35 minutes

This is the version we use for our famous Warm Tempeh Reuben Sandwich. We simply put the sauce on our tempeh and bake it. Please refer to the "Sauces and Marinades" section, pages 200–13 for more marinades.

> 1 pound tempeh, sliced into sandwich-size pieces
> 1¹/₃ cup apple cider or apple juice
> 3 tablespoons shoyu or tamari
> 3 tablespoons prepared mustard, preferably grainy
> 1 teaspoon ground cumin
> 1 teaspoon ground caraway
> 1 clove garlic, minced
> Pinch of cayenne pepper
> ¹/₃ cup olive oil

The Dragon Bowl & Other Basics

❖ Preheat oven to 350°F.

❖ Prepare marinade by whisking all ingredients except tempeh together.

* Lay tempeh in a baking dish large enough to hold all the pieces in a single layer.
* Pour marinade over the tempeh to barely cover.
* Cover the dish and bake for 35 minutes.
* Uncover and bake 5 to 10 minutes longer, or until tempeh is nearly dry.

tofu

YIELD: 3 to 4 servings   COOKING TIME: 8 to 10 minutes

Tofu is a key element in the soy protein base of most vegan diets. At Angelica Kitchen we use it in dozens of ways. It's an absolute mainstay of our cuisine. Here, we offer our recipe for basic quick-simmered tofu, followed by baked, marinated tofu. You can build a meal around either of these variations.

1 pound firm tofu
1 tablespoon peeled, finely chopped fresh ginger
3 tablespoons shoyu or tamari
3 cups water

* Rinse the tofu, pat dry, and cut into $1/2$-inch cubes.
* Combine the tofu with the ginger, shoyu, and water in a 2-quart saucepan and bring to a boil.
* Lower the flame and allow the tofu to simmer gently uncovered for 5 minutes.

How Tofu Is Made

1. The farmer grows, harvests, and delivers the soybeans.
2. The beans are rinsed and washed, then soaked for twelve to fifteen hours (overnight).
3. Next day, the beans are drained and rinsed, then conveyed into a "bean disintegrator," a fancy name for a grinder, and ground up with triple-filtered water (the "rewash" from Step 6). The grind is called "slurry."
4. The slurry is pumped into a steam-injection cooker, which is essentially a very large pressure cooker, and cooked at about 240°F for 4 to 5 minutes.

(continued)

(continued)

5. The cooked slurry is cooled down to below the boiling point and spun in a centrifuge to separate the milk from the pulp, which is known by its Japanese name, *okara*. The milk is pumped to a holding tank.

6. The *okara* is then spun in the centrifuge again; the resulting liquid, called "rewash," is pumped back for use in the bean grinder. The *okara* is used for livestock feed.

7. The soy milk is drawn off into curdling barrels and the precipitating agent is added. At Fresh Tofu they use *nigari*, also known as sea bitterns, which comes in the form of flakes that are dissolved in water.

   The process takes about thirty to forty minutes and this is where the skill comes in. The tofu maker's goal is to create big billowy curds; he or she has to have an eye for the subtle variations that occur in soybeans from one field or farm to the next, from one day or week to the next.

8. Next the whey is drained off and the curds are poured into forming boxes that are lined with a cheesecloth-like fabric. They're pressed for fifteen to twenty minutes. Presto! From soaked beans, in a little over an hour, you have fresh tofu.

9. The large slabs of tofu are then cut into smaller blocks, placed in a water trough, and chilled, at which point they're ready for packaging and refrigeration or to be made into other products.

Tofu makers categorize their product according to firmness. The longer the curd is pressed, the more water is extracted and the firmer it will be. Fresh Tofu likes to make a firm product, which is considered more versatile.

How firm should tofu be? It's a matter of personal preference. If you want to make tofu firmer, press it between plates, the top one weighted; if you want to make it softer, it can be mixed with some liquid in a blender or food processor.

Fresh Tofu produces a "Japanese-style" tofu, meaning it's made with nigari. Chinese-style tofu, which is softer, is made with a different coagulant, calcium chloride. The Japanese style has less calcium, but Gary believes it has better flavor.

The Dragon Bowl
& Other Basics

baked tofu with lemon-rosemary marinade

YIELD: 4 servings   COOKING TIME: 40 to 50 minutes

This is the version used for our famous Tofu Sandwich with Roasted Vegetables and Basil–Walnut Pesto (see page 165). We love the combination of lemon and rosemary. The balsamic vinegar lends a pleasant sweetness to this marinade, which has an amazingly rich flavor with very low fat.

To prepare the tofu for baking, we press it for 20 minutes to firm it up by extracting excess water. Normally, you would buy it in the store firm and cook it as is. But if you like it even firmer and chewier, try taking the extra step of pressing it between two plates with a quart container of liquid on top to weight it down, discarding the water that's squeezed out. For sandwiches, we omit the pressing and the tofu remains softer.

Serving suggestions: Cut baked tofu into cubes and toss into a salad or serve with noodles in Dashi broth (see page 129), garnished with sliced scallions and toasted sesame seeds.

1 pound firm tofu, rinsed, patted dry, and cut into 1/2-inch slices
3 tablespoons of freshly squeezed lemon juice, strained
1 tablespoon balsamic vinegar
2 tablespoons tamari
1/2 teaspoon minced fresh rosemary
Pinch of freshly ground white pepper
1 1/2 tablespoons olive oil

* Preheat oven to 350°F.
* Slice the tofu into thirds horizontally.
* Stack the slices and cut them crosswise to make 12 triangles.
* Place the tofu in a single layer in a baking dish.
* In a bowl, whisk together the remaining ingredients for the marinade.
* Pour the marinade over the tofu.
* Bake for 30 to 40 minutes, or until the tofu is nicely browned and the marinade has been absorbed.

kamut, spelt berries, and wild rice

YIELD: 4 to 6 servings   COOKING TIME: 1 hour

It doesn't get much more "whole grainy" than this! A lively, festive-looking fall dish, it is warm and offers deep colors and a great texture. Among the grains, spelt and kamut are both relatively high in protein.

Serving suggestion: Alongside a salad for a hearty lunch.

Try this: Use as a stuffing for roasted squash.

1/2 cup kamut berries
1/2 cup spelt berries
1/2 cup wild rice
6 cups water
1 teaspoon plus pinch of sea salt
3 tablespoons extra virgin olive oil
1/2 cup finely chopped onion
2 cups finely chopped mushrooms
1/4 cup finely chopped celery
1/4 cup peeled and finely chopped carrots
1 tablespoon chopped fresh herbs such as rosemary, sage, or thyme
2 tablespoons chopped chives

- Rinse the grains in a strainer under cold water.
- Place the grains in a 3-quart pressure cooker with water and 1 teaspoon of salt, bring to pressure, reduce heat to simmer, and cook for 50 minutes.
- While the grains cook, warm the oil in a sauté pan.
- Add all of the vegetables and herbs (except for the chives) plus a pinch of salt.
- Cook gently over low heat until tender, about 30 minutes, stirring occasionally to prevent sticking.
- When the grains are cooked, drain well and toss them in a bowl with the vegetables.
- Season with salt and freshly ground pepper to taste, stir in the chives, and serve.

Alternate cooking method:

- Soak the grains for 8 hours in 1 quart of cold water. Drain and rinse.
- Bring 2 quarts of water to a boil, add the grains and the of salt. Simmer over moderate heat for 1 hour.
- Drain and proceed as above.

The Dragon Bowl
& Other Basics

three-grain pilaf

YIELD: 4 to 6 servings   COOKING TIME: 35 to 40 minutes

In a traditional pilaf, the rice or grain is first sautéed with diced aromatic vegetables (for example, onions, leeks, carrots, celery, scallions) to brown it, then stock or water is added, and the dish is simmered on top of the stove or baked until done. Here is our interpretation of this Near Eastern favorite.

Serving suggestions: This is a wonderfully versatile dish that goes well with dishes like the Curried Chickpea and Vegetable Stew, the layered Autumn Tempeh and Vegetable Stew, and the Moroccan-Style Tagine (pages 171, 172, 176).

1 cup white basmati rice
¹/₂ cup millet
¹/₂ cup quinoa
³/₄ teaspoon sea salt
¹/₂ cup scallions, minced (white
*   and tender green part only)*
2 tablespoons olive oil
3 cups water or vegetable stock

* Preheat oven to 350°F.
* Combine the grains with the salt, scallions, and oil in a heavy-bottomed 2-quart saucepan with a tight-fitting lid. Cook uncovered over a medium flame, stirring constantly, until the grains begin to brown and are fragrant and toasty, about 5 to 7 minutes.
* Add the water and bring to a boil.
* Cover and bake in the oven for 30 minutes.
* Remove from the oven and allow to rest for 5 minutes.
* Fluff with a fork and it's ready to serve.

Appetizers and Condiments

pear-apple chutney

YIELD: 4 cups   COOKING TIME: 1 hour

Chutneys add spark to simple dishes such as rice and lentils. This is one of our favorites. It has a nice fresh ginger flavor but is not overly hot or spicy. It can keep well for up to three weeks in the fridge, tightly covered in a container with minimum air.

Try this: Make a sandwich with Charmoula-marinated tempeh (page 211) and the Pear-Apple Chutney.

> *1 star anise (optional)*
> *4 cloves*
> *2 sticks cinnamon*
> *1 bay leaf*
> *3 cardamom pods*
> *1 piece of cheesecloth, approximately 10 inches square*
> *1 tablespoon olive oil*
> *1 tablespoon peeled, minced ginger*
> *1 cup diced onions*
> *2 cups apple cider*
> *3 tablespoons apple cider vinegar*
> *2 tablespoons maple syrup*
> *1/2 cup currants*
> *3 cups peeled, diced apples*
> *3 cups peeled, diced pears*

❖ Place the star anise, cloves, cinnamon, bay leaf, and cardamon pods in cheesecloth and tie with kitchen twine to form a neat bundle. This is known as a sachet.

❖ Place the olive oil in a heavy 3-quart saucepan over medium heat. Sauté the ginger and onions with a pinch of salt for 8 minutes or until softened.

❖ Add the spice sachet, apple cider, apple cider vinegar, maple syrup, currants, apples, and pears.

❖ Bring to a boil, lower the flame, and simmer uncovered for 1 to 1 1/2 hours or until thickened. Remove and discard the spice sachet. Allow chutney to cool before serving.

Appetizers
& Condiments

hijiki-cucumber salsa

YIELD: 2¹/₂ cups   COOKING TIME: 10 minutes

Hijiki by itself in a bowl with shoyu or tamari, some rice wine vinegar, and a sprinkling of sesame seeds makes a superb salad or even main dish. It is one of the more intense sea vegetables, so a little bit goes a long way. This salsa, with the moderating influence of the cucumbers, the cilantro and the various other seasonings, and just a couple of tablespoons of hijiki, is a delicious way to get accustomed to that flavor.

Try this: Substitute arame for the hijiki; it has a different texture, not as chewy, and a lighter taste of the ocean.

2 tablespoons dried hijiki
1 large or 2 medium cucumbers, peeled, seeded, and finely diced
¹/₄ cup finely sliced scallion
¹/₄ cup cilantro, leaves and stems, firmly packed and finely chopped
1 teaspoon minced garlic
1 large jalapeño pepper, stemmed, seeded, and minced
1 tablespoon ginger, peeled and minced
2 tablespoons brown rice vinegar
2 tablespoons mirin
2 teaspoons sea salt

❖ Bring 1 quart of water to a boil in a 2-quart saucepan and add the hijiki.

❖ Lower the heat and simmer for 10 minutes.

❖ Drain the hijiki in a strainer and run cold water over it until it's thoroughly chilled.

❖ Drain well and toss the remaining ingredients in a bowl and add the hijiki.

❖ Allow the salsa to sit for 5 minutes, adjust seasoning, and serve.

hummus, angelica style

YIELD: 4 cups

COOKING TIME: up to 3 hours
(not including soaking)

Our hummus, visitors from Israel have told us, is the best they've ever had! The key is the freshly prepared ingredients—fresh lemon juice, freshly ground cumin, and so forth.

When Peter first came to work at Angelica, one of the first things he did was eliminate as many of the pre-ground spices as possible, insisting that we grind everything fresh every day. You can do it at home with a coffee grinder, a suribachi, or a mortar and pestle. It does make a huge difference.

Hummus is one of those dishes that allows chefs a lot of leeway to express their individuality. We encourage you to experiment and come up with your own signature version of this Middle Eastern classic. First, you might want to try adjusting the quantities of lemon and garlic. Then you can try adding roasted peppers, roasted garlic, chopped cilantro, toasted whole sesame seeds, ground caraway, or coriander seeds.

Cooking suggestions: If the chickpeas are taking a long time to soften up, add a pinch of baking soda. (The harder the water, the more difficult it is for any kind of beans to soften up.) Pressure cooking is by far the best means to soften chickpeas. We generally pressure cook for 45 minutes, then open up the cooker to check them, and cook for another 15 minutes or so if necessary. If you want the chickpeas to hold some of their shape for a salad, don't pressure cook them for more than about 30 minutes.

> 1 1/2 cups dried chickpeas, sorted
> 6 cups water
> 1/2 cup tahini
> 2/3 cup freshly squeezed lemon juice, strained
> 2 cloves garlic, halved lengthwise
> 1 teaspoon ground cumin
> 3/4 teaspoon sea salt
> Pinch of cayenne pepper
> 3/4 cup water (or reserved chickpea cooking liquid)

* Soak the chickpeas for 8 hours in 6 cups of cold water.
* Drain the chickpeas, place in a 2- to 3- quart saucepan, and cover with fresh water by 2 inches.
* Bring to a boil, lower the heat, cover, and simmer for 2 to 3 hours or until the peas are tender.
* Drain and reserve cooking liquid.

*Appetizers
& Condiments*

* Combine chickpeas, tahini, lemon juice, garlic, cumin, salt, and cayenne in a food processor fitted with a steel blade.
* With the machine running, gradually add the water (or cooking liquid), processing until the mixture is creamy and smooth. If the sides become caked with bits of unpureed chickpeas, stop and scrape them down with a rubber spatula.
* Taste and adjust seasonings.
* Serve with warm pita bread and a few black olives.

Alternate cooking method:

* Place the chickpeas in a 2- to 3-quart pressure cooker with enough water to cover by 1 inch and cook for 45 minutes. Drain, reserve cooking liquid, and proceed with instructions above.

NOTE: $1^1/2$ cups dried, soaked chickpeas yield 3 cups cooked ones. You can substitute canned organic chickpeas; Eden is a recommended brand.

kimchee

YIELD: 2 cups   PREPARATION TIME: 30 minutes

We call this our "faux-chee" because it's a much simpler, quicker recipe than the ubiquitous Korean condiment that's traditionally sealed in large containers, buried in the ground to ferment and dug up as needed. We loved the idea, but . . .

Recently one of our regular customers came back from a business trip to Seoul, during which she dined at some of the city's top restaurants. She had our quick kimchee and enthusiastically told Peter she liked it better than anything she had there. This recipe is incredibly quick and easy to carry out and it yields a truly refreshing, spicy condiment. It can keep up to four days in the refrigerator.

Serving suggestion: This spicy, refreshing pickled cabbage concoction can provide a welcome accent to most simply prepared grains and noodles. We've found it goes particularly well with the Baked Sweet Ginger Tofu and Rice, page 213, and also as a topping for the Oden Stew, page 175.

Try this: Toss all of the ingredients together and place them in an oriental salad press. (Note: An oriental salad press is a plastic container with a screw-top that presses down, causing the vegetables to yield a brine and keeping them submerged in that brine.) Press for one hour before serving.

1 head Napa cabbage, approximately 1 pound
1 whole scallion, finely sliced

(continued)

(continued)

    1¹/₂ *teaspoons sea salt*
    1 *teaspoon peeled, minced ginger*
    1 *teaspoon minced garlic*
    ¹/₂ *teaspoon cayenne pepper*
    2 *tablespoons rice vinegar*
    1 *tablespoon mirin*

❖ Rinse the cabbage and remove bruised or discolored outer leaves.

❖ Quarter the cabbage lengthwise and remove the core, then slice it crosswise into ¹/₄-inch strips.

❖ Toss the cabbage with scallions and sea salt in a medium-sized mixing bowl. Knead and press the cabbage with your hands to work in the salt.

❖ Add the ginger, garlic, cayenne pepper, rice vinegar, and mirin. Mix well and allow to rest for at least 10 to 15 minutes before serving.

lemon-date chutney

YIELD: 6 cups   COOKING TIME: 45 minutes

This is a sweeter, thicker, more intensely flavored chutney than the Pear-Apple Chutney. We serve this ambrosia with stews, for example the Curried Chickpea and Vegetable Stew (page 171), over basmati rice. It's also great as a dip with toasted chapati or pita wedges that are lightly brushed with olive oil and baked in the oven till crisp.

Try this: Use it as a dipping sauce for cubes of tempeh baked in Charmoula. You get a nice contrast of the sweet and spicy flavors.

    2 *strips lemon peel*
    1 *bay leaf*
    1 *(2-inch) piece cinnamon stick*
    4 *whole cloves*
    4 *whole cardamom pods*
    2 *pinches sea salt*
    1 *piece of cheesecloth, approximately 10 inches square*
    1 *tablespoon olive oil*
    2 *cups diced onions*
    2 *tablespoons peeled, minced ginger*
    1 *small jalapeño pepper, stemmed, seeded, and minced*
    3 *cups dates, pitted and finely chopped*
    2 *cups water*
    2 *cups apple cider*
    ¹/₂ *cup freshly squeezed lemon juice, strained*

Appetizers
& Condiments

❖ Combine the lemon peel, bay leaf, cinnamon stick, cloves, cardamom pods, and a pinch of the sea salt in the cheesecloth and tie closed with kitchen twine into a neat bundle.

❖ Place the olive oil in a heavy-bottomed 3-quart saucepan, and sauté the onions, ginger, and jalapeño pepper with a pinch of sea salt for 8 to 10 minutes. Add the dates, water, apple cider, fresh lemon juice, and cheesecloth bundle; bring to a boil over high heat. Lower heat and simmer for 1 hour or until thickened, stirring occasionally to prevent sticking.

lentil-walnut pâté

YIELD: 4 cups   COOKING TIME: 30 minutes

This pâté is an Angelica Kitchen signature dish. It is also multicultural, with a hint of Japan from the umeboshi and miso and a Mediterranean influence from the olive oil. (Lentils, by the way, are found across the globe—you could call them a "world food.")

Always make plenty of this item. It is an excellent way to introduce the possibilities of vegan haute cuisine. It pleases all kinds of palates, vegetarians and non-vegetarians alike. Serve it at parties; it's guaranteed to impress your guests.

Note: Walnuts come whole, in halves, or as "syrupers," which means coarsely chopped. You can use any of the three for this recipe but the syrupers are definitely more convenient. Always be sure the nuts are fresh. Rancidity, of course, ruins the recipe, so be sure to taste the nuts before proceeding with the recipe.

You can opt to mash the pâté in a mortar or suribachi instead of using a food processor, in which case it will have a rougher, more rustic consistency.

Umeboshi paste is salty and sour, so in a pinch you could substitute some red wine vinegar mixed with salt or some pickled vegetables.

Try this: Spread pâté on slices of sourdough bread, broil for about one to two minutes, and serve warm. Substitute pecans for the walnuts.

Serving suggestions: Serve in small scoops on lettuce leaves, garnished with sliced scallions, accompanied by thinly sliced baguettes, chips, or crackers. It can also be spread on bread and topped with roasted vegetables and lettuce to make a sandwich.

²/₃ cup dried green lentils, sorted
1 large bay leaf
2 cups walnuts
1 tablespoon extra virgin olive oil
3 cups diced onions

(continued)

113

(continued)

> 1 tablespoon minced garlic
> 1 tablespoon mirin
> 1 tablespoon plus 1 teaspoon umeboshi paste
> 1¹/₂ tablespoons barley miso
> 1 tablespoon dried basil

* Preheat the oven to 350°F.
* Rinse lentils in strainer under cold running water.
* Place lentils in a 2-quart saucepan with bay leaf and enough water to cover by 2 inches.
* Bring to a boil. Lower heat, cover and simmer until the lentils are tender, about 30 to 40 minutes.
* Meanwhile, roast the walnuts on a cookie sheet until they turn a shade darker, about 6 to 8 minutes.
* Pour the nuts into a colander and let them cool.
* Drain the lentils. (You may want to reserve the cooking liquid for soup or stock.)
* Optional: Rub the walnuts together between the palms of your hands to remove the skins. Set aside. Walnut skins will impart a slightly bitter taste.
* Sauté the onions and garlic in olive oil in an 8-inch skillet over a medium flame, stirring frequently, until lightly browned, about 10 to 15 minutes.
* Combine the walnuts, lentils, onion mixture, and the remaining ingredients in a food processor fitted with a steel blade and puree until smooth.
* Spoon into a bowl and refrigerate until cool.
* The pâté will keep 3 to 5 days refrigerated in a tightly sealed container.

mushroom phyllo turnovers

YIELD: 2 dozen turnovers   **COOKING TIME:** 1 hour

These turnovers are party finger food, a delicious pass-around appetizer that is enshrined in the Angelica Hall of Fame. It is one of the most popular dishes that ever appeared on the menu, but eventually we had to retire it because we couldn't make it cost effective. It is a genuine gourmet health treat. The turnovers can be refrigerated for up to a day or frozen for up to three months before baking.

*Appetizers
& Condiments*

1 tablespoon extra virgin olive oil
¹/₂ pound mushrooms, finely chopped
1 onion, finely chopped
3 cloves garlic, minced
¹/₂ tablespoon fresh sage, minced
³/₄ pound fresh spinach, stemmed and chopped fine
1 tablespoon umeboshi paste
*1 tablespoon chickpea miso (any other light miso is an acceptable
    substitute)*
¹/₂ tablespoon balsamic vinegar
¹/₂ tablespoon freshly squeezed lemon juice, strained
Pinch of freshly ground black pepper
³/₄ pound firm tofu, crumbled
¹/₂ pound phyllo sheets
Vegetable oil for brushing phyllo

NOTE: Phyllo comes in sheets that are about 12 inches square.

❖ Preheat the oven to 400°F.

❖ Place the olive oil in a 10- to 12-inch sauté pan over medium heat.
Sauté the mushrooms, onion, garlic, and sage in olive oil until
softened, about 10 minutes.

❖ Add spinach and cook covered until tender, about 1 to 2 minutes.

❖ Add umeboshi paste, miso, balsamic vinegar, lemon juice, pepper,
and tofu.

❖ Simmer until heated through.

❖ Pour mixture into a bowl and cool.

❖ Cut the phyllo sheets in half lengthwise to make rectangles about
12 inches wide by 6 inches high.

❖ Brush the top of each phyllo rectangle lightly with vegetable oil, then
fold in half lengthwise, and brush the top with oil again.

❖ Place 1 tablespoon filling at the bottom corner (either right or left) of
the folded rectangle of phyllo. Fold the phyllo in the same manner as
you would fold a flag, end over end to make triangular shapes, until
you have a triangle-shaped multi-layered turnover.

❖ Repeat the procedure until you have 2 dozen turnovers.

❖ Brush the turnovers with oil, place them on a cookie sheet close
together but not touching, and bake in the oven for about 15 minutes
or until crisp and lightly browned.

mushroom glaze

YIELD: approximately 1 cup   COOKING TIME: 1 hour, 20 minutes

We used to present the turnovers with this sauce, which we called a glaze (a fancy word for a clear sauce) spread across the plate underneath. The turnovers are great served solo but if you're feeling a little ambitious, try creating this sauce and serving it in a small bowl on the side for dipping. Once you have tasted this sauce, you will imagine many uses for its simple, luscious flavors.

> 2 pounds button mushrooms, quartered (about 10 cups)
> 1 onion, peeled and chopped
> 4 cloves garlic
> 6 tablespoons olive oil
> 1/2 teaspoon sea salt plus additional for seasoning
> 4 cups water
> 3 or 4 sprigs thyme
> 4 tablespoons minced fresh parsley
> Sea salt and freshly ground black pepper

❖ Preheat the oven to 400°F.

❖ Toss the mushrooms with onions, garlic, 2 tablespoons of oil, and the sea salt in a large mixing bowl.

❖ Spread mushrooms evenly over 2 cookie sheets and roast them in the oven for 25 to 30 minutes or until they are deep brown and caramelized.

❖ Scrape the vegetables into a 3-quart saucepan. Add 4 cups of water, thyme, and parsley and bring to a boil over high heat. Reduce the flame to low. Simmer for 40 minutes, uncovered.

❖ Place a strainer over a 2-quart saucepan. Pour the mushroom-vegetable mixture into the strainer and press hard with a wooden spoon to extract as much broth as possible. Discard the vegetables.

❖ Cook the broth over high heat until it is reduced to 1 cup. (At this point you may freeze the glaze for up to 3 months, without oil. When ready to use, thaw and continue with recipe.)

❖ Line a strainer with a layer of damp cheesecloth. Strain the mushroom reduction into a small mixing bowl and whisk in the remaining oil.

❖ Season with additional sea salt and freshly ground black pepper to taste.

NOTE: The dip will keep refrigerated for up to 3 days in a tightly sealed container.

Washing Mushrooms

Put the mushrooms in a colander and rinse quickly under cold running water. Immediately pat dry with a clean towel. If there's not much dirt, just shake them well without wetting them. The soil that sometimes clings to organically grown cultivated mushrooms is generally very clean and there's no need to worry if traces of it go into the cooking pot.

Appetizers & Condiments

basil–walnut pesto

YIELD: 4 cups   COOKING TIME: 15 minutes

Since it doesn't rely on either pine nuts or Parmesan cheese, our pesto is lighter than the traditional Genovese version but it still has a classic flavor. As usual, be sure to start with top quality fresh garlic, fresh lemon juice, and the finest extra virgin olive oil, assuring yourself a good result.

Serving suggestions: This pesto can be used in a cold pasta salad with sliced fresh tomatoes at the height of their season. It works well as a sandwich spread or on mashed potatoes. You can also put it on hot pasta if you like. In that case, thin it with a little of the pasta cooking water before mixing it in.

Try this: Substitute toasted almonds or pumpkin seeds for the walnuts.

> $1^1/_2$ cups walnuts
> 2 cups firmly packed fresh basil leaves
> 2 cups firmly packed fresh parsley
> 2 cloves garlic, halved lengthwise
> 3 tablespoons freshly squeezed lemon juice, strained
> $^1/_2$ cup extra virgin olive oil
> $1^1/_4$ cup olive oil
> Sea salt and freshly ground black pepper

* Preheat oven to 350°F.
* Spread the walnuts on a cookie sheet and toast in the oven for 8 minutes.
* Remove the walnuts to a strainer and allow to cool.
* Wash basil and parsley leaves. Spin dry.
* Rub the walnuts against the side of the strainer and shake to remove as much bitter skin as possible.
* Place the walnuts into the bowl of a food processor fitted with a steel blade and pulse to a coarse meal.
* Add the basil, parsley, garlic, and lemon juice and process until smooth.
* With the motor running, add the oils in a thin steady stream.
* Season with salt and pepper to taste and pulse to combine.

quick crispy pickled vegetables

YIELD: 8 cups   COOKING TIME: 15 minutes   REST TIME: 12 hours

When it's harvest time and you have an excess of fresh vegetables, pickling is a delightful way to preserve them. Here is a simple, quick way to do it. (We call it quick because it only takes overnight as opposed to other pickling recipes that may take days or weeks.)

Pickles are a worldwide condiment that adds zest and variety to any meal, stimulates the appetite and aids digestion. This recipe is what you get with our Pickle Plate at the restaurant. We always include garlic kelp, a product of our friends at Maine Sea Coast Vegetables. You can add any vegetable that has good fiber content, including fiddlehead ferns, cucumbers, pink radishes, daikon, corn off the cob, okra, ramps—even mushrooms. Don't try asparagus, though, because it turns mealy.

For the brine:
1 quart water
⅓ cup brown rice vinegar
3 tablespoons kosher salt
1 tablespoon minced garlic
1 sprig dill
Pinch of cayenne pepper

2 quarts mixed vegetables such as cauliflower, carrots, celery, string beans, red onions, green cabbage, summer squash, cut in bite-size pieces

❖ Combine the ingredients for the brine in a non-reactive 3-quart stainless steel saucepan.

❖ Bring to a boil, lower the flame, and simmer for 2 to 3 minutes.

❖ Place the vegetables in a glass jar just large enough to hold the vegetables.

❖ Allow the brine to cool, then pour it into the jar with the vegetables, cover, and refrigerate overnight.

❖ Pickles are ready after 12 hours. Keep refrigerated.

NOTE: These pickles will keep for 3 to 4 weeks.

*Appetizers
& Condiments*

The Angelica Pickle Plate: Quick Crispy Pickled Vegetables, Spiced Beets, and Garlic Kelp Pickles (from Maine Coast Sea Vegetables).

pumpkin pâté

YIELD: 3 cups   COOKING TIME: 1 hour

Butternut squash also works well for this recipe but is generally only available in fall and winter. Kabocha is another tasty squash that can be had year round in most places; you can also use buttercup or red kuri.

Helpful hint: Steam the whole squash for a couple of minutes to soften up the skin and make it easier to peel. Winter squash, particularly kabocha, has a fairly hard skin. As an alternative, you can bake the squash, which intensifies its flavor. Coat the outside with some oil, put it in a pan with a little water, and bake in a 350°F oven until soft—about forty-five minutes to an hour.

Save the kabocha peels and toss them in with your onions, celery, thyme, garlic, and so forth when you make vegetable stock. They're a great addition.

Chopped fresh sage adds a distinctive aroma. It marries perfectly with the onions; they're two strong flavors that in this case balance and compliment each other. Sage, by the way, is reputed to banish neurotic house guests and other unwanted spirits.

Try this: Substitute walnuts, pumpkin seeds, or pecans for the sunflower seeds. Substitute sweet potato or steamed carrot for the pumpkin.

1/2 cup sun-dried tomatoes, dry packed
3/4 pound onions, peeled and chopped
1 tablespoon minced garlic
1/4 cup olive oil
1/2 teaspoon sea salt plus additional for seasoning
2 tablespoons finely chopped fresh sage
1 pound winter squash, peeled, seeded, and chopped into 1-inch pieces
1/2 cup sunflower seeds
Sea salt and freshly ground black pepper

❖ Preheat the oven to 350°F.

❖ Bring 2 cups of water to a boil in a small (1-quart) saucepan. Add the sun-dried tomatoes, remove from the heat, and set aside to swell for about 20 minutes.

❖ Sauté the onions and garlic in oil over medium heat with 1/2 teaspoon of salt for 8 to 10 minutes.

❖ Reduce the heat to low. Add the sage and continue to cook for 15 to 20 minutes over low heat, stirring occasionally. Do not allow to brown.

❖ Steam the pumpkin squash until tender, about 15 minutes.

❖ Place the sunflower seeds on a cookie sheet and toast in the oven for 10 minutes.

Appetizers
& Condiments

* Allow the seeds to cool, then grind to a powder—in a clean electric coffee grinder if possible. (It can also be done by hand in a suribachi.)
* Drain the tomatoes.
* Combine all the ingredients in a food processor fitted with a steel blade and puree. Season with salt and pepper to taste.
* Serve on thinly sliced toasted baguettes.

red onion and beet marmalade

YIELD: 3 cups   COOKING TIME: 1¹/₂ hours

This is a versatile "picnicky" kind of relish that, with its maple syrup, vinegar, and onions, is sweet, sour, and savory. It is an absolutely gorgeous, dazzling deep bright red and adds a brilliant dash of color to liven up any presentation. It can keep about five to seven days properly covered and refrigerated.

Serving suggestions: Try it on a croquette or with a marinated tofu sandwich. It also goes well with pan-fried seitan or tempeh or as a topping for a salad of leafy and/or bitter greens such as dandelion, arugula, watercress, or chicory. The sweet-and-sour flavor helps counter any bitterness in those fresh greens.

> 2 tablespoons olive oil
> 2 cups finely chopped red onion
> 2 tablespoons maple syrup
> 1 tablespoon rice vinegar
> ¹/₂ cup freshly squeezed orange juice, strained
> 2 tablespoons freshly squeezed lemon juice, strained
> ¹/₂ teaspoon cayenne pepper (optional)
> 1 pound beets (mixed red and gold)
> Sea salt and freshly ground black pepper

* Place the oil in an 8-inch skillet over medium heat. Sweat the onions for 5 to 7 minutes, stirring. (Do not let them brown.)
* Add maple syrup, rice vinegar, orange juice, lemon juice, and cayenne pepper, bring to a boil, lower heat, and cook gently for 10 to 15 minutes more.
* While the onions cook, pressure-cook the beets for 10 minutes. (Alternately, start cooking the beets earlier in boiling water, and let them cook for 40 to 50 minutes or until tender.)
* Cool the beets in cold water and peel.
* Cube the beets and combine them with the onion mixture in a food processor.
* Pulse several times to blend. Season with salt and pepper to taste.

ruby kraut

YIELD: 10 cups

PREPARATION TIME: 45 minutes
REST TIME: 3 to 5 days

This recipe calls for one important piece of equipment not necessarily found in every home kitchen: a 1-gallon glazed ceramic crock. Not to fear, though, you can also make it in a glass jar.

It's important to use salt that has no additives and no off flavors. We used to use sea salt but it didn't seem to work as well as kosher salt, which we find simply makes the best kraut.

Ruby kraut is a stunning magenta color; as the cabbage ferments, its color turns brighter and brighter due to the lactic acid that develops. It's also very good for you because of beneficial bacteria from fermentation.

5 pounds red cabbage, tough outer leaves removed and rinsed
3 level tablespoons kosher salt
1 (3-gallon) glazed ceramic crock

❖ Your vessel of choice MUST be sterilized. Wash it with boiling water or run it through a dishwasher.

❖ Quarter, core, and finely slice the cabbage.

❖ Toss the cabbage with the salt in a large bowl.

❖ Pack it into the crock and pound it with the end of a wooden rolling pin or a baseball bat for a few minutes to bruise it. This is not gratuitous violence. It releases the cabbage juice by breaking down its fiber and jumpstarts the fermentation process.

❖ Place a plate or other flat object that is close to diameter of the crock on top of cabbage.

❖ Cover the crock with a clean plastic bag. Place a clean weight, such as a 1-gallon jar filled with water or a couple of bricks, on top of the plastic bag.

❖ Leave the cabbage to ferment at 70–75°F for 3 to 5 days. Make sure the cabbage is always submerged in the brine that forms.

❖ After the third day, taste the kraut. It should have a pleasing sour taste and a crunchy texture. It should not taste salty; if it does, allow the kraut to ferment another day or two.

❖ Transfer the kraut to a sterilized glass or heavy plastic container with a tight-fitting lid.

NOTE: The kraut will keep for 8 to 10 days refrigerated.

Appetizers
& Condiments

BILL KING, KRAUT GURU

At Angelica Kitchen we feel blessed to have friends like Bill King. An internationally renowned sculptor and refreshingly down-to-earth fellow with a wry sense of humor, Bill is also our kraut guru. He started coming to the restaurant in the late 1980s and soon became a regular, particularly after an accident in 1990 landed him in the New York Eye and Ear Infirmary a couple blocks away. While he was recuperating, his sweetie Connie Fox would come to Angelica Kitchen to procure sustenance for the bedridden Bill.

I first met Bill on the occasion of a dinner at the home of Scott Chaskey and Megan Boyd, Connie's daughter. It was love at first sight. He gave me some of his homemade sauerkraut as a token of thanks for "saving his life." (Who knows if he would have survived that hospital food . . .) As soon as I tasted that kraut, I knew it was something special—simple, delicious, beautiful, and fun. When I asked him if he would make some for the restaurant, he said it was the best commission he'd ever had. This from a man who's won the Louise Nevelson Lifetime Achievement Award, had sculpture on the lawn of the White House, and is former president of the American Academy of Design.

Kraut was a staple of Bill's macrobiotic diet in the 1980s and when he got tired of paying retail prices for it, he started making his own, first from green cabbage and later from the red, which was equally tasty but with even more aesthetic appeal. Bill's recipe calls for chopping the cabbage, putting it in a large ceramic crock, and then mashing it down with the butt end of a two-by-four. As he says, "You have to abuse it."

Bill's sculptures of marionette-like human figures, which mirror his own tall, angular physique, are on display all over New York, the United States, and the world. There is a sixty-foot trio of them at the Orlando Airport in his native Florida. There are also two at Angelica Kitchen. The one resting on top of the vestibule at Angelica Kitchen was made specifically for that spot. It has one arm extended, offering an olive branch to the people who are waiting for tables—typical of Bill's sensitivity, wit, and charm. See one of Bill's sculptures "La Vendeuse" in the photo on page 197.

sea vegetable topping

YIELD: approximately 3 cups   COOKING TIME: 1¹/₂ hours

We're calling this a topping because we use it on green salads, but it's also a key ingredient inside our Sam or I Sandwich. It's versatile, fun, tasty, and colorful; it adds nutrition and flavor to all kinds of dishes. This recipe should simply serve to stimulate your imagination for the many possible uses of sea vegetables, some of the most beneficial, deserving, and versatile foods on the planet.

Serving suggestions: Atop any salad or included in just about any sandwich; as an accompaniment to any grain; combined with mashed tofu to make a filling for a tart; mixed with fresh corn off the cob or fresh chopped green beans to make a salad. You can stir in chopped fresh peppers, scallions, olive oil, and lemon and serve it as an appetizer, side dish, or main course. And the list goes on . . .

¹/₂ cup dried arame
¹/₂ cup dried hijiki
¹/₂ tablespoon olive oil
2 tablespoons sliced scallions
1¹/₂ tablespoons freshly squeezed lemon juice, strained
3 tablespoons apple cider
¹/₄ teaspoon salt
Pinch of cayenne pepper

❖ Place the sea vegetables in a medium-size bowl with water to cover by 3 inches and soak until plumped, about 1 hour.

❖ Drain and rinse.

❖ Place the oil in a sauté pan over low heat and sauté the sea vegetables for 15 minutes.

❖ Add the remaining ingredients plus enough water to barely cover.

❖ Cook over medium heat until barely moist.

Appetizers
& Condiments

sun-dried tomato–walnut tapenade

YIELD: 3 cups   COOKING TIME: 30 minutes

This recipe was devised for the Taste of the Nation event, put on by Share Our Strength to help raise money to feed the hungry. The event was a roaring success and so was the tapenade.

Serving suggestions: For appetizers: grill or pan-sauté mini-polenta triangles until golden brown, serve them topped with tapenade; make crostini by toasting sourdough bread slices and spread tapenade on top; use as a spread or dip for celery or endive. Mix with cold pasta for a salad; toss with hot pasta and steamed vegetables. Use as a sandwich spread with marinated tempeh or tofu and sprouts or lettuce.

1 quart water
2 cups sun-dried tomatoes
$^1/_4$ cup walnuts, toasted and finely chopped
1 clove garlic, crushed
1 tablespoon salt-packed capers, rinsed well (capers cured in brine
    may be substituted; drain them)
2 teaspoons fresh tarragon, leaves only, chopped
3 tablespoons balsamic vinegar
$^1/_2$ teaspoon finely grated orange zest
$^3/_4$ teaspoon sea salt
3 tablespoons mirin
Freshly ground black pepper
1 tablespoon extra virgin olive oil

❖ Preheat oven to 350°F.

❖ Bring 1 quart of water to a boil in a 2-quart saucepan.

❖ Add the tomatoes, remove from the heat, and set aside covered for up to 20 minutes or until tomatoes are soft.

❖ While the tomatoes are soaking, spread the walnuts on a cookie sheet and toast in the oven for 8 minutes. Let them cool.

❖ Drain the tomatoes and discard the cooking water.

❖ Combine all ingredients in a food processor along with 2 tablespoons water and pulse to form a rough paste, somewhere between chunky and smooth.

black olive tapenade

YIELD: 2 cups   PREPARATION TIME: 30 minutes

This is our vegan version of the classic Nicoise dish (the Nicoise tapenade uses anchovies), with a few interesting twists, namely using rice wine instead of brandy or cognac, which is what they would use in France, and adding lemon zest. It is intensely flavored—a little bit goes a long way—and works well in any number of variations. Try adding capers, green olives, or artichoke hearts. You can vary the texture of your tapenade, leaving it in the processor for less time for a chunkier result. It keeps well up to two weeks, especially if you top off its storage container with some olive oil.

Serving suggestions: For an hors d'oeuvre, spread the tapenade on thin slices of daikon sprinkled with parsley; on toasted bread topped with sun-dried tomatoes or sprouts; or simply serve it as a dip for crudités. You can also serve it with roasted vegetables or in a sandwich with Baked Tofu with Lemon-Rosemary Marinade (page 105). It can double as a pasta sauce if you add extra olive oil and toss a small amount of it with the pasta, thinning it with a bit of the cooking water. Thinned with additional lemon juice and olive oil, it can be used as a salad dressing. You can even swirl it into mashed potatoes.

How's that for versatility?

Note: If you buy pitted olives it's very important to check them for pits because every so often there is one that still has a pit. The best way is to process the olives in the food processor briefly and listen for that telltale clicking or clacking sound.

Try this: At the restaurant we frequently add capers to this recipe. Our favorites are the ones that come salt-packed from Gaeta Imports; they need to be soaked in fresh water for 10 minutes to remove excess salt. For a more assertive tapenade, try adding 1 tablespoon of capers.

> *1 cup finely chopped onions*
> *3 tablespoons finely chopped garlic*
> *1 tablespoon finely chopped fresh thyme (leaves only)*
> *3 tablespoons extra virgin olive oil*
> *Pinch of sea salt*
> *1/4 teaspoon cayenne pepper*
> *2 tablespoons mirin*
> *2 tablespoons freshly squeezed lemon juice, strained*
> *1 teaspoon minced lemon zest*
> *2 cups Kalamata olives, pitted*

❖ Combine the onions, garlic, thyme, and olive oil in an 8-inch skillet, add a pinch of sea salt, and cook gently over a medium flame until the onions are soft and fragrant, about 8 minutes.

Appetizers
& Condiments

- Add the cayenne, mirin, lemon juice, and lemon zest and simmer for 2 minutes.
- Combine the onion mixture with the olives in a food processor fitted with a steel blade. Puree until smooth.

JOHN FUSCO, GAETA IMPORTS

John Fusco, owner of Gaeta Imports, Angelica Kitchen's purveyor of olive oil for close to ten years, is one of my favorite entrepreneurs. He's a dynamic guy who runs his business with enthusiasm and care. Since Italy and the United States don't share organic certification standards, we must rely on the integrity of our supplier. We use John's products with confidence and pride because his high standards are right in line with the restaurant's.

Of the oil we use, olive oil's influence is the greatest. It is a source of healthy fat, and it imparts a luscious consistency and flavor to foods, particularly the top grade extra virgin, which has 1 percent or less acidity.

Gaeta Imports, which John founded in 1985, also supplies Angelica's with light olive oil, balsamic vinegar, capers, and olives. It is an unusual enterprise not only because of its high standards, but also because it's a special kind of family business: The olive oil is produced by John's relatives using the time-honored, chemical-free methods of their ancestors from olives grown in their own orchards situated in Gaeta, a town on the coast of Italy between Rome and Naples. These orchards are world famous for their superior olives. In 1921, John's grandfather immigrated from Italy and started a grocery store in lower Manhattan. He kept the family connection alive and now John carries on the tradition.

tofu sour cream

YIELD: 2¹/₂ to 3 cups   PREPARATION TIME: 15 minutes

Here is another extremely versatile, all-purpose condiment. This is the type of recipe that's been around the vegetarian community for a long time, but it really is only as good as your fresh ingredients and your execution and interpretation of it.

Try this: You can create a number of interesting variations by adding 1¹/₂ tablespoons of a fresh herb such as dill, cilantro, basil, mint, or tarragon—or even a mix of equal parts mint and cilantro. Try tossing some jalapeño peppers with olive oil and a few garlic cloves, roast them in the oven, chop them, and add them to the tofu cream. Or simply mix in some roasted garlic. You can also make "faux aioli" by mixing saffron, roasted garlic, cayenne, and lemon juice with the tofu, then drizzling in some oil as you process the mixture.

Serving suggestions: Use it as a dip for raw vegetables or toss it with freshly sliced cucumbers and serve it as a vegetarian raita. We use dollops of it on top of crispy phyllo turnovers.

Note: The food processor is an important piece of equipment to achieve the right consistency here. Be sure to blend the tofu mixture very well so it's totally smooth. After a few years of frequent use, your processor blade will become dull, so don't forget to replace it. A sharp new blade makes a big difference.

> 1 pound firm tofu, rinsed and patted dry
> ¹/₄ cup freshly squeezed lemon juice, strained
> ¹/₃ cup olive oil
> 1¹/₂ tablespoons freshly chopped herbs (optional)
> 4 teaspoons rice vinegar
> 1¹/₂ teaspoons sea salt
> ¹/₄ teaspoon white pepper

❖ Combine ingredients in a food processor fitted with a steel blade and process until creamy.

*Appetizers
& Condiments*

Soups

BASIC BROTHS AND STOCKS

Note: With the exception of the Miso Soup and the Creamy Watercress, Leek, and Potato Soup, any of the following soups can be kept in an airtight container in the refrigerator for up to three days or frozen for up to three months.

angelica-style dashi

YIELD: 4 to 6 servings   COOKING TIME: 1 hour

Dashi is the traditional vegetable stock made from shoyu, kombu, shiitake mushrooms, and ginger root that is the basis for much of Japanese cuisine. There are two classic versions: one is kombu-dashi; the other has dried bonito (tuna) flakes. Our version—a delightful, energizing, no-fat pick-me-up—is enlivened with mirin and brown rice vinegar. (Treat yourself by paying a visit to the Asian markets where you live and stocking up on Japanese ingredients.)

Serving suggestions: Generally, we serve dashi hot as a broth for soba or udon noodles. It can also be thickened by boiling it down and used as a base for sauces. In the hot summer months, try serving it chilled.

> 2 quarts cold water
> 1 (4- to 5-inch) piece dried kombu
> 2 cups dried shiitake mushrooms
> 6 tablespoons brown rice vinegar
> $^1/_2$ cup mirin
> $^3/_4$ cup shoyu or tamari
> $^1/_4$ cup ginger juice

* Combine 2 quarts water and kombu in a 3-quart saucepan and bring to a boil.
* Remove the kombu and save it for another use such as cooking beans. (It will keep, wrapped in plastic in the refrigerator, for up to 2 days.)
* Add the mushrooms, reduce the heat to low, and simmer gently uncovered for 1 hour.
* Stir in the remaining ingredients.
* Strain the broth, reserving the mushrooms for another use. (Use them sliced to garnish a bowl of noodles or simply toss them into your vegetable soup.)

gingered root-vegetable consommé

YIELD: 3 quarts   COOKING TIME: 2¹/2 to 3 hours

This invigorating consommé is made in three stages. First vegetables are roasted in the oven. Second, the roasted vegetables are simmered in water and strained. Finally, fresh vegetables, ginger, and herbs are added to the roasted vegetable stock, and it is simmered and strained to create a richly flavored consommé. The consommé can be served as is or you can simmer any number of vegetables, including diced carrots, celery, or parsnips, until tender. Snipped chives or minced parsley added just before serving add a fresh herbal accent.

For the roasted vegetable stock:
1 pound parsnip
2 pounds carrots
1 pound burdock
2 pounds onions
2 heads garlic
2 tablespoons olive oil
4 quarts water

❖ Preheat the oven to 425°F.

❖ Peel parsnip and carrots, scrub burdock. Cut into 1-inch chunks.

❖ Peel and roughly chop the onions. Separate the garlic into cloves, leaving the skin intact.

❖ Toss the vegetables with the oil in a bowl. Place them on a cookie sheet and roast for 30 minutes, stirring from time to time.

❖ Combine the roasted vegetables with 4 quarts cold water in an 8-quart stock pot.

❖ Bring to a boil, lower flame, and gently simmer for 1 hour.

❖ Strain the stock into a bowl. Wash the pot and return the stock to it.

For the consommé:
1 head garlic, sliced in half horizontally
4 ounces fresh ginger root
2 pounds carrots, peeled and finely diced
2 pounds onions, peeled and finely diced
2 stalks celery, finely diced
2 sprigs parsley
4 sprigs fresh thyme
3 quarts roasted vegetable stock
2 quarts cold water
Soy sauce

To Make Ginger Juice

• Line a plate with a 10-inch square piece of cheesecloth.

• Rinse a 3- to 4-inch piece of fresh, plump ginger root and grate on the fine side of a box grater (or use an oriental ginger grater) onto the plate.

• Gather the corners of the cheesecloth together and twist into a tight bundle.

• Squeeze the bundle to extract the juice, allowing it to run into a cup.

Soups

* Separate the garlic into cloves, leaving the skins intact.
* Peel and slice the ginger into thin rounds.
* Combine the vegetables, ginger, parsley, and thyme with the roasted vegetable stock in a pot. Add 2 quarts cold water and bring to a boil.
* Lower flame and simmer uncovered for 1 to 1^1/$_2$ hours or until the stock has reduced to 3 quarts.
* Line a sieve with 2 layers of damp cheesecloth and strain the stock into a clean container.
* Add salt or soy sauce to taste.

kombu vegetable bouillon

YIELD: 2 quarts   COOKING TIME: 1^1/$_2$ hours

This deeply comforting broth is served on its own before dinner to help calm the soul and stimulate the appetite. Sipping a cup of Kombu bouillon is a beautiful segue from the hustle and bustle of your busy day—a sure signal that it's time to sit down, relax, and enjoy a meal. As with the other broths, it can double as a base for sauces.

> 1^1/$_2$ cups peeled, chopped onions
> 1 large carrot, sliced into ^{1}/$_2$-inch-thick rounds
> 1 cup chopped celery (1 or 2 stalks with leaves)
> ^{1}/$_2$ cup peeled, diced parsnips
> 2 cloves garlic
> 2 slices fresh ginger, each about the size of a quarter
> 1 sprig fresh thyme
> 2 leaves fresh sage
> 1 (3-inch) piece dried kombu
> 8 cups water

* Combine all of the ingredients with 8 cups of water in a 4-quart soup pot and bring to a boil.
* Adjust the flame as low as possible and simmer covered for 1^1/$_2$ hours.
* Strain the broth into a clean container.

SUGGESTION: The vegetables can be pureed and added to a soup (but be sure to discard the thyme stems and kombu).

chickpea-garlic soup with rosemary and olive oil

YIELD: 4 to 6 servings　　　　　　　COOKING TIME: 1 hour

Here is a recipe that is as simple to make as it is delicious. Some people glance at this recipe and envision liquid hummus, dense and heavy. Wrong! This soup is light, lemony, and smooth. The combination of fresh herbs and mellow garlic flavor give it an irresistible flavor. As you may recall from the mashed potato recipe in the previous chapter, the key to a pleasantly mild garlic flavor is to carefully peel the cloves and leave them whole.

Note: This version calls for $1/4$ cup lemon juice, but you can vary the amount according to taste.

> *2 cups dried chickpeas, sorted, soaked overnight*
> *6 cups water*
> *1 stalk celery*
> *1 bay leaf*
> *1 branch fresh rosemary*
> *3 to 4 fresh sage leaves*
> *$1/4$ cup extra virgin olive oil*
> *2 cups diced onions*
> *$1/4$ cup garlic cloves*
> *$1/4$ cup freshly squeezed lemon juice, strained*
> *Sea salt and freshly ground black pepper*

- Rinse chickpeas and combine them in a 3-quart pressure cooker with 6 cups of water, celery, bay leaf, rosemary, and sage.
- Bring to full pressure, lower heat, and cook for 45 minutes.
- Meanwhile, warm the olive oil in a heavy 3-quart saucepan over low heat.
- Stir in onions and garlic; continue to cook over the lowest possible heat, stirring from time to time, until the chickpeas are done, up to 40 minutes.
- When chickpeas are done, remove and discard the celery and herbs, then add the chickpeas, along with 3 cups of the cooking water, to the onions and garlic.
- Puree the soup with lemon juice, salt, and pepper to taste.

Soups

Alternate cooking method:

- If you aren't pressure cooking the chickpeas, simmer them in a 3-quart saucepan for 1^1/$_2$ to 2^1/$_2$ hours, covered.
- Meanwhile, cook the onion-garlic mixture for up to 45 minutes over the lowest possible heat.
- When the chickpeas are tender, add the onion mixture to them.
- Puree the soup with lemon juice, salt, and pepper to taste.

creamy carrot and sweet potato soup

YIELD: 4 to 6 servings   COOKING TIME: 30 minutes

We have made hundreds of soups at the restaurant, with many real gems. It would be difficult to pick the all-time greatest, but this is definitely one of the most popular. It has a bright, cheery color. It's earthy, warming, and comforting, has a delicate sweetness, and fills you up without being heavy (with a huge hit of vitamin A).

Suggested garnishes: Tofu sour cream, nori strips, snipped chives, croutons, parsley.

> 2 cups diced onions
> 3 cups diced carrots
> 2 cups peeled, diced sweet potatoes
> 2 tablespoons olive oil
> 1 tablespoon each of cumin seeds, fennel seeds, caraway seeds, and coriander seeds, ground to fine powder
> 2 teaspoons salt plus additional for seasoning
> Freshly ground black pepper
> 6 cups water

- Combine the vegetables, oil, and seasonings in a heavy-bottomed 3- to 4-quart saucepan over medium heat. Cook for 7 to 8 minutes.
- Lower the flame, cover, and cook for 5 to 10 minutes, stirring occasionally. The vegetables should cook gently; do not let them brown.
- Add 6 cups of water and raise the heat to bring to a boil.
- Lower the heat and simmer the soup until the vegetables are soft, approximately 20 minutes.
- Puree the soup and add additional water to thin it if desired. In place of water, you can thin the soup with apple cider, which yields a sweeter taste.
- Season with salt and pepper to taste.

"Creamy" Soups

For lack of a better word, we use the adjective "creamy" to describe soups like this one that have a smooth consistency. Of course, this has nothing to do with dairy; the soups are simply pureed, which renders them creamy in appearance and mouth-feel. You can use a hand food mill, a handheld mixer, or a blender for this procedure. It can't be done with a potato masher. Caution: If you use a food processor, strain off the liquids first, add the solids to the food processor, and then drizzle in the liquids gradually so as to avoid excess spillage. Peter highly recommends a small handheld mixer, a relatively new invention that is useful and efficient.

creamy watercress, leek, and potato soup

YIELD: 4 to 6 servings   COOKING TIME: 45 minutes

If the previous carrot-sweet potato concoction was a great way of "eating orange," this soup is the way to "ingest green." It has a beautiful emerald color. It should be served the same day it's prepared to take advantage of the freshness of the watercress.

Good watercress is crunchy and has a sharp peppery flavor, which is balanced in this recipe by the potatoes and the olive oil. Watercress is traditionally available in the spring. It has long been cause for concern among mothers and grandmothers because it grew on the sides of streams where it could pick up parasites. With modern cultivation methods, this is no longer a worry.

Serving suggestion: This recipe is a twist on the classic French leek-and-potato cream soup known as Vichyssoise, which is served cold. You can do the same, with some thinly sliced cucumbers arranged on top.

Try this: Substitute mizuna, tatsoi, baby mustard greens, or spinach for the watercress.

> *¹/₄ cup and 2 tablespoons extra virgin olive oil*
> *2 large leeks, white part only, washed and chopped to yield 3 cups*
> *3 to 4 cloves garlic*
> *Pinch of sea salt*
> *1 pound potatoes, peeled and diced*
> *2 bunches watercress, washed, drained, and coarsely chopped*
> *1 tablespoon chopped fresh tarragon, leaves only*
> *Freshly squeezed lemon juice to taste*
> *Sea salt and freshly ground black pepper*

❖ Combine the ¹/₄ cup oil, leeks, and garlic in a heavy-bottomed 3-quart saucepan over medium heat.

❖ Simmer for 2 to 3 minutes.

❖ Add pinch of salt, lower flame, cover, and cook 15 minutes longer, stirring from time to time.

❖ Meanwhile, prep potatoes, add them to the pan, add enough water to cover, and bring to a boil.

❖ Lower flame and simmer until potatoes are tender, about 20 to 25 minutes.

❖ Add the watercress to the soup and simmer 1 to 2 minutes longer.

❖ Add tarragon and remaining olive oil. Puree the soup until creamy.

❖ Stir in lemon juice. Season with salt and pepper to taste.

❖ If the soup is too thick, thin with additional water to desired consistency.

Soups

134

curried golden split pea soup

YIELD: 4 to 6 servings   COOKING TIME: 1 hour, 10 minutes

Of all the millions of gallons of split pea soup served in America each year, the vast majority is made from green split peas. For our split pea soup, we make a statement by choosing the "golden" variety with its warm, vibrant yellow color. Green split peas, by the way, are perfectly good to eat; ditto red lentils, acceptable substitutes here that simply have a less vibrant color when cooked.

At Angelica Kitchen, we always like to heighten the sensual experience of eating and celebrate the diversity of nature by serving attractive, colorful dishes. It makes the meal more fun—imagine all those colors going down into your belly . . .

This soup really benefits from the use of freshly made curry powder. Once you try it, you'll never go back to the store-bought kind.

Serving suggestion: For a meal in a bowl, try adding steamed basmati rice and a dollop of Pear-Apple Chutney (page 108).

1¹/₂ cups dried yellow split peas
8 cups water or vegetable stock
1 (3-inch) piece of dried kombu
1¹/₂ cups diced onions
1 cup peeled, diced carrots
¹/₂ cup diced celery
2 tablespoons olive oil
1 tablespoon Homemade Curry Powder (see Curried Chickpea and
    Vegetable Stew, page 171)
1 teaspoon sea salt plus additional for seasoning
Chopped fresh cilantro for garnish (parsley can be substituted)

* Rinse the peas, strain, and combine with 8 cups of water and kombu in a 3-quart saucepan.
* Bring to a boil over high heat.
* Lower the heat, cover, and simmer gently for 1 hour or until the peas become a puree.
* While the peas simmer, combine the remaining ingredients in an 8-inch heavy-bottomed skillet or saucepan over medium heat.
* Sauté for 3 to 5 minutes, stirring.
* Lower the heat, cover, and sweat for 15 minutes.
* Deglaze the sauté pan with ¹/₂ cup of water and pour the contents of the pan into the peas.
* Simmer gently for 10 minutes, add additional salt to taste if desired.
* Serve sprinkled with cilantro (or parsley).

Leek Tops

The tough green tops of the leeks make great soup stock. Simply wash and coarsely chop them, then combine with an equal amount of sliced carrot and celery (especially the leaves), fennel, garlic, and fresh herbs. Simmer in enough water to cover by 2 inches for 45 minutes to 1 hour, then strain.

kamut and wild mushroom soup

YIELD: 4 to 6 servings   COOKING TIME: 1 hour, 10 minutes

The first question that usually arises with respect to this recipe is "What is kamut?" It's an age-old grain whose name comes from the ancient Egyptian word for wheat. Known as "the great-grandfather of grains," it is high in protein, features a delicious nutty flavor, and has never been hybridized. Kamut cooks up plump and chewy and goes well with many kinds of mushrooms. The more varieties of mushrooms you can muster for this recipe, the more flavor and texture you can capture. It's hearty and substantial—just the thing for a snowy winter day.

> 3/4 cup kamut, soaked in 3 cups water for 8 hours or overnight
> 6 cups water
> 1 cup diced onion
> 1/2 cup chopped carrots
> 1/2 cup chopped celery
> 1/2 cup chopped cabbage
> 2 cups thinly sliced mixed mushrooms, fresh shiitake, chanterelle,
>   cremini, portobello, lobster, black trumpet, and so forth (if wild
>   mushrooms are unavailable, substitute an equal amount of
>   domestic white mushrooms)
> 1 clove garlic, minced
> 1 tablespoon extra virgin olive oil
> 1 teaspoon sea salt
> 2 tablespoons minced fresh dill
> 2 tablespoons shoyu or tamari

* Strain the kamut and combine with 6 cups of water in a heavy 3-quart saucepan over high heat. Bring to a boil.
* Lower the flame, cover the pot, and simmer for 45 minutes or until the kamut is tender.
* While the kamut simmers, sauté the onions, carrots, celery, cabbage, mushrooms, garlic, olive oil, and salt in a heavy-bottomed 10-inch skillet or saucepan over medium heat for 3 to 5 minutes, stirring.
* Lower heat, cover the pan, and sweat for 15 minutes.
* When kamut is tender, add the vegetables, dill, and shoyu.
* Swirl 1/2 cup water into the skillet, deglaze, then pour into the soup pot.
* Simmer for an additional 10 minutes.

Deglazing

When aromatic vege-tables are sautéed in oil with seasonings, they leave behind a flavorful glaze on the bottom of the pan. Add a bit of water or stock and scrape up the glaze with a wooden spoon or rubber spatula while the pot is still on the burner and add it to the soup.

Soups

136

minestrone al pesto

YIELD: 4 to 6 servings   COOKING TIME: 45 minutes

Here is another traditional bean-and-vegetable number dressed up
Angelica style, in this case by adding a dollop of pesto on top of each
bowl just before serving.

Try this: For the pesto, substitute basil or mint for half of the parsley.
You can add various different vegetables to the soup—string beans or
Swiss chard, for example. It's also a good place to put your leftover pasta.

Serving suggestion: For a quick meal in a bowl, add a piece of
toasted sourdough bread to the soup.

For the soup:
2 onions, peeled and coarsely chopped
1 tablespoon olive oil
Pinch of sea salt
1 celery stalk, sliced lengthwise and coarsely chopped
2 carrots, sliced lengthwise and cut into $1/4$-inch half moons
2 cups winter squash such as butternut or buttercup, peeled and cut
   into $1/2$-inch cubes
4 fresh sage leaves, roughly chopped (or substitute $1/2$ teaspoon
   dried sage)
2 to 3 cups cooked beans (Great Northern, chickpea, or pinto)
5 cups water
$2/3$ cup minishells or elbow macaroni
Sea salt and freshly ground black pepper

For the pesto:
1 cup fresh Italian parsley (leaves only)
2 small or 1 large clove garlic, minced
$1/4$ cup walnuts
$1/3$ cup extra virgin olive oil
Sea salt and freshly ground black pepper

❖ In a heavy 3-quart saucepan, sauté onions in oil with pinch of salt for
   2 minutes.

❖ Add remaining vegetables plus sage and cook for 10 more minutes
   over medium heat. You may add 1 or 2 tablespoons of water if needed.

❖ Add beans and 5 cups of water and bring to a boil over high heat.

❖ Reduce the heat to low, cover, and gently simmer for 20 minutes.

❖ While the soup simmers, make the pesto. Combine the parsley,
   garlic, and other ingredients in a blender or food processor and
   puree until creamy.

(continued)

(continued)

❖ Uncover the soup pan, stir in the pasta, and simmer for 10 minutes more or until the pasta is fully cooked.

❖ Season with salt and pepper to taste.

❖ Ladle the soup into bowls and place a dollop of pesto into each one.

miso soup

YIELD: 6 servings   COOKING TIME: 25 minutes

Soup made from miso, which is fermented soybean paste, is a staple in Japanese and vegetarian restaurants the world over. It is an extremely healthy food, providing easily digestible protein and beneficial live bacteria, cleansing the blood, and aiding digestion.

I have been approached numerous times over the years by customers who exclaim that this is the best miso soup they've ever tasted. Our secret? We use super high-quality Miso Master Mellow Barley Miso. John and Jan Belleme, the original owners of the company, went to Japan to study miso making with the masters. When they came back, they searched for a climate that replicated ideal miso-making conditions in Japan. This turned out to be in the foothills of the Smoky Mountains in western North Carolina. They settled in a little town called Rutherfordton and set up a traditional miso-making operation. They no longer own the company, but it continues to churn out a superior product.

Serving suggestions: Dress up your miso soup by adding millet or steamed vegetables or more sea vegetables.

> 1 (2-inch) piece dried wakame
> 1 (3-inch) piece dried kombu
> 4 cups water
> 1 carrot, cut into matchstick-size pieces
> 1 onion, sliced into thin crescents
> 7 tablespoons barley miso (miso of choice can be substituted)
> 1 cup tofu, cut into 1/2-inch cubes
> Sliced scallion for garnish

❖ Soak the wakame in 2 cups of cold water until soft, about 15 minutes.

❖ Combine the kombu with 4 cups of water in a 2-quart saucepan and bring to a simmer.

❖ Gently cook for 2 minutes.

❖ Remove the kombu and reserve for another use (chopped into a stew or cooked with any grain or bean).

❖ Strain the wakame soaking water into the saucepan and add the carrots and onions.

Soups

* Chop the wakame into bite-size pieces and add them to the saucepan. Bring the soup to a simmer, cover, and cook gently until vegetables are tender, approximately 25 minutes.
* In a small bowl, dissolve the miso in $^1/_2$ cup of strained soup stock. Return this miso back to the pot.
* Add the tofu and simmer for 1 minute. Do not allow to boil.
* Serve garnished with scallions.

NOTE: Longer cooking or boiling destroys miso's beneficial micro-organisms.

squash potage

YIELD: 6 to 8 servings   COOKING TIME: 45 minutes

Potage is the traditional French term for a pureed soup that's often enriched with cream or eggs. In this case, the starchy flesh of the squash, blended or processed, yields a mouth-watering velvety consistency. Squash is technically a fruit since, like tomatoes and other fruits that are thought of as vegetables, it has its seeds on the inside. This recipe features another fruit flavor, apple cider, to create a hearty fall or winter dish. Any hard-skinned winter squash such as buttercup, butternut, hokkaido, kuri, turban, or hubbard works equally well in this recipe.

Try this: For an even smoother, more elegant soup, strain it through a fine sieve.

   2 tablespoons olive oil
   1 large onion, coarsely chopped (to yield about 2 cups)
   1 teaspoon sea salt plus additional for seasoning
   1 tablespoon fresh ginger, peeled and minced
   1 cinnamon stick
   3 cloves garlic
   6 leaves fresh sage (to yield 1 teaspoon minced)
   $^1/_2$ cup apple cider or more to taste
   3 pounds winter squash, peeled, seeded, and chopped (to yield about
      2 quarts)
   $^1/_2$ cup peeled, sliced carrots
   4 cups water or vegetable stock
   Sea salt and freshly ground black pepper

* Warm the oil over medium heat in a heavy-bottomed 3-quart saucepan. Add the onions along with 1 teaspoon salt and sweat, covered, uncovering to stir occasionally, for about 10 minutes.
* Add the ginger, cinnamon, garlic, and sage and continue to cook for 5 minutes.

(continued)

(continued)

❖ Stir in the apple cider and bring to a boil.

❖ Add the squash, carrots, and 4 cups of water. Bring to a boil, then lower the heat, cover, and cook for 20 minutes or until the squash is falling apart.

❖ Remove the cinnamon stick and puree with a handheld mixer until the mixture is creamy.

❖ Add additional cider and salt and some freshly ground black pepper to taste.

❖ Serve piping hot.

triple lentil soup

YIELD: 4 to 6 servings   COOKING TIME: 1 hour

This is a classic lentil soup with a twist: it has three different types of lentils—green, red, and French (aka gray). The green lentil is the largest of them and it comes whole. The red (aka Egyptian) comes peeled. French lentils are very small and they cook up tender. A lentil qualifies as a pulse, the ancient biblical term for the dried seed of a legume. There are many varieties of lentils, particularly in India, where they use up to 60 different types for dahl, an Indian dish whose name also means "lentil."

> *1 tablespoon extra virgin olive oil*
> *1¹/₂ cups diced onions*
> *Pinch of sea salt*
> *1 clove garlic, crushed*
> *¹/₂ cup diced celery (with leaves)*
> *1 cup diced carrots*
> *1 bay leaf*
> *2 teaspoons minced fresh herbs (sage, thyme, or rosemary;*
> *   1 teaspoon dried herbs can be substituted)*
> *¹/₃ cup of each: dried green lentils, red lentils, French lentils*
> *1 (3-inch) piece dried kombu*
> *6 cups water or vegetable stock*
> *Freshly squeezed juice of ¹/₂ lemon, strained*
> *Sea salt and freshly ground black pepper*
> *Finely sliced scallion for garnish*

❖ Warm the olive oil over medium heat in a heavy-bottomed 3- to 5-quart soup pot.

❖ Add the onions and a pinch of salt and cook for 8 to 10 minutes, stirring occasionally.

Soups

140

* Add the garlic, celery, carrots, bay leaf, and herbs and sauté for 5 minutes.
* Sort through the lentils and discard any foreign matter. Rinse briefly in a strainer under cold running water.
* Add the lentils, kombu, and 6 cups of water to the soup pot and bring to a boil.
* Lower the heat, cover, and simmer for 40 to 50 minutes or until the lentils are tender.
* Remove and discard the kombu and bay leaf.
* Stir in the lemon juice and season with salt and pepper to taste.
* Simmer for 3 minutes.
* Serve garnished with scallion.

Salads and Dressings

SIDE SALADS

carrot-mint salad

YIELD: 4 servings   PREPARATION TIME: 30 minutes

This quick, refreshing summer salad is based on a traditional Moroccan recipe. Fresh ingredients and simple preparations are always crucial but especially with salads. There's nothing quite like freshly dug carrots, which are featured in this recipe along with two complimentary flavors— mint and garlic. A touch of sweetness is provided by the currants. They work much better than raisins, which are standard fare in carrot salads but bigger and lumpish.

For presentation, we love the bright orange carrots, flecked with the green and black of the herbs and currants. Try to highlight these colors by arranging the salad over a bed of light-colored baby Bibb lettuce on a white plate.

1/4 cup freshly squeezed lemon juice, strained
1/2 teaspoon sea salt
1 to 2 cloves garlic, minced
Pinch of freshly ground white pepper
3 tablespoons extra virgin olive oil
1 pound carrots, peeled and coarsely grated
2 tablespoons finely chopped chives
3 tablespoons fresh mint, leaves only, minced
3 tablespoons currants

❖ Whisk together the lemon juice, salt, garlic, pepper, and oil.

❖ Add the carrots and toss.

❖ Add the chives, mint, and currants. Serve over tender lettuce, such as Bibb or butter lettuce.

Salads & Dressings

red and green slaw

YIELD: 4 to 6 servings   PREPARATION TIME: 40 minutes

This slaw is low in fat, high in flavor, and has a wonderful crunchy texture. It's one of the fastest salads to prepare, a quick snack or light meal when you're on the run.

Note: Make sure to use top-quality organic unpasteurized apple cider vinegar; otherwise, you don't get the real taste or the enzymes.

> 8 cups shredded cabbage (red or green or combination)
> 2 carrots, coarsely grated
> 1 teaspoon sea salt
> 2 scallions, finely sliced
> 2 tablespoons apple cider vinegar
> 2 tablespoons fresh dill, finely chopped
> 1 teaspoon caraway or fennel seeds, lightly toasted
> 1 tablespoon olive oil

❖ Remove the outer tough leaves of the cabbage, quarter it, and remove the core. Lay cut-side down on cutting board and cut crosswise in fine strips. You can also grate it with a mandolin-style slicer or chop it in a food processor fitted with the slicing blade.

❖ Combine the cabbage, carrots, and salt in a large mixing bowl.

❖ Add the scallions, vinegar, dill, and seeds. Toss well.

❖ Add the oil and toss again. Chill for 20 minutes and adjust the seasonings before serving.

fresh sea vegetable salad with rice wine vinaigrette

YIELD: 4 servings   PREPARATION TIME: 45 minutes

This salad makes good use of fresh sea vegetables. My best advice is to ask your local fresh fish supplier about possible sources. Another possibility is to reconstitute the dry version of sea vegetables in water, then proceed as stated in the recipe.

> *For the salad:*
> 2 ounces fresh dulse
> 2 ounces fresh sea lettuce or wakame
> 2 ounces fresh sea beans or haricots de mer
> 2 cups cucumber, peeled, seeded, and cut into 1/2-inch cubes

(continued)

(continued)

1 cup red radish, coarsely grated
1 cup peeled carrot, coarsely grated
2 tablespoons chopped fresh cilantro
2 tablespoons finely sliced scallions
$^1/_2$ tablespoon sesame seeds, lightly toasted in a skillet over medium
  heat until they start to pop

For the vinaigrette:
1 tablespoon mirin
2 tablespoons rice vinegar
$^1/_2$ cup apple cider
2 tablespoons olive oil

For the garnish:
1 orange, peeled and diced
Clover sprouts

* Soak the sea vegetables in enough cold water to cover for 15 minutes.
  Drain and gently squeeze dry.
* Coarsely chop the sea vegetables and place them in a mixing bowl.
* Add the cucumber, radish, carrot, cilantro, scallions, and sesame seeds.
* In a separate bowl whisk together the ingredients for the vinaigrette.
* Add the vinaigrette to the vegetables and toss to coat.
* Spoon onto individual plates and garnish with diced oranges and
  clover sprouts.

NOTE: Fresh sea vegetables sometimes have tiny calcium deposits
clinging to them. This is especially true for sea lettuce. After soaking,
carefully pick through and scrape off any of these deposits, then
proceed.

mixed sprout salad with mint vinaigrette

YIELD: 4 to 6 servings   PREPARATION TIME: 50 minutes

Here is Angelica Kitchen's answer to the raw-food trend, a sprouty,
crunchy, fiber-filled delight. If you can't find onion sprouts, use alfalfa or
clover ones. Many farmers markets have a stand with an impressive array
of fresh sprouts. They would love to have your business, and you theirs!

(continued)

Salads & Dressings

Fresh Sea Vegetable
Salad with Rice Wine
Vinaigrette.

(continued)

For the salad:
2 cups mung bean sprouts
2 cups snow pea shoots or sunflower sprouts
1 cup finely sliced red cabbage
1 cup finely sliced green cabbage
1 cup peeled, julienned daikon
1 cup peeled, julienned carrot

For the mint vinaigrette:
4 tablespoons chopped mint
¹/₂ cup apple cider or apple juice
¹/₄ cup rice vinegar
2 tablespoons mirin
2 tablespoons shoyu or tamari
1 tablespoon olive oil

Garnishes:
¹/₂ cup peanuts
1 bunch watercress, washed with tough stems removed
1 cup onion sprouts

* Preheat the oven to 350°F.

* Spread the peanuts on a cookie sheet and toast for 10 minutes.

* Remove peanuts from oven, allow to cool, then chop coarsely.

* Toss the salad vegetables and sprouts together in a mixing bowl.

* In a separate bowl, whisk together the mint, apple cider, vinegar, mirin, shoyu, and olive oil.

* Toss the salad with the vinaigrette.

* Serve over the watercress, sprinkled with peanuts and topped with onion sprouts.

sea caesar salad

YIELD: **4 to 6 servings**   PREPARATION TIME: 1 hour

Here is another of our perennially popular menu items, a delicious, nutritious way of introducing some sea vegetables into your system. The creamy-style dressing makes use of tofu and miso. This recipe was developed by the late, great Frank Arcuri, who was a consultant and occasional guest chef at Angelica Kitchen. Frank was a true maven who made many contributions to the restaurant.

1 large head romaine lettuce

Salads & Dressings

For the croutons:
2 cups sourdough bread, preferably day-old, cut into ¹/₂-inch cubes
  (remove crust first if it is very dark)
1 tablespoon extra virgin olive oil
1 tablespoon fresh thyme leaves or 1 teaspoon dried ones
Pinch of freshly ground black pepper

For the garnish:
1 cup dulse
2 sheets nori

For the dressing:
1 tablespoon minced garlic
2 teaspoons Dijon mustard
2 teaspoons umeboshi (pickled plum paste)
3 tablespoons balsamic vinegar
3 tablespoons freshly squeezed lemon juice, strained
1 tablespoon light miso
¹/₄ pound silken tofu (if not available, soft tofu can be substituted)
¹/₃ cup olive oil
²/₃ cup extra virgin olive oil

❖ Preheat the oven to 350°F.

❖ Discard any tough or bruised outer leaves of the lettuce, wash in cold water, spin dry, and chill in the refrigerator.

❖ To make the croutons, toss the bread cubes, 1 tablespoon of olive oil, thyme leaves, and black pepper together in a bowl. Spread the cubes on a cookie sheet and toast in the oven for 15 minutes or until light brown and crunchy. Remove from oven and allow to cool.

❖ Spread dulse on a cookie sheet and toast in the oven for 10 minutes or until crispy.

❖ Grind dulse to a powder in a suribachi or spice grinder, then set aside.

❖ Using a pair of scissors, cut the nori lengthwise into 4 pieces.

❖ Stack the pieces and snip crosswise into ¹/₈-inch strips, then set aside.

❖ To make the dressing, combine the garlic, mustard, umeboshi paste, vinegar, lemon juice, miso, and tofu in a blender or food processor and blend until creamy.

❖ Slowly add the oils and blend until fully emulsified.

❖ Toss the romaine with an amount of dressing to taste, then sprinkle with dulse powder and sourdough croutons.

❖ Top with nori strips and serve.

NOTE: Dried sea vegetables will keep indefinitely in an airtight container.

carrot-ginger-dill dressing

YIELD: 2 cups   PREPARATION TIME: 20 minutes

This dressing is colorful, tangy, and delicious. The carrots lend a sweetness and the ginger contributes a pleasing bite. It goes well with just about any green salad and also with steamed greens such as kale, collard greens, and bok choy. The sweet-and-sour notes from the apple cider vinegar are an excellent compliment to any bitterness in the greens.

> 1 tablespoon finely diced onion
> 1 cup firmly packed peeled, grated carrots
> 2 teaspoons peeled, minced fresh ginger
> 1/4 teaspoon mustard powder
> 2 teaspoons rinsed, finely chopped fresh dill
> 2 teaspoons shoyu or tamari
> 2 tablespoons apple cider or apple juice
> 4 tablespoons apple cider vinegar
> 6 tablespoons olive oil
> 1 teaspoon toasted sesame oil

❖ Combine all of the ingredients in a blender and puree until creamy.

angelica house dressing

YIELD: 1 cup   PREPARATION TIME: 15 minutes

For those who avoid vinegar, here is our fresh-tasting tahini-based herbal dressing, a basic menu item for as long as anyone can remember. It features a salty-and-sour taste from the umeboshi (pickled plums) and a creamy smoothness from the tahini. Due to the fresh ingredients, it doesn't keep for more than about two days. It's mild and delicate, low in acidity. Many people apply it to the Dragon Bowl. It also works well with any salad that includes grains and can be tossed with pasta.

> 1/2 cup firmly packed fresh parsley, washed, dried, and chopped
> 1 whole scallion, rinsed and sliced
> 1/4 cup tahini
> 1 tablespoon umeboshi paste
> 1/2 cup water

❖ Combine all of the ingredients in a blender and puree until smooth.

Salads & Dressings

basic vinaigrette

A great all-purpose vinaigrette is essential for salads, steamed greens served hot or cold, green beans, asparagus, cauliflower, and many other vegetables. Here is our version. Enjoy creating your own variations by using different herbs or mustards. Stick to one dominant flavor or combination, though; don't get too adventurous and "overspice" it.

> 1 pint olive oil
> 1 pint extra virgin olive oil
> 5 ounces apple cider vinegar
> 3 tablespoons shoyu or tamari
> 1^1/$_2$ tablespoons mirin
> 5 tablespoons maple syrup
> 6 ounces apple cider
> 1 tablespoon prepared mustard
> ^{1}/$_2$ teaspoon sea salt
> 1 teaspoon freshly ground black pepper
> 4 tablespoons chopped fresh herbs (parsley, basil,
>   and tarragon)

❖ Place all ingredients, except oils and herbs, in a stainless steel mixing bowl large enough to accommodate at least 1^1/$_2$ quarts of liquid.

❖ Thoroughly whisk all of these ingredients until homogenous.

❖ Combine both oils and, while whisking, slowly drizzle oils into existing mixture until the vinaigrette is emulsified.

❖ Add herbs, and mix to incorporate.

❖ Allow vinaigrette to "rest" for 10 minutes or so to let the flavors "marry" and develop. Taste and adjust seasoning to your palate.

❖ This is known as a temporary emulsion, in that after a short period of time the oil and vinegar will separate. All you need to do is place the vinaigrette back in a mixing bowl and whisk until re-emulsified.

❖ You could also use a blender or food processor to make this vinaigrette instead of a whisk and mixing bowl.

❖ Can remain in refrigerator, covered tightly, for two weeks.

balsamic variation

YIELD: ¹/₂ cup   PREPARATION TIME: 10 minutes

A small amount of rice vinegar in this version tones down the balsamic vinegar, which has a strong sweet component. Likewise, in the rosemary variation, we use light olive oil to balance the strength and weight of the extra virgin olive oil.

> 1 teaspoon Dijon-style mustard
> 1¹/₂ tablespoons balsamic vinegar
> ¹/₂ tablespoon rice vinegar
> Pinch of sea salt
> Pinch of freshly ground black pepper
> 6 tablespoons extra virgin olive oil

❖ Combine the mustard, vinegars, salt, and pepper in a small bowl.

❖ Slowly beat in the oil with a fork or small whisk until emulsified.

rosemary variation

YIELD: ³/₄ cup   PREPARATION TIME: 15 minutes

We serve this one warm over mesclun greens in the autumn. Whisk together the ingredients in a small saucepan and allow it to warm up over low heat. Serve over spinach or mesclun for a wilted salad; don't overdress because the greens will become soggy.

> 2 tablespoons red wine vinegar
> 1 tablespoon Dijon-style mustard
> ¹/₂ teaspoon minced garlic
> 1¹/₂ teaspoons fresh rosemary, minced
> 6 tablespoons extra virgin olive oil
> 4 tablespoons olive oil
> Sea salt and freshly ground black pepper

❖ Combine the vinegar, mustard, garlic, and rosemary in a small bowl.

❖ Slowly beat in the oil with a fork or small whisk until well emulsified.

❖ Season with salt and pepper to taste.

Salads & Dressings

black bean salad

YIELD: 4 to 6 servings   PREPARATION TIME: 1¹/₂ hours

Like the other salads in this section, this one is equally suitable for lunch, picnics, or buffets. The black beans, lime juice, jalapeño, and cilantro give it a decided Mexican accent. It also has a festive appearance, with the contrasting red onions, orange carrots, and green celery sprinkled like confetti on a background of dark-colored beans.

Warning: Be sure to wash your hands with soap and water after handling the jalapeños or, alternately, wear rubber gloves. Any trace of this pepper in your eyes is unforgettably painful.

Serving suggestion: This salad goes well with Angelica's fluffy Southern-Style Cornbread (page 158) or, for a change of texture, some crispy tortilla chips. Try it for lunch, perhaps alongside a bowl of your favorite soup with a crusty piece of peasant bread on the side.

For the salad:
2 cups dried black beans
6 cups water
1 cup (approximately ¹/₄ lb.) each of the following:
   • *celery (1 large stalk) cut into ¹/₈-inch-thick slices*
   • *summer squash, cut into ¹/₈-inch-thick slices*
   • *red onions, cut into ¹/₈-inch-thick slices*
   • *carrots, cut into ¹/₈-inch-thick slices*

For the vinaigrette:
¹/₂ cup freshly squeezed lime juice, strained
1¹/₂ tablespoons stemmed, seeded, and minced jalapeño pepper
2¹/₂ teaspoons sea salt
2 teaspoons minced garlic
1 teaspoon lime zest
¹/₄ cup chopped fresh cilantro
¹/₂ cup olive oil

❖ Sort through the beans and remove any stones or broken beans.

❖ Rinse the beans in several changes of cold water and drain.

❖ Combine the beans with 6 cups of water in a 3- to 4-quart pressure cooker. Bring to full pressure, lower the flame, and cook for 35 to 40 minutes. Release the pressure and drain the beans in a colander. Cool under cold running water and set aside.

(continued)

(continued)

❖ Combine the vegetables in a steamer and steam for 2 to 3 minutes or until crisp-tender.

❖ Chill in a bowl of cold water for 1 minute. Drain and set aside.

❖ In a large mixing bowl combine the lime juice, jalapeño pepper, sea salt, garlic, lime zest, and cilantro. Whisk in the olive oil and stir in the steamed vegetables and the black beans.

❖ Season with sea salt and black pepper to taste.

Alternate cooking method for beans:

❖ Simmer beans in a pot. The beans can also be cooked conventionally in a pot as per the instructions in the Basic Beans recipe on page 89.

warm potato salad with herbed mustard vinaigrette

YIELD: 4 to 6 servings   PREPARATION TIME: 1 hour

We like to toss the potatoes with the vinaigrette while they're still warm so they absorb the dressing well. The dish can be served immediately or allowed to cool to room temperature, which is when we think it's best. If you store it overnight in the fridge, allow time for it come to room temperature before serving; served cold, it is less flavorful.

Yukon Gold potatoes are recommended for their nice firm flesh. Red potatoes (a.k.a. "new" or "waxy") also work well, but not russet (baking) because their mealier flesh tends to turn mushy.

Serving suggestions: Try the potato salad alongside barbecued tofu or tempeh kebabs or with grilled seitan. It's also a good accompaniment to sautéed broccoli with a crusty piece of peasant bread.

For the salad:
2 pounds Yukon Gold potatoes, scrubbed and cut into 1-inch cubes
1 1/2 cups sliced celery
1 1/2 cups sliced red onions

For the vinaigrette:
1/2 cup apple cider vinegar
2 teaspoons sea salt
1 teaspoon freshly ground black pepper
4 teaspoons whole grain mustard
1 plump clove garlic, minced
1/2 cup extra virgin olive oil

Salads & Dressings

For the garnish:
2 tablespoons finely chopped fresh tarragon (dill can be substituted)
2 tablespoons minced fresh parsley

❖ Steam the potatoes in a 3- to 4- quart saucepan equipped with
  steamer basket and lid for 15 to 20 minutes or until tender. Remove
  and set aside.

❖ Steam the celery and red onions for 3 to 4 minutes. Combine the
  potatoes, celery, and red onions in a large mixing bowl and set aside.

❖ Combine the vinegar, salt, pepper, mustard, and garlic in a mixing
  bowl. Whisk in the oil, adding it in a steady stream.

❖ Gently fold in the potatoes, carrots, celery, and red onions until
  thoroughly mixed. Cool at room temperature for 10 minutes,
  allowing the potatoes to absorb the vinaigrette.

❖ Sprinkle with parsley and tarragon or dill, and serve.

roasted vegetable salad with toasted cumin vinaigrette

YIELD: 4 to 6 servings   PREPARATION TIME: 1¹/₂ hours

Cumin, one of the key ingredients in Indian curries as well as some
Mexican dishes, is perfumed, a tad exotic, and considered a digestive aid.
Be sure to toast and grind it yourself; it's worth the extra effort. In this
recipe, we use cumin in two forms: ground and toasted whole. The
ground cumin infuses the vinaigrette with flavor while the whole toasted
seeds add an interesting texture to the salad.

For the salad:
3 cups carrots, approx. 3/4 pound, peeled and cut into 1-inch cubes
1/2 cup garlic cloves, blanched and drained
3 cups sliced red onions
1 head cauliflower, cut into florets
2 cups red bell peppers, cut into 2-inch slices
2 cups button mushrooms, dusted with a damp towel and left whole
2 large fennel bulbs, trimmed and cut into 1-inch cubes
1 teaspoon sea salt
Freshly ground black pepper
2 tablespoons olive oil

For the vinaigrette:
1 teaspoon sea salt
1 tablespoon cumin seed, toasted and ground

(continued)

153

(continued)

> 1 teaspoon cumin seed, toasted and left whole
> 4 tablespoons balsamic vinegar
> 2 tablespoons extra virgin olive oil
> 2 tablespoons finely chopped fresh parsley

❖ Preheat the oven to 400°F.

❖ Steam the carrots in a 3-quart saucepan equipped with a steamer basket and lid for 3 minutes or until tender.

❖ Blanch the garlic cloves in boiling water for 1 minute and drain.

❖ In a large mixing bowl, combine the carrots, garlic, red onions, cauliflower, red peppers, button mushrooms, fennel, sea salt, black pepper, and light olive oil. Toss well and spread in a single layer on a baking sheet.

❖ Roast in the oven for 35 to 40 minutes, stirring occasionally.

❖ Meanwhile, combine the sea salt, cumin seed (both ground and whole), and balsamic vinegar in a large mixing bowl and whisk in the olive oil.

❖ Add the roasted vegetables to the bowl and toss to coat with the cumin vinaigrette.

❖ Sprinkle with chopped parsley and serve warm or at room temperature.

wild rice salad

YIELD: 4 to 6 servings   PREPARATION TIME: 2 hours

Wild rice is a luxurious, special-occasion grain, which is why this dish is perfect for a picnic or a potluck dinner. The presentation is dramatic, a virtual riot of texture, flavor, and color contrasts. You have tangy sun-dried tomatoes, sweet raisins or currants, and crunchy toasted almonds. Black, red, and green are the dominant colors.

Suggestion: Prepare the rice the day before you make this salad so it can be well-chilled.

> *For the salad:*
> 1 cup wild rice, rinsed
> 1/2 teaspoon sea salt
> 3 cups water
> 2/3 cup slivered almonds
> 3/4 cup sun-dried tomatoes, plumped in hot water
> 3/4 cup carrots, sliced into 1/8-inch-thick pieces
> 1/2 cup red onions, sliced into 1/8-inch-thick pieces
> 3/4 cup celery, sliced into 1/8-inch-thick pieces
> 3/4 cup yellow bell peppers, sliced into 1/8-inch-thick pieces
> 1/2 cup currants

Salads & Dressings

For the vinaigrette:
¹/₄ cup freshly squeezed lemon juice, strained
2 tablespoons chopped fresh dill
¹/₄ cup balsamic vinegar
¹/₄ cup olive oil
Sea salt and freshly ground black pepper
2 tablespoons chopped fresh parsley

❖ To make the salad, combine the rice, sea salt, and 3 cups of water in a 2-quart saucepan and bring to a boil. Lower the flame, cover, and allow rice to simmer for 1 hour or until the water has been absorbed.

❖ Transfer the rice to a bowl to cool to room temperature, then cover and refrigerate several hours or overnight.

❖ Toast the almonds in a 350°F oven for 10 minutes and set aside to cool.

❖ Bring 2 cups of water to a boil and pour over the sun-dried tomatoes. Allow them to plump for 15 to 20 minutes.

❖ Steam the carrots and onions for 2 to 3 minutes or until crisp-tender. Chill in a bowl of cold water for 1 minute. Drain and set aside.

❖ Drain the tomatoes and cut into strips.

❖ Combine the lemon juice, dill, and balsamic vinegar in a large mixing bowl. Whisk in the olive oil, sea salt, and black pepper to taste.

❖ Stir in the rice, carrots, red onions, celery, slivered almonds, yellow bell peppers, and currants.

❖ Add the parsley, toss with the vinaigrette, adjust the seasonings, and serve.

Breads, Spreads, Muffins, and Sandwiches

BREADS

amaranth-sunflower-spelt bread

YIELD: 6 to 8 servings   BAKING TIME: 1$^1/_2$ hours

The ancient grain amaranth is what gives this bread its moist, rich, light character. Amaranth is tiny and crunchy as opposed to some of the larger, heavier grains such as rice or kamut.

This is a highly nutritious bread that cries out for a leguminous accompaniment. Try cutting it into thick wedges and serving it along-side your favorite bean dish. Peter loves to cook it in a cast-iron skillet, because you can bring it straight to the table that way and serve it pip-ing hot. The bread has a satisfying, complex texture in part because some of the sunflower seeds are mixed into the batter while others are sprinkled on top.

Try this: For a savory addition, arrange some sautéed leeks, onions, or chopped black olives on top of the bread before baking.

1 cup of water
$^1/_2$ cup amaranth
3/4 teaspoon sea salt
3/4 cup sunflower seeds
1$^1/_2$ cups whole spelt flour (whole wheat flour can be substituted)
$^1/_2$ cup cornmeal
1$^1/_2$ teaspoons baking powder
3/4 teaspoon baking soda
1 cup soy milk
6 tablespoons olive oil
3 tablespoons apple cider vinegar
1 tablespoon maple syrup

❖ Place 1 cup water and $^1/_4$ teaspoon sea salt in a 1-quart saucepan and bring to a boil.

❖ Add amaranth, lower flame, and cover. Simmer for 45 minutes or until water is absorbed.

* Preheat oven to 350°F. Spread the sunflower seeds on a baking sheet and toast for 8 to 10 minutes. Remove from the oven and allow to cool.
* Whisk together the whole spelt flour, cornmeal, baking powder, baking soda, $^1/_2$ cup of sunflower seeds, and remaining sea salt in a medium-size mixing bowl.
* In a separate bowl, whisk together the soy milk, amaranth, olive oil, apple cider vinegar, and maple syrup.
* Combine the wet and dry ingredients together. Mix thoroughly but do not overmix. Batter will be thick but pourable.
* Lightly oil a 9- by 10-inch round pie plate.
* Pour in the batter and sprinkle with the remaining $^1/_4$ cup of sunflower seeds.
* Bake for 45 minutes or until a toothpick comes out clean.

angelica cornbread

YIELD: 6 to 8 generous pieces   BAKING TIME: 1 hour, 15 minutes
or 1 small loaf

This is another of Angelica's signature dishes. One of the restaurant's great traditions, it's been on the menu since Day One. Despite the name, it is not what most people expect when they order bread. It's a lumpy, moist, chewy, fiber-filled whole-grain loaf that features cornmeal, brown rice, and rolled oats. If you want energy to burn, have it for breakfast. We get letters from all over the world asking for the recipe. Some people consider it more of a curiosity than anything else. We strongly suggest you try it and find out where you stand.

   1 recipe Basic Brown Rice (page 94)
   1$^1/_3$ cups rolled oats
   1$^1/_3$ cups cornmeal
   $^1/_2$ tablespoon sea salt
   3 cups apple cider or apple juice
   $^1/_4$ cup unrefined corn oil plus more for brushing the baking pan
   2 tablespoons sesame seeds

* Preheat the oven to 350°F.
* In a large mixing bowl, combine the cooked rice, rolled oats, cornmeal, sea salt, apple cider (or juice), and corn oil. Mix well using a wooden spoon or whisk.
* Lightly oil a 9 x 5 x 3-inch loaf pan and sprinkle with sesame seeds. This prevents the bread from sticking to the pan and adds a delicious toasty sesame flavor.

(continued)

(continued)

- ❖ Fill the pan with batter, smoothing the top with a spatula.
- ❖ Bake on the middle rack of the oven for 1 hour and 15 minutes or until a toothpick comes out clean.
- ❖ Allow to cool before serving.
- ❖ Serve with spread of choice and top with sprouts or grated vegetables.

southern-style cornbread

YIELD: 8 servings   BAKING TIME: 25 minutes

Not to be confused with our "Angelica Cornbread" (see previous page), this is our vegan version of a good, old-fashioned, fluffy southern cornbread. It is true comfort food, an extremely popular menu item, mostly ordered as a side dish to accompany our daily entrée specials. We sell at least 500 servings of it a week, which translates to about 25,000 pieces of bread per year. Try this recipe and you'll realize there's no need for the lard and eggs you find in traditional cornbread.

Serving suggestions: This bread is the perfect accompaniment to chili, barbecued tempeh, or basic beans. I like to take a thick slice, open it up and put it in a bowl; ladle some pinto beans on top, then finish off with a dollop of mustard.

> 1 cup cornmeal
> 1/2 cup whole wheat pastry flour
> 1/2 cup unbleached white flour
> 2 teaspoons baking powder
> 1/4 cup minced scallions
> 1 cup soy milk
> 1/4 cup olive oil
> 1/4 cup maple syrup
> 1/2 teaspoon sea salt

- ❖ Preheat the oven to 350°F. Oil an 8- to 10-inch round ovenproof glass or cast iron skillet.
- ❖ Whisk together the cornmeal, whole wheat pastry flour, unbleached white flour, baking powder, and scallions in a mixing bowl.
- ❖ In a separate mixing bowl, combine the soy milk, olive oil, maple syrup, and sea salt.
- ❖ Combine the wet and dry ingredients. Mix thoroughly with a wooden spoon; do not overmix.

Breads, Spreads, Muffins, & Sandwiches

- Pour into the oiled baking dish and bake for approximately 25 minutes or until toothpick comes out clean.
- Set aside to cool.
- Slice into wedges and serve.

sweet potato biscuits

YIELD: about 10 biscuits   BAKING TIME: 30 to 35 minutes

We serve these savory biscuits with barbecued tempeh, cole slaw, baked beans, pickled vegetables, and sautéed greens. Their beautiful golden color dresses up a meal and they're scrumptious served hot.

  1 cup unbleached white flour
  1 cup whole wheat pastry flour
  $^1/_2$ tablespoon baking powder
  $^3/_4$ teaspoon baking soda
  $^3/_4$ teaspoon sea salt
  $^1/_4$ teaspoon black pepper
  $^3/_4$ cup pecans, toasted and chopped (optional)
  3 cups sweet potatoes, peeled and cut into 1-inch chunks
  3 tablespoons freshly squeezed lemon juice, strained
      (vinegar can be substituted)
  2 tablespoons maple syrup
  $^1/_3$ cup olive oil
  1 cup soy milk
  $^1/_2$ cup water

- Preheat the oven to 350°F.
- Steam sweet potatoes until soft, about 20 minutes, and allow to cool.
- In a large bowl, whisk together flours, baking powder, baking soda, salt, pepper, and pecans.
- Puree sweet potatoes, lemon juice, maple syrup, olive oil, soy milk, and water.
- Fold wet ingredients into dry ingredients.
- Lightly oil 2 cookie sheets.
- Place $^1/_2$-cup scoops of batter 3 inches apart on the cookie sheets.
- Bake for 30 to 35 minutes or until a toothpick comes out clean.
- Biscuits are okay to freeze for up to three months.

SPREADS

carrot-ginger butter

YIELD: 3 cups   COOKING TIME: 20 minutes

Carrots and ginger are a natural pairing—in soup, muffins, and juice and in this delectable fat-free spread. Fresh organic carrots are nothing if not sweet. The peppery bite of the ginger balances that sweetness, brightening the flavor of the carrots. This spread works well on any bread or biscuit. It's also a key ingredient in our carrot muffins. Well-sealed and refrigerated, it can keep up to five days.

> *2 pounds carrots, scrubbed and cut into 1-inch chunks*
> *1 cup apple cider or apple juice*
> *Pinch of sea salt*
> *1 (2-inch) piece fresh ginger root, to yield 1 tablespoon of juice*

❖ Place the carrots, apple cider (or juice), and salt in a pressure cooker. Bring to full pressure over a high flame, lower the flame, and cook for 20 minutes.

❖ Run cold water over the pressure cooker to bring down the pressure.

❖ Drain the carrots; the cooking liquid can be used for soup or as a tea.

❖ Grate the ginger and squeeze it through cheesecloth or press through a strainer to yield 1 tablespoon of juice.

❖ Puree the carrots and ginger juice in a food processor fitted with a steel blade until creamy. Alternatively, pass the carrots through a food mill then stir in the ginger juice.

❖ Serve spread on bread of choice and garnish with sprouts or grated vegetables.

Alternate cooking method for carrots:

❖ Combine them with 2 cups apple cider or juice in a saucepan and bring to a boil.

❖ Reduce the heat, cover, and simmer for 40 minutes or until the carrots are totally soft.

Breads, Spreads, Muffins, & Sandwiches

miso-tahini spread

YIELD: 2 cups   PREPARATION TIME: 10 minutes

This savory spread—smooth,salty, and rich—goes well with all different kinds of breads. In combination with one of the daily breads, this is one of our most popular side orders.

Serving suggestion: Use it as a sandwich spread with toasted sourdough, roasted vegetables, and lettuce.

Possible additions: Orange zest or a squeeze of lemon or chopped chives or roasted garlic.

Note: Make sure the tahini is well mixed before using. If it sits for any length of time, oil separation may occur. Simply stir it to a smooth consistency and proceed. This recipe yields a rather thick spread. If you like it thinner, add $^1/_4$ to $^1/_2$ cup additional water when pureeing.

> $^1/_3$ cup mellow barley miso
> $^1/_2$ cup water
> $1^1/_3$ cup tahini

❖ Combine the miso with $^1/_2$ cup water in a food processor or suribachi.

❖ Puree until creamy.

❖ Add tahini and process until smooth.

❖ Cover and refrigerate. It will keep up to 5 days.

❖ Spread on bread of choice and top with sprouts or grated vegetables.

onion butter

YIELD: $1^1/_2$ cups   COOKING TIME: $3^1/_2$ to 4 hours

All you need for this recipe is a few good onions and some time. That's time, folks, not thyme . . . It is one of our simplest and most delicious recipes. It's also fat-free. All the negative connotations of eating onions—harsh taste, bad breath, indigestion—melt away when you caramelize them. Caramelizing involves a long, slow, steady cooking process that brings out the natural sugars in a vegetable, turning it a sweet, toasty brown.

This is another tremendously versatile spread. If you're in a hurry or need a quick snack, try making what we call a "waiter sandwich"—sourdough bread with Miso-Tahini Spread and Onion Butter.

Try this: For an appetizer, toast sliced sourdough baguettes, spread with onion butter, and top with sauteed mushrooms and/or roasted peppers.

>   *3 pounds onions, peeled and thinly sliced to yield 3 quarts*

(continued)

(continued)

❖ Place the onions in a heavy-bottomed 3- to 4-quart pot with a tight-fitting lid.

❖ Heat over as low a flame as possible. Cook 3 to 4 hours, stirring occasionally, until the onions have completely melted into a dark caramelized mass.

❖ Place the onions in a food processor fitted with a steel blade and puree until smooth.

❖ Serve on bread of choice topped with sprouts or grated vegetables.

❖ The butter will keep for up to 7 days refrigerated.

MUFFINS

carrot-walnut muffins

YIELD: 12 large muffins   BAKING TIME: 30 minutes

The secret to these delicious muffins is a double-carrot whammy. Whereas the batter for most carrot breads merely contains shredded or grated carrots, this one also has pureed carrots by way of the Carrot-Ginger Butter. This means they're not only dense and satisfying, but also moist and intensely "carroty." They are loaded with beta-carotene, which is known to be good for vision and is an anti-cancer agent, as well.

> 4 cups whole wheat pastry flour
> 1 teaspoon sea salt
> 4 teaspoons baking powder
> 4 teaspoons cinnamon
> 1¹/₃ cups walnuts, chopped
> 1 cup raisins
> ²/₃ cup apple cider or apple juice
> ²/₃ cup maple syrup
> ²/₃ cup olive oil
> 1¹/₃ cups Carrot-Ginger Butter (see recipe page 160)
> ²/₃ cup peeled, grated carrots

❖ Preheat the oven to 350°F.

❖ Lightly oil a 12-cup muffin tin.

❖ Whisk flour, salt, baking powder, and cinnamon together in a mixing bowl. Add the walnuts and raisins.

*Breads, Spreads,
Muffins, &
Sandwiches*

- In a separate bowl, whisk together cider or juice, maple syrup, oil, Carrot-Ginger Butter, and grated carrots.
- Using a wooden spoon or rubber spatula, stir the wet mixture into the dry one. Combine but do not overmix. The batter will be thick.
- Fill each muffin cup to capacity.
- Bake for 35 minutes or until a toothpick comes out clean.
- Allow the muffins to cool before removing them from the tin.

oatmeal-sunflower-currant muffins

YIELD: 12 large muffins   BAKING TIME: 35 minutes

These are superb breakfast muffins. Their mouth-watering chewy texture comes from the oats, while the sunflower seeds lend a nice crunchiness. Peter thinks they may be the tastiest muffins on the menu. Who's to argue? They are a true down-home, healthy treat, loaded with fiber from the whole wheat pastry flour, rolled oats, and sunflower seeds.

Currants: There are two types of currants: a small dark raisin-like dried grape that is most often used in baked goods, and the small berry that comes in black, red, and white varieties and is used for jams, jellies, and preserves.

> 4 cups whole wheat pastry flour
> 2/3 cup sunflower seeds
> 1 cup rolled oats
> 4 teaspoons baking powder
> 4 teaspoons cinnamon
> 1 cup currants
> 1 teaspoon sea salt
> 2 cups apple cider or apple juice
> 2/3 cup maple syrup
> 2/3 cup olive oil

- Preheat oven to 350°F.
- Lightly oil a 12-cup muffin tin.
- Whisk the flour, sunflower seeds, rolled oats, baking powder, cinnamon, currants, and salt together in a mixing bowl.
- In a separate bowl, whisk together the apple cider, maple syrup, and olive oil.
- Using a wooden spoon or rubber spatula, stir the wet mixture into the dry mixture and combine without overmixing.

(continued)

(continued)

❖ Allow the batter to rest for 5 minutes before filling the muffin tin. The oats will absorb some of the liquid ingredients and the batter will thicken.

❖ Fill each muffin cup to capacity.

❖ Bake for 35 minutes or until a toothpick comes out clean.

❖ Allow the muffins to cool before removing them from the tin.

pear-ginger muffins

YIELD: 12 large muffins   BAKING TIME: 35 minutes

These muffins are a ginger lover's delight, with a refreshing zing that perfectly complements the sweetness of the fruit. They feature chunks of juicy pears and whole wheat flour. You can substitute ripe peaches or apples. If you go the apple route, be sure to peel them.

Note: In the case of thin-skinned pears such as Bartlett or Comice, you don't need to peel them if they're ripe. If they're the tougher-skinned Bosc pears, they will need to be peeled.

> 4 cups whole wheat pastry flour
> 4 teaspoons baking powder
> 1 tablespoon ginger powder
> 1 teaspoon sea salt
> ²/₃ cup pear juice
> ²/₃ cup maple syrup
> ²/₃ cup olive oil
> 1 tablespoon vanilla extract
> 2²/₃ cups pears, peeled (optional) and diced

❖ Preheat oven to 350°F.

❖ Lightly oil a 12-cup muffin tin.

❖ Whisk the flour, baking powder, ginger powder, and salt together in a mixing bowl.

❖ In a separate bowl, whisk together the juice, syrup, and oil.

❖ Stir pears and vanilla into wet mix.

❖ Stir the wet mixture into the dry mixture with a wooden spoon. Mix until combined; do not overmix.

❖ Fill each muffin cup to capacity.

❖ Bake 35 minutes or until a toothpick comes out clean.

❖ Allow the muffins to cool before removing them from the tin.

Corn Oil

Unrefined corn oil is rich and fairly heavy. If you add a small amount of it to the batter for muffins, it combines with the olive oil to lend a pronounced toasty, buttery flavor. Although we use corn oil spar-ingly, we find it does go particularly well with corn-based baked products.

Breads, Spreads, Muffins, & Sandwiches

SANDWICHES

tofu sandwich with roasted vegetables and basil–walnut pesto

YIELD: 4 to 6 sandwiches   COOKING TIME: 50 minutes

Here is a classic vegan sandwich with a Mediterranean flair. It is absolutely guaranteed to be finger-licking good. You can also add zucchini, peppers, eggplant, mushrooms—any soft vegetable in season.

If you eat this sandwich with one of our soups, it's enough for a big lunch or dinner.

Note: The ingredients for this sandwich are best when used fresh, but if you want to make them in advance so you can put together sandwiches quickly on demand—often a necessity in families with kids—the tofu preparation can keep up to a week, covered and refrigerated, the vegetables for up to two days.

> 1 recipe Baked Tofu with Lemon-Rosemary Marinade (page 105)
> 1 recipe Oven-Roasted Onions and Carrots (page 168)
> 1 recipe Basil–Walnut Pesto (page 117)

To assemble the sandwich:

❖ Spread bread of choice with pesto.

❖ Layer roasted vegetables, marinated tofu, and a leaf of lettuce.

❖ Cut in half and serve.

hot open-faced tempeh sandwich

YIELD: 4 servings   COOKING TIME: 35 minutes

During the mid-nineties sandwiches were introduced to our menu. This vegan variation on an American classic has become a fixture. It's a hearty cold-weather crowd-pleaser, appropriate for lunch or dinner; you can definitely serve this one at your Super Bowl party. It has probably won over more skeptical carnivores than any other item on our menu.

> *For the tempeh:*
> 1 pound tempeh
> 1/3 cup olive oil
> 2/3 cup apple cider or apple juice

(continued)

How to Assemble the "Sam or I Sandwich"

Spread 2 pieces of bread evenly with Soba Sensation Sauce (page 209), top with a slice of Baked Tofu with Lemon-Rosemary Marinade (page 105), and a tablespoon or two of the following: Ruby Kraut (page 122), finely grated daikon, Sea Vegetable Topping (page 124), and lettuce.

(continued)

> $^1/_4$ *cup shoyu or tamari*
> $^1/_4$ *cup brown rice vinegar*

For the sandwich:
> 1 recipe Brown Rice Gravy with Roasted Mushrooms or Herbed
>   Mushroom Gravy (pages 202, 204)
> 1 recipe Mashed Potatoes with Garlic and Rosemary (page 91)
> 1 bunch spinach, large stems removed, washed and dried
> 1 sourdough baguette
> 1 recipe Ruby Kraut or Quick Crispy Pickled Vegetables
>   (pages 122, 118; optional)

To bake the tempeh:

❖ Preheat the oven to 350°F.

❖ Slice the tempeh into 12 pieces, 2 by 3 inches and approximately $^1/_3$-inch thick. Use a straight-edged knife as a serrated one will tear the tempeh.

❖ Choose a lasagna-style baking dish that will hold the tempeh in a single layer.

❖ Whisk the olive oil, apple cider, shoyu, and brown rice vinegar together and pour over the tempeh to barely cover.

❖ Bake on the middle rack of the oven for 35 minutes or until the marinade has been absorbed.

To assemble the sandwich:

❖ Cut $^1/_4$-inch thick slices of baguette.

❖ Remove large stems from the spinach. Wash in several changes of cold water. Dry and coarsely chop. Arrange the spinach on 4 plates.

❖ Place five baguette slices artfully on top of the spinach, then a piece of tempeh atop each bread slice.

❖ Scoop a mound of mashed potatoes on each plate.

❖ Smother each tempeh piece and the mound of potatoes with gravy.

❖ Sprinkle the sandwich with Ruby Kraut, the potatoes with chopped parsley, and garnish each plate with Quick Crispy Pickled Vegetables.

Hot Open-faced
Tempeh Sandwich

oven-roasted onions and carrots

YIELD: 2¹/₂ cups   COOKING TIME: 25 minutes

We use this onion-carrot mixture for our marinated tofu sandwich. It works well between two slices of bread on its own, as a side dish, or even as a main course served over rice or any other favorite grain.

In the summer, replace half the steamed carrots with raw zucchini slices. Bear in mind, though, that different vegetables require different amounts of time in the oven depending on their density and/or cellular structures. Carrots are hard and don't give up their water easily, so steaming them in advance helps reduce the roasting time as well as the amount of fat you have to use. Cauliflower, on the other hand, roasts very quickly and will not need to be steamed or parboiled before roasting. Zucchini, which has a fairly high water content and is relatively soft, roasts even more quickly than cauliflower.

Try this: Serve the vegetables over grains or rice topped with Brown Rice Gravy (page 202) or a bean sauce. Cool them, toss with balsamic vinegar and freshly chopped basil, and serve as a topping for salad.

> 1 quart onions (approx. 1 pound), sliced into ¹/₃-inch-thick rings
> 3 cups carrots (3/4 pound), cut on the diagonal into slices ¹/₄ inch thick and 2 inches long
> Freshly ground black pepper to taste
> 1 tablespoon olive oil

* Preheat oven to 400°F.
* Steam the onions and carrots for 3 minutes in a 2-quart saucepan, fitted with a steamer basket and tight-fitting lid.
* Toss the onions, carrots, and pepper together in a bowl.
* Spread the vegetables on an oiled cookie sheet and roast for 15 to 20 minutes or until lightly browned.
* Allow the vegetables to cool at room temperature.

Breads, Spreads, Muffins, & Sandwiches

tempeh reuben sandwich

YIELD: 4 to 6 sandwiches   COOKING TIME: 45 minutes

Voila—another boss sandwich: satisfying, hearty, and all-vegan. The keys to this sandwich are the Russian Dressing and the sauerkraut. You can make your own organic sauerkraut, but it takes up to a month and there are some very good brands on the market. (We recommend Eden.)

This recipe is vastly improved if you serve the kraut and the tempeh warm, which is how we do it at the restaurant. If the dressing is kept cold, this makes for a nice contrast. Heat up the sauerkraut in any kind of pot on the stove. Unless it's just been baked, warm the tempeh, covered, in a 250°F oven for 10 minutes.

1 recipe Baked Tempeh with Soy-Mustard Marinade (page 102)
1 (32-ounce) jar of prepared organic sauerkraut
Russian Dressing (see below)

For the Russian Dressing:
$^1/_2$ pound soft tofu
1 tablespoon freshly squeezed lemon juice
3 tablespoons rice syrup
1 tablespoon olive oil
1 teaspoon prepared mustard
1 tablespoon minced red onion
$^2/_3$ cup sun-dried tomatoes, soaked and finely chopped
$^1/_3$ cup minced dill pickles
$^1/_2$ teaspoon sea salt plus additional for seasoning

❖ Combine the tofu, lemon juice, rice syrup, olive oil, and mustard in a food processor fitted with a steel blade and puree until creamy.

❖ Add tomatoes, pickles, red onions, and salt.

❖ Pulse a few times to combine.

❖ Spread bread of choice with Russian Dressing.

❖ Layer with tempeh, organic sauerkraut, and a leaf of lettuce.

❖ Cut in half and serve.

Entrées: Daily Seasonal Creations

braised seitan with onions and fresh herbs

YIELD: 4 to 6 servings   COOKING TIME: 1 hour

This is a substantial main course that provides a good wallop of protein and is an ideal fall or winter meal.

Serving suggestion: With Mashed Potatoes with Garlic and Rosemary (page 91).

Try this: To make a breaded version, brush the seitan slices liberally with olive oil and dredge them in toasted sourdough breadcrumbs seasoned with dried thyme, basil, and oregano. Then bake in a 350°F oven for half an hour. Since the seitan is already cooked, all you are really doing is crisping the breadcrumb coating. Serve smothered with Herbed Mushroom Gravy (page 204).

> 2 pounds seitan
> 2 pounds onions, cut in ¹/₄-inch crescents
> 1 tablespoon minced garlic
> 1 to 2 tablespoons minced fresh herbs such as rosemary, sage, or thyme
> Pinch of sea salt
> ¹/₄ teaspoon freshly ground black pepper
> ¹/₃ cup olive oil
> 3 tablespoons mirin or dry sherry
> Water or vegetable stock

* Preheat the oven to 350°F.

* Combine the onion, garlic, herbs, salt, and pepper with the olive oil in a 10-inch sauté pan. Cook over high heat until the vegetables begin to sizzle.

* Reduce the heat to low, add the mirin, cover, and simmer for 20 to 30 minutes or until the onions are very soft. Stir often to prevent sticking.

* Slice the seitan into ¹/₂-inch-thick pieces.

* Spread half of the onion mixture on the bottom of a baking dish, layer the seitan slices, and spread the remaining onions on top.

* Add enough water or stock to barely cover the onions and bake uncovered until the flavor of the onion and herbs have permeated the seitan and the onions are lightly browned on top.

curried chickpea and vegetable stew

YIELD: 4 to 6 servings   COOKING TIME: 1¹/₂ to 2 hours

This dish offers endless potential for experimentation. First of all, you can try different proportions of spices for the curry mix. When you grind spices for fresh curry powder, the aromas are delightfully intoxicating and—who knows—you might just discover some new taste sensations. Try it once according to the ingredients list below, then plan on changing the vegetables according to season, varying the grains, and playing around with the curry mix.

Note: The chickpeas need to be soaked in 5 cups of cold water, in advance.

homemade curry powder

YIELD: ¹/₂ cup

¹/₄ cup coriander seed
1 tablespoon cumin seed
1¹/₂ tablespoons black peppercorns
2-inch-long piece of cinnamon stick, broken into pieces
¹/₂ tablespoon cardamom pods
³/₄ teaspoon fenugreek seeds
2 tablespoons ground turmeric
1 tablespoon ground ginger

❖ Place the coriander seeds, cumin seeds, peppercorns, cinnamon stick, cardamom pods, and fenugreek seeds in a dry 8-inch skillet. Cook over medium heat, stirring and shaking the pan until the spices are toasty, approximately 3 minutes. Let the spices cool.

❖ Grind the spices to a fine powder using a clean coffee mill or mortar and pestle. Pour them into a bowl and stir in the tumeric and ginger.

❖ Store in an airtight container.

For the curry:
1¹/₂ cups dried chickpeas, sorted and soaked in 5 cups cold water for 8 hours
2 cups diced onions
2¹/₂ tablespoons Homemade Curry Powder
3 tablespoons olive oil
¹/₂ cup diced celery
1 cup diced carrots
2 cups scrubbed, diced potatoes
Water or vegetable stock
1¹/₂ cups diced zucchini

(continued)

When you're preparing
the curry powder for
this recipe—or for that
matter any spice or
combination of spices—
don't forget an impor-
tant Angelica Kitchen
rule of thumb: Always
grind your own.
Whether you grind one
spice or eight, it's a
complete revelation
that will change the
way you cook. It's like
the difference between
coffee made from
freshly ground beans
and the preground,
canned stuff. No com-
parison! To grind the
spices, use either a
coffee grinder or do it
by hand with a mortar
and pestle or suribachi.
They'll retain their vivid
flavor for up to a month;
after that they begin to
fade. Keep them in a
tightly covered con-
tainer away from light.

(continued)

> *2 cups cauliflower cut in florets*
> *1 bunch spinach, washed, dried, and coarsely chopped*
> *Sea salt*

- Soak chickpeas in the cold water for 8 hours or overnight.
- Drain the chickpeas, place them in a pressure cooker with water to cover by 1 inch, and cook for 40 minutes. Drain the chickpeas and set aside, reserving the cooking liquid.
- Place the onions, curry powder, and olive oil in a 3-quart heavy-bottomed saucepan over medium heat. Sauté the onions for 10 minutes, stirring frequently to prevent browning.
- Add the celery, carrots, potatoes, chickpeas, and reserved cooking liquid plus enough water or (stock) to equal 4 cups. Bring to a boil, lower flame, cover, and simmer for 30 minutes.
- Add the zucchini and cauliflower, uncover, and cook for 10 more minutes.
- Season with sea salt to taste and simmer for 5 more minutes.
- Add spinach and cook for 2 minutes or until spinach is wilted.
- Serve over Three-Grain Pilaf or Basic Brown Rice (pages 107, 94).

autumn tempeh and vegetable stew

YIELD: 4 to 6 servings   COOKING TIME: 1 hour

This is an example of the unique and traditional nishimi-style Japanese cooking where ingredients are layered in a pot and simmered. The stock or water is poured down the side of the pot and left to cook unstirred, so as not to disturb the layers. This method allows a mysterious harmony of flavors and textures to develop, determined largely by the nature of the ingredients and their placement in the pot. Seaweed, by virtue of its watery habitat, has a kind of floating energy that will tend to rise up from the bottom of the pot. Carrots and burdock grow as roots with a downward energy that seeks the depth of the earth for water and nutrients; they form the top layer of the pot. Onions and squash grow, up, down, and sideways; they form the middle layer of the pot.

> *For the vegetables:*
> *2 (6-inch) pieces dried kombu*
> *2 teaspoons olive oil or light sesame oil*
> *4 cups water*
> *2 onions, cut into 1-inch chunks*
> *4 cups squash such as kabocha, buttercup, Hokaido or red kuri,
>   seeded and cut into 2-inch chunks (about 1 1/2 pounds)*

¹/₄ cup garlic cloves
6 fresh sage leaves
2 turnips, cut into 2-inch chunks
2 carrots, cut into 2-inch chunks
¹/₂ pound burdock, cut into 2-inch chunks
2 teaspoons sea salt plus additional for seasoning
Freshly ground black pepper

For the tempeh:
1 pound tempeh, cut into 1-inch cubes
2 tablespoons mirin
3 tablespoons shoyu
3 tablespoons olive oil
1 teaspoon minced fresh rosemary

❖ Preheat the oven to 350°F.

❖ Soak the kombu in 4 cups of water while you prep the vegetables. After about 15 minutes, remove the kombu from the water and cut into 1-inch squares, reserving the water.

❖ Coat the bottom of a heavy 4- to 5-quart casserole with the oil and spread the kombu along the bottom.

❖ Spread individual layers of onions, squash, garlic, sage leaves, turnips, carrot, and burdock. Make sure all ingredients are layered separately in that order.

❖ Sprinkle 2 teaspoons of sea salt over the top of the vegetables and gently pour the reserved kombu water down the side of the pot without disturbing the layers.

❖ Place the casserole over high heat and bring to a boil. Reduce heat to low, cover, and simmer 45 minutes to 1 hour.

❖ While the stew simmers, prepare marinade by whisking together the mirin, shoyu, and olive oil, then stir in the rosemary.

❖ Toss the tempeh cubes with the marinade and divide them among 2 10-inch ovenproof glass pie plates or place in 1 large lasagna pan.

❖ Cover the pan with foil and bake for 30 minutes. Uncover and continue to bake for 15 more minutes, stirring to brown evenly.

❖ Remove the tempeh from the oven and stir into the stew. By this time the squash will have fallen apart. Stir it to create a thick sauce around the root vegetables and tempeh.

❖ Season the stew with sea salt and freshly ground black pepper to taste.

❖ Serve over soft polenta, Millet, Angelica Style, or Three-Grain Pilaf (pages 93, 92, 107).

CARL AND RENEE KRUMMENOEHL, CRICKLEWOOD TEMPEH

Cricklewood, Angelica Kitchen's tempeh supplier, is an excellent example of the kind of cottage industry with which we enjoy doing business. The mom-and-pop operation is owned by Carl and Renee Krummenoehl and is situated on their property in Mertztown, Pennsylvania. It had its beginnings about twenty years ago when the couple moved to the country seeking a healthier lifestyle—they found much more: a vocation.

Carl and Renee started small, making tempeh by incubating it in a Styrofoam box in the house. They next shifted production to a converted shed out back. Their current operation is triple the size but still manages to stay small and hands-on. Today Cricklewood produces about 70,000 pounds of tempeh a year, roughly 1 percent of the tempeh market. (There are only seven or eight tempeh manufacturers in North America.)

Like tofu, tempeh is a soybean product, and all the beans Carl and Renee use are New York State grown, non-hybridized, and organic.

The production of tempeh relies upon Rhizopus oligosporus, a microscopic spore or mold that feeds on the soybeans, fermenting or "pre-digesting" them, a process that makes them much easier for the human body to assimilate. Rhizopus grows on a number of different bases including sweet potatoes, wheat, and rice. Cricklewood purchases small amounts of the culture, then cultivates second-generation batches in highly controlled, sterilized conditions. Tempeh production begins by grinding up the soybeans, soaking them overnight, and then cooking them for about an hour. Carl and Renee make 100-pound batches in a huge stockpot. The beans are cooled and dried mechanically, then inoculated with the rhizopus culture, and finally placed in perforated plastic bags in an incubator where they gradually ferment into tempeh. In about twelve hours the rhizopus begins feeding on the beans, initiating the fermentation process, which generates quite a bit of heat. Depending on the weather, the temperature in the incubator can be anywhere from seventy to one hundred degrees.

As Carl explains, the key to making tempeh is patience. The fermentation process can't be rushed and it must be carefully monitored. If the temperature in the incubator gets too high, the rhizopus shuts down and the batch is ruined. The entire process takes about twenty-four hours, during which time the factory

Entrées:
Daily Seasonal
Creations

takes on an appetizing, yeasty smell reminiscent of a bakery. When the process is complete, the fermented beans are solidly bound together by microscopic mycelium, a network of thread-like tubes that is the rhizopus's fungal growth. This is tempeh at its best, aromatic and delicious.

Many larger producers use vacuum-packing, a process that kills the beneficial enzymes. At Cricklewood, in contrast, the fresh tempeh is cooled, carefully packaged, and then frozen, which keeps the enzymes inactive but alive. So ask for Cricklewood to have an authentic, satisfying tempeh experience.

oden (asian root-vegetable stew)

YIELD: 4 to 6 servings   COOKING TIME: 1 hour

A highlight of Japanese country cooking, oden is generally a five-root stew. Our version adheres to that tradition. This is my favorite winter stew and it features several fundamental ingredients of Japanese cuisine—kombu, shoyu, ginger, and rice wine (mirin). If you like, you can include additional root vegetables such as white turnips, jerusalem artichokes, celeriac (celery root), and parsley root. And oden is good for what ails you: It's a blood purifier and fortifier. For authenticity, cook it in a black iron kettle over a fire in the middle of your hut.

  2 teaspoons olive oil
  2 cups diced onions (1 large)
  6 cups water
  Approximately 6 oz. each of the following 5 ingredients:
    1 cup burdock, scrubbed and cut into 1-inch pieces
    1 cup carrots, scrubbed and cut into 1-inch pieces
    1 cup daikon, scrubbed and cut into 1-inch pieces
    1 cup rutabagas, scrubbed and cut into 1-inch pieces
    1 cup parsnips, scrubbed and cut into 1-inch pieces
  4 to 6 dry shiitake mushrooms
  1 (3-inch) piece dried kombu
  5 slices ginger, each the size of a quarter
  ¹/₂ cup shoyu or tamari
  2 tablespoons mirin
  ¹/₄ cup kuzu
  1 tablespoon toasted sesame oil
  2 tablespoons sliced scallions for garnish

(continued)

(continued)

❖ In a heavy 3-quart saucepan, sauté the onions and burdock in the olive oil over medium heat for 10 minutes.

❖ Add 6 cups of water and bring to a boil over high heat. Add the carrots, daikon, rutabagas, parsnips, shiitake mushrooms, kombu, ginger, mirin, and tamari.

❖ Lower the flame and simmer covered for 30 to 40 minutes or until the vegetables are tender. Remove the ginger and discard.

❖ Remove the kombu and shiitake mushrooms, slice into bite-size pieces, and return to the pot.

❖ Dissolve the kuzu in $^1/_4$ cup cold water; stir into the stew and simmer for 1 or 2 minutes longer.

❖ Stir in the sesame oil.

NOTE: You should never cook with toasted sesame oil because high heat will release free radicals in the oil, making it toxic. Use toasted sesame oil as a last-minute addition; treat it like a flavor enhancer such as salt or vinegar.

❖ Serve with noodles or rice, accompanied by baked, marinated tofu, kimchee, and scallion garnish.

moroccan-style tagine

YIELD: 6 to 8 servings   COOKING TIME: 45 to 50 minutes

Thomas Jefferson used the phrase "enlightened experimentality." We try to apply this concept in the kitchen. We like to take a cosmopolitan, eclectic approach, finding inspiration in many different cuisines of the world. A tagine is a Moroccan stew of meat or poultry and vegetables that is cooked long and slow. Though we took creative license in interpreting this dish, as we are wont to do, we kept intact the typical Moroccan spicy/sweet blend of flavorings.

Serving suggestions: At Angelica, we love to introduce people to different types of grains. Tagines are almost always served over couscous, but this recipe also goes very well with a mix of grains such as teff, basmati rice, and millet, the last of which is wonderfully light when toasted and cooked dry. (It also would work well with a flat bread.)

> 1 teaspoon coriander seeds
> $^1/_2$ teaspoon cumin seeds
> $^1/_2$ teaspoon caraway seeds
> $^1/_2$ teaspoon fennel seeds

(continued)

Entrées:
Daily Seasonal
Creations

Oden (Asian Root-
Vegetable Stew)

(continued)

    3 cloves
    1 cinnamon stick
    ¹/₂ tablespoon turmeric
    1 teaspoon cayenne pepper
    3 cups roughly chopped onion
    2 tablespoons chopped garlic
    ¹/₄ cup extra virgin olive oil
    2 strips orange peel
    2 strips lemon peel
    2 cups diced carrots
    2 cups diced turnips
    2 teaspoons sea salt plus additional for seasoning
    3 cups cooked chickpeas (or 2 cans organic chickpeas, drained)
      Note: See Curried Chickpea and Vegetable Stew (page 171)
      for instructions on how to pressure-cook chickpeas.
    2 teaspoons peeled, minced ginger
    1 (28-ounce) can organic whole peeled tomatoes and their juice
    2 small zucchini cut in medium-size dice, about 2 cups
    ¹/₂ head cauliflower, cut in florets (about 2 cups)
    ¹/₂ cup firmly packed Kalamata olives, pitted and halved
    ¹/₂ cup chopped fresh cilantro for garnish

❖ Grind the coriander, cumin, caraway, fennel, cloves, and cinnamon to a fine powder in a spice mill or with a mortar and pestle. Set aside in a small dish and stir in the cayenne pepper and turmeric.

❖ Place the onions, garlic, and olive oil in a 4-quart casserole over medium heat. Sauté for 5 minutes or until the onions are translucent.

❖ Add the ground spices, fruit peels, carrots, ginger, turnips, and 2 teaspoons of salt. Cover and reduce the heat to low. Simmer 10 minutes more.

❖ Add the chickpeas, tomatoes, and their juice and simmer for 10 minutes.

❖ Add the zucchini and cauliflower and continue to cook uncovered for 15 to 20 minutes more.

❖ Remove the orange and lemon peels. Add the chopped olives and simmer 3 minutes longer.

❖ Season with additional salt to taste and serve garnished with chopped cilantro.

Entrées:
Daily Seasonal
Creations

three sisters (posole)

YIELD: 6 to 8 servings

COOKING TIME: 2 hours,
plus 1 hour for bean soaking

In Native American culinary tradition, the three sisters are squash, corn, and beans. This recipe calls for four different kinds of beans, winter squash, and corn in the form of hominy, aka posole. Whole hominy is the hulled, unground version of field corn that is the basis for all North American corn dishes such as tortillas, tamales, and arepas. Peter and Leslie learned how to dehull field corn from John Mohawk, Ph.D., a Turtle Clan Seneca and professor of American studies at the State University of New York at Buffalo, who is developing food products based on the traditional crops of the Iroquois. We love introducing people to a traditional ingredient like hominy; and we highly recommend you add it to your regular inventory of grains. It has its own signature chewy texture, which is retained nicely in a stew.

1 cup whole hominy
$^1/_2$ cup dried pinto beans
$^1/_2$ cup dried anasazi beans
$^1/_2$ cup dried black beans
$^1/_2$ cup dried kidney beans
2 quarts water
$^1/_4$ cup olive oil
3 cups chopped onions
1 tablespoon chopped garlic
1 cinnamon stick
2 bay leaves
1 jalapeño pepper, stemmed, seeded, and chopped (rubber gloves
    advised)
$1^1/_2$ tablespoons ground cumin
3 leaves fresh sage, chopped
$^1/_2$ cup diced celery
3 cups diced carrots
3 cups diced turnips
3 cups winter squash such as kuri, hubbard, or kabocha, peeled,
    seeded, and cubed
1 (32-ounce) can peeled organic tomatoes and their juice
Sea salt and freshly ground black pepper
Chopped fresh cilantro for garnish

❖ Sort through the beans and hominy to discard any broken ones or stones. Place the beans and hominy in a 3- to 4-quart saucepan and cover with 2 quarts water.

❖ Bring to a boil over high heat. Reduce the heat to low and simmer 2 minutes.

(continued)

(continued)

❖ Remove the pan from the heat and allow to sit for 1 hour so the beans and hominy can swell.

❖ Meanwhile, prep the other vegetables.

❖ When the beans and hominy have soaked, drain and rinse them in a strainer. Place them in a 3- to 4-quart pressure cooker with 5 cups of water, bring to pressure, lower heat to simmer, and cook for 30 minutes.

❖ Place the $^1/_4$ cup olive oil in a stove top casserole over medium heat and sauté the onions, garlic, cinnamon, bay leaves, jalapeño pepper, cumin, and sage for 10 minutes, stirring frequently, then add the remaining vegetables and tomatoes. Reduce the heat to low.

❖ Quick-release the pressure cooker by running cool water over the top, then add the beans along with their cooking liquid to the casserole.

❖ Simmer over low heat, covered, for 1 hour or until everything is tender.

❖ Add salt and pepper to taste and continue to cook another 15 to 20 minutes or until thickened.

❖ Served topped with Tofu Sour Cream (page 128) and chopped cilantro.

classic vegetable lasagna

YIELD: 10 to 12 servings   COOKING TIME: 2 hours

This is perfect party food. It looks great as the centerpiece for a buffet and is excellent reheated as a leftover. It can be assembled up to the point of putting the tofu cheese layer on top and frozen for up to a month. (Be sure to defrost before baking, though.) Leftover or frozen, it doesn't lose any of its flavor; in fact, the taste may even improve.

Try this: Substitute a traditional tomato sauce for our famous No-mato Sauce or try the Béchamel with Basil Garlic to create a white lasagna.

For the filling:
2 quarts mushrooms, wiped clean with a damp towel and thinly
    sliced
8 tablespoons extra virgin olive oil
2 teaspoons sea salt plus additional for seasoning
1 pound tempeh, cut into $^1/_2$-inch cubes
3 tablespoons shoyu or tamari
1 quart peeled and diced onions (approx. 1 pound)
2 quarts firmly packed greens of choice (kale, collards, or mustard
    greens), washed and chopped
1 cup Kalamata olives, pitted and chopped

For the tofu ricotta:
1½ *pounds firm tofu, rinsed and patted dry*
8 *tablespoons olive oil*
3 *tablespoons finely chopped fresh herbs such as tarragon, basil,*
  thyme, or rosemary
⅓ *cup freshly squeezed lemon juice, strained*
½ *teaspoon freshly ground black pepper*

For the lasagna:
1½ *cups No-mato Sauce (page 206)*
  Note: *We recommend you make half of the recipe to yield 1 quart*
  of sauce and simply reserve the unused portion for another dish.
1 *pound whole wheat lasagna noodles*

To make the filling:

❖ Preheat the oven to 400°F.

❖ Toss the mushrooms with 2 tablespoons of oil and 1 teaspoon of sea salt, then spread them on a cookie sheet and roast for 30 minutes.

❖ Toss the tempeh with the tamari and 3 tablespoons of oil. Spread the cubes on a cookie sheet and roast for 30 minutes.

❖ Meanwhile, place the onions in a 8- to 10-inch sauté pan in 3 tablespoons of oil with 1 teaspoon of sea salt over medium heat and sauté for 8 to 10 minutes or until lightly browned.

❖ Steam the greens in a pot equipped with a steamer basket over high heat for 6 to 8 minutes or until tender. Remove the greens to a plate until cool enough to handle, then chop finely.

❖ Spoon roasted tempeh and mushrooms into a large mixing bowl.

❖ Add the onions, greens, and olives. Toss well.

❖ Season with salt and pepper to taste.

To make the tofu ricotta:

❖ Combine all the ingredients in a food processor fitted with a steel blade and puree until smooth.

To make the lasagna:

❖ Lower the oven temperature to 350°F.

❖ Bring 4 quarts of water with 1 tablespoon of sea salt to a boil. Turn off the heat and soak the lasagna noodles for 5 minutes or until pliable and slightly soft, then drain.

❖ Spread 1 cup of No-mato Sauce in the bottom of a 9- by 13-inch lasagna pan.

❖ Cover the sauce with a single layer of noodles, slightly overlapping.

(continued)

(continued)

❖ Spread half of the tempeh-vegetable filling over the noodles. Top with a layer of noodles.

❖ Spread the remaining ¹/₂ cup of sauce over the noodle layer. Spread the remaining tempeh-vegetable filling on top, then add the final layer of noodles.

❖ Spread the tofu ricotta on top of the final layer of noodles.

❖ Bake for 1 hour or until the tofu ricotta is light brown and firm.

❖ Allow the lasagna to rest for 10 minutes before serving.

enchilada with mole

YIELD: **8 servings**   COOKING TIME: 1¹/₂ hours

One of the keys to an authentic mole is to include some chocolate, which gives it the typical sumptuous dark brown color and consistency. This recipe is adopted from one brought from Mexico by Salvador Lima, one of our talented chefs at Angelica. Our version calls for one very non-traditional Mexican ingredient, tamari, which gives it a rich depth of flavor.

Note: Sprouted wheat tortillas should be available at any health food store. We use the Alvarado Street brand, which are quite large.

For the mole sauce (yields 2 quarts):
2 cups ancho chilis
¹/₂ cup olive oil
¹/₂ cup sesame seeds
¹/₂ cup peanuts
¹/₂ cup almonds, slivered or chopped
¹/₂ cup raisins
7 cups water
1¹/₂ ounces bittersweet chocolate broken into pieces
Sea salt

For the seitan and vegetables:
¹/₃ cup olive oil
3 cups diced onions
1 tablespoon minced garlic
2 cups diced carrots
2 cups seeded and diced red bell peppers
2 cups thinly sliced mushrooms
1 tablespoon ground cumin
2 bay leaves
1 teaspoon dried thyme
2 cups seitan (page 96), coarsely ground in a food processor

Entrées:
Daily Seasonal
Creations

2 cups cooked pinto beans
Shoyu or tamari to taste
Lemon juice to taste
6 sprouted wheat tortillas
1 recipe Tofu Sour Cream (page 128)

To prepare the mole sauce:

❖ Place the chiles in a pot with water to cover and bring to a boil. Remove from the heat and soak until soft, about 15 minutes.

❖ Cool under cold running water. Drain completely, remove stems, and scrape out and discard the seeds.

❖ Place the olive oil in a frying pan over medium heat to warm. Add sesame seeds, peanuts, almonds, and raisins. Stir and continue to toast over a low heat for 10 to 15 minutes.

❖ Combine the chiles and nut mixture in a food processor and while the motor is running add enough of the water to form a smooth puree. Pour the puree into a saucepan, add the remaining water, and bring to a boil over medium heat.

❖ Reduce the heat to low and simmer, uncovered, for 20 minutes. Stir in the chocolate and continue to cook 5 to 10 more minutes until thickened.

❖ Season with sea salt to taste.

To prepare the seitan and vegetables:

❖ Preheat the oven to 375°F.

❖ Place the olive oil in a heavy 10- to 12- inch sauté pan over medium heat. Cook the onions with $1/2$ teaspoon of salt for 8 to 10 minutes or until translucent.

❖ Add the garlic, carrots, peppers, mushrooms, cumin, bay leaves, and thyme. Reduce heat to low, cover, and cook 20 minutes longer, stirring often to prevent sticking.

❖ Coarsely grind the seitan in a food processor. Add ground seitan, beans, tamari, and a squeeze of lemon to the vegetables. Cook 5 minutes over medium heat, adding a little water if the mixture starts to stick. Remove from the heat. Discard bay leaves.

To assemble:

❖ Thinly coat the bottom of a lasagna pan with about $3/4$ cup of mole.

❖ Pour 1 quart of the mole into a second lasagna pan or skillet large enough to accommodate a tortilla. Dip both sides of a tortilla in the mole and place it on a plate.

(continued)

(continued)

❖ Spoon 3/4 cup of the vegetable filling onto the tortilla and roll into a cigar shape. Lay the rolled enchilada in the first lasagna pan. Continue to dip, fill, and roll tortillas until all the filling is used. You should be able to form a single layer of approximately 6 to 8 enchiladas.

❖ Spread 1/2 cup mole sauce over the enchiladas. Cover with foil (shiny side down) and bake for 25 minutes.

❖ While the enchiladas bake, transfer what is left of the mole to a 2-quart saucepan and gently reheat.

❖ Prepare Tofu Sour Cream with cilantro (page 128).

❖ To serve, slice the enchiladas in half. It is essential to do this while they are still in the pan. Serve with additional mole, tofu sour cream, a simple green leaf salad with lemon and olive oil, and some thinly sliced radishes.

greek phyllo casserole with beets, spinach, and potatoes

YIELD: 4 to 6 servings   COOKING TIME: 1 hour

This dish is a real treat for beet-and-potatoes lovers!

With its delicious, flaky baked phyllo topping and smooth layer of mashed potatoes underneath, it is a study in balance and contrast. The lemon juice balances the sweetness of the beets, and together they cut through the richness of the potatoes. When you slice the casserole, you will enjoy the festive color combination. We like to call these kinds of dishes haute peasant cuisine. In this case, it's a sophisticated version of rustic Greek country fare.

Serving suggestion: Line plate with French Lentil Sauce (page 204), ladle piece of casserole over sauce, and top with Tofu Sour Cream with dill (page 128).

> 1 1/2 pounds yellow-flesh potatoes (peeling is optional)
> 1 pound beets
> 4 cups thinly sliced onions
> 2 tablespoons minced garlic
> 2 tablespoons minced fresh oregano (1 teaspoon dried oregano may be substituted)
> 2 tablespoons extra virgin olive oil
> 2 tablespoons freshly squeezed lemon juice, strained
> 2 pounds fresh spinach, washed and large stems removed
> Sea salt and freshly ground black pepper to taste
> 1/2 cup olive oil, for brushing phyllo and pan
> 8 ounces phyllo

Entrées:
Daily Seasonal
Creations

- Steam the potatoes until tender, about 15 minutes, in a 3- to 4-quart saucepan equipped with steamer basket until tender.
- Pressure-cook the beets for 15 minutes. Alternately, boil them in a 3-quart saucepan for 45 minutes to 1 hour or until tender.
- Preheat the oven to 400°F.
- Place the onions, garlic, oregano, and olive oil in a 10-inch sauté pan over low heat and cook for 10 to 15 minutes or until soft.
- Combine the potatoes and onions in a bowl and mash. Set aside.
- Cool and peel the beets under cold running water. Cut into ^{1}/8-inch-thick rounds. Toss them in a bowl with lemon juice and salt and pepper to taste and set aside.
- Steam the spinach until just wilted, about 1 to 2 minutes. Refresh in a bowl of cold water, squeeze dry, and chop. Season with salt and pepper to taste.
- Oil a 10 x 10-inch ovenproof glass dish. Lightly brush 3 sheets of phyllo with oil and layer in the bottom of the pan.
- Spread potato mixture evenly over the phyllo.
- Spread the spinach over the potatoes and cover with 2 sheets of lightly oiled phyllo, then spread a layer of beets.
- Cover the beets with 10 sheets of phyllo, each sheet lightly oiled. With the tip of a sharp knife, cut through the top layers of phyllo (stopping just short of the filling) into even 4- by 6-inch portions. This will make it much easier to divide up the casserole after baking.
- Bake for 30 minutes or until golden brown.
- Slice through and serve.

Greek Phyllo Casserole with Beets, Spinach, and Potatoes and French Lentil Sauce

LILI AND ANTHONY ANAGOSTOU, POSEIDON CONFECTIONERY

When Angelica Kitchen's chefs began to create some wonderful recipes that called for phyllo, the Greek pastry that consists of multiple layers of super-thin dough, we sought out Poseidon Confectionery, makers of authentic, fresh phyllo made in the time-honored traditional manner. Since Poseidon didn't use organic flour, we supplied it from our regular source, Community Mill and Bean. As far as we know, it was the first time authentic phyllo had been made from organic dough. Now, Angelica's goes through about forty pounds of phyllo every couple of weeks.

Poseidon had its beginnings in 1923 when Demetrios Anagostou immigrated to America from the island of Corfu in Greece and founded the bakery on the west side of Manhattan. His family has been operating it continuously since then, even at the same location—629 Ninth Avenue between 44th and 45th Streets. The business remains in good hands: Anthony Anagnostou has been making phyllo since he was sixteen, and his wife Lili runs the world-famous Ninth Avenue Food Festival.

Lili and Tony produce the best Greek pastries in New York, if not the entire country. They are also the last bastion of the traditional method of making phyllo. Most of Poseidon's phyllo is sold to restaurants or used in their own traditional Greek pastries including baklava (walnut-honey pastries) and spanakopitas (spinach pies). A small amount is sold to walk-in customers in

Entrées:
Daily Seasonal
Creations

one-pound wraps. Poseidon's customers include some of New York's top gourmet restaurants—Clementine, Chanterelle, Union Square Cafe, and Gramercy Tavern. Poseidon supplies three Turkish restaurants with phyllo, but ironically, the Greek ones all use the factory-produced version made with preservatives.

Poseidon's phyllo is both light and luxurious, rich and delicate. It's made from wheat flour, water, and salt and nothing else. The trick is to add the exact proportion of salt that will allow the dough to retain just the right amount of moisture to stay strong yet supple enough to be rolled into those exquisitely thin sheets. After the dough is made, it's formed into huge balls, which are then broken up into smaller balls that weigh about one and three-quarters pounds each. A large, old rolling pin is used to carefully roll each ball into a tissue-thin layer that fills the surface of a muslin-covered, five-foot square table. The key to the phyllo-maker's art is to be relaxed, to pull the dough in a smooth, continuous motion, not to grab or jerk it. Once the dough reaches the desired thickness, it's cut into eighteen-inch squares and stacked in layers of thirty. Depending on the humidity, the sheets may be hung on racks to dry or placed in a drying oven. Poseidon's phyllo lasts for between three days and a week if properly wrapped and refrigerated. It can also be frozen.

chickpea, rice, and vegetable casserole

YIELD: 4 to 6 servings   COOKING TIME: 1¹/₂ hours

This is a Western-style dish with decidedly Indian flavors, strikingly colorful and hearty. An excellent one-dish main course and a good choice for potluck suppers, it is also good reheated as leftovers.

  1 cup basmati rice
  2¹/₂ cups of water
  4 tablespoons olive oil

(continued)

(continued)

> 1^1/$_2$ *teaspoons sea salt*
> ^{1}/$_2$ *teaspoon turmeric*
> 3/4 *cup chickpea flour*
> 12 *ounces mushrooms, thinly sliced (approximately 5 cups)*
> 2 *cups thinly sliced onions*
> 1^1/$_2$ *tablespoons curry powder (for homemade, see recipe for Curried*
>   *Chickpea and Vegetable Stew, page 171)*
> 2 *cups peeled, thinly sliced carrots*
> 1 *pound fresh spinach, large stems removed and thoroughly washed*

- Place the rice with 2^1/$_2$ cups of water, 1 tablespoon olive oil, and ^{1}/$_2$ teaspoon of sea salt in a 2-quart saucepan over high heat.
- Bring to a boil, cover, lower heat, and simmer for 20 minutes or until water has been absorbed.
- While the rice simmers place the turmeric, 1 teaspoon of sea salt, 1 tablespoon of olive oil, and 3 cups of water in another 2-quart saucepan over high heat.
- Bring to a boil, then whisk in the chickpea flour.
- Reduce the heat to low and cook for 20 minutes, stirring occasionally to prevent sticking.
- Lightly oil a 10 x 10-inch ovenproof baking dish and press an even layer of cooked rice on the bottom. Set aside.
- Place the mushrooms, onions, curry powder, and 2 tablespoons of olive oil in a skillet over medium heat and sauté until lightly browned, about 10 minutes. Spread an even layer of this mixture over the rice.
- Steam the carrots for 5 minutes or until soft and layer over mushrooms.
- Steam the spinach until just wilted, about 1 to 2 minutes. Cool in a bowl of cold water, squeeze dry, and chop.
- Season with salt and pepper to taste and layer over the carrots.
- Pour the chickpea mixture in the bowl of a food processor fitted with a steel blade and puree until creamy. (Alternately, puree in the pot with a handheld mixer.) Pour over spinach and smooth with a wet spatula.
- Preheat the oven to 350°F.
- Refrigerate the casserole until the chickpea topping is firm, about 20 minutes.
- Bake for 40 minutes, cut into squares, and serve topped with Lemon-Date Chutney (page 112).

Entrées:
Daily Seasonal
Creations

shepherd's pie

YIELD: 6 to 8 servings   COOKING TIME: 2 hours

Shepherd's Pie is classic comfort food, originally devised as a way to make good use of leftover meat and potatoes. Here is a healthy vegan version of this old-time favorite, a one-dish meal (with pickles on the side) that will impress vegetarians and non-vegetarians alike. It has a biscuit-bottom crust, lentils for a hearty protein base, and features shiitake mushrooms, which lend their subtle but distinctive flavor to the dish and give it a pleasantly chewy consistency.

For the filling:
3 ounces dry shiitake mushrooms
1 cup green lentils, sorted and rinsed
2 bay leaves
2 cups diced onions
1 cup diced carrots
1 cup diced celery
2 tablespoons olive oil
1 teaspoon each of minced fresh sage, rosemary, and thyme
2 tablespoons shoyu or tamari
1/2 teaspoon freshly ground black pepper

For the topping:
1 recipe Mashed Potatoes with Garlic and Rosemary (page 91)

For the crust:
1²/3 cup whole wheat or whole spelt flour
1/2 teaspoon baking soda
1/2 teaspoon baking powder
1/2 teaspoon sea salt
2/3 cup plain soy milk
3 tablespoons cider vinegar
1/3 cup olive oil

❖ Place the shiitake mushrooms and 4 cups of water in a 2-quart saucepan over high heat. Bring to a boil, reduce the heat to low, and simmer 45 minutes or until mushrooms are tender.

❖ Remove the pan from the heat and set aside while you prepare the vegetables and the lentils.

❖ Place the lentils, bay leaves, and 4 cups of water in a 2-quart saucepan over high heat. Bring to a boil, reduce the heat to low, cover, and simmer 30 minutes or until the lentils are tender.

(continued)

(continued)

- ❖ Prepare Mashed Potatoes with Garlic and Rosemary while the lentils cook. (When the potatoes are done, mash them in a bowl and set aside.)
- ❖ Discard the bay leaves and drain the lentils. Reserve the cooking liquid for a soup if you like. Set the lentils aside in a bowl.
- ❖ Place the onions, carrot, celery, and oil in a sauté pan over medium heat and cook for 8 to 10 minutes or until the vegetables begin to soften. Stir often to prevent sticking.
- ❖ Drain the mushrooms, reserving 3/4 cup of their cooking juices.
- ❖ Slice away and discard any tough stems from the mushrooms and chop them into 1/2-inch pieces.
- ❖ Add herbs, shoyu, pepper, 3/4 cup of reserved shiitake liquid, and mushrooms to the vegetable pan. Raise the heat and bring to a boil. Reduce heat and simmer uncovered until almost dry, about 25 minutes.
- ❖ Add the vegetable-mushroom mixture to the lentils and stir to combine.
- ❖ Preheat oven to 325°F.

To prepare the crust:

- ❖ Whisk the dry ingredients for the crust together in a mixing bowl.
- ❖ Whisk the wet ingredients together in a separate bowl.
- ❖ Stir the wet into the dry to form a dough. Lightly oil a 10-inch glass ovenproof pie pan Spread the dough in the pie pan, pressing down with damp fingers to form a crust. Make sure the dough is evenly distributed across the bottom and along the sides of the pan.
- ❖ Fill the crust with the lentil-vegetable mixture. Top with mashed potatoes, smooth with a wet spatula, and brush lightly with olive oil.
- ❖ Bake on the middle shelf of the oven for 45 minutes or until golden brown.
- ❖ Remove the pie from the oven and let it rest for 5 minutes before slicing to serve.

baked sweet dumpling squash with chestnut stuffing and anasazi bean sauce

YIELD: 6 to 8 stuffed squash   COOKING TIME: 2 hours

This recipe was created for one of our Thanksgiving menus. With the squash and chestnuts, it is beautiful, festive, and most definitely appropriate for a late fall or winter celebration. The original recipe called for sauce made from Scarlet Runners, a fairly rare heirloom bean that is not readily available organic, so we substituted anasazi beans. The dumpling

is a miniature hard-skinned orangish-yellow squash that is the ideal size for single servings. If it's not available, you can substitute other fall or winter squash.

Note on chestnuts: Chestnuts come in three forms. In the autumn, they're fresh, unpeeled, and have to be blanched to remove the outer skin. They also come either dried and pre-peeled, in which case they have to be soaked for several hours to reconstitute, or jarred, preserved in liquid. The latter type is available at Italian gourmet specialty shops.

Note on preparation: This is a rather complex recipe with many steps. To simplify things, we recommend baking the cornbread, soaking the chestnuts, and preparing the stock two days in advance. Prepare the stuffing and soak the beans the day before; make the bean sauce and prepare and stuff the squash the same day.

chestnut stuffing

YIELD: 6 cups   COOKING TIME: 2 hours

$^{1}/_{2}$ cup dried chestnuts, soaked 4 to 6 hours, excess skins removed and drained (see note below if using fresh chestnuts)
3 cups cubed Southern-Style Cornbread (page 158), cut into 1-inch cubes
2 cups cubed sourdough bread, or other bread of choice, cut into 1-inch cubes
$^{1}/_{2}$ cup pecans
1 cup finely diced yellow onions
1 cup finely diced red onions
1 tablespoon olive oil
$1^{1}/_{2}$ teaspoons sea salt
2 cloves garlic, minced
2 teaspoons minced shallots
1 teaspoon dried thyme
1 cup finely diced celery
$1^{1}/_{2}$ cups vegetable stock (page 130)
$1^{1}/_{2}$ tablespoons minced fresh sage
$1^{1}/_{2}$ tablespoons minced fresh thyme
Sea salt and freshly ground black pepper

NOTE: To remove the outer peel of fresh chestnuts, score with tip of sharp knife and blanch for 1–2 minutes in boiling water. Drain, cool nuts, then peel.

❖ Place the chestnuts in a small saucepan, cover with water by 1 inch, and simmer until soft, about 40 minutes. Remove from liquid, break into coarse pieces, and set aside.

(continued)

(continued)

❖ Spread the cubes of cornbread and sourdough on a baking sheet and toast in a 350°F oven until golden, about 15 minutes. Set aside.

❖ Spread the pecans on another baking sheet and toast in the oven for 8 minutes. Set aside to cool them, then coarsely chop.

❖ Place the onions with olive oil and salt in a skillet over low heat and cook until the onions begin to sweat and become translucent. Add garlic, shallots, dried thyme, and celery and cook until vegetables are tender, about 15 minutes.

❖ Add the toasted bread cubes, slowly adding up to 1¹/₂ cups stock as needed to moisten bread and prevent it from sticking. Add chestnuts, pecans, and fresh herbs and mix together.

❖ Remove the pan from the heat and season to taste with salt and pepper.

anasazi bean sauce

YIELD: **8 cups**   COOKING TIME: 1¹/₂ **hours**

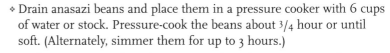

1¹/₂ *cups dried anasazi beans, sorted and presoaked*
6 *cups water or vegetable stock*
1 *cup diced onion*
2 *cloves garlic*
¹/₂ *fresh jalapeño pepper, stemmed, seeded, and minced*
2 *teaspoons sea salt plus additional for seasoning*
2 *tablespoons olive oil*
¹/₂ *cup diced carrots (1 medium carrot)*
¹/₂ *cup diced celery (1 rib)*
2 *teaspoons dried cumin, ground*
1 *teaspoon dried thyme*
1 *teaspoon dried rosemary*
¹/₂ *teaspoon dried sage*
3/4 *cup diced parsnip (¹/₄ pound)*
3/4 *cup diced sweet potatoes*
1 *teaspoon freshly squeezed lemon juice, strained*
Pinch of cayenne pepper

❖ Drain anasazi beans and place them in a pressure cooker with 6 cups of water or stock. Pressure-cook the beans about 3/4 hour or until soft. (Alternately, simmer them for up to 3 hours.)

❖ In the meantime, place the onion, garlic, jalapeño, cumin, thyme, rosemary, sage, and a pinch of salt with the olive oil into a 3- to 4-quart saucepan over low heat. Cover and cook for 10 to 15 minutes or until the vegetables are soft. Add the carrots and celery and cook for another 5 minutes.

* Add cooked beans along with parsnips, sweet potatoes, remaining salt, lemon juice, and a pinch of cayenne. Simmer together for about 30 minutes until the flavors "marry" and the root vegetables have partially decomposed and form a thick gravy around the beans.

the squash

COOKING TIME: 45 minutes

* Preheat the oven to 350°F.
* Wash, dry, and lightly oil 6 dumpling squash. Place them in a baking pan with 2 cups of water. Bake uncovered 45 minutes or until tender but still slightly firm. Cool, slice off their tops, and scoop out the seeds.
* Remove the squash from the pan and set aside.
* Drain the baking pan and brush lightly with olive oil

To assemble the dish:

* Spoon the filling into the prebaked squash and return them to the pan; bake uncovered until top has begun to crisp, about 20 minutes.

To serve:

* Ladle $^1/_2$ cup bean sauce onto plate, top with baked squash. Garnish with chopped fresh herbs such as cilantro, parsley, or chives.

five-grain croquettes

YIELD: 16 (2-inch) croquettes   COOKING TIME: 50 minutes

In this top-of-the-line whole-grain fantasy, a blend of four delicate grains is bound together by sushi rice. Regular brown rice will not work; it just doesn't have the right consistency. These tasty, filling morsels can benefit from any number of sauces and work equally well as an appetizer or main dish.

> $^1/_2$ cup white organic sushi rice or jasmine rice
> 2 tablespoons amaranth
> 2 tablespoons teff
> 2 tablespoons quinoa
> 2 tablespoons millet
> $2^1/_2$ cups of water
> 1 teaspoon sea salt
> 1 cup minced onion
> $^1/_2$ finely diced red bell pepper, seeds and membranes removed
> $^1/_4$ cup finely diced celery
> 2 tablespoons extra virgin olive oil
> $^1/_4$ teaspoon freshly ground black pepper

❖ Preheat the oven to 350°F.

❖ Place all the grains in a strainer and rinse under cold running water. Drain thoroughly and place grains in a 2-quart saucepan with $2^1/_2$ cups of water and $^1/_2$ teaspoon salt. Bring to a boil over high heat, lower the heat, cover, and simmer for 30 minutes or until all water is absorbed.

❖ While the grains cook, place the vegetables with the olive oil, remaining salt, and pepper in an 8-inch sauté pan over medium heat. Cook 8 to 10 minutes, stirring occasionally to prevent sticking.

❖ Reduce the heat to low, cover, and continue cooking for 10 to 15 minutes or until the vegetables are very tender. Do not brown; you may need to add a tablespoon or two of water to prevent this.

❖ When the grains are finished cooking, spoon them into a medium-size mixing bowl. Add the vegetables and mix thoroughly. Set the grain and vegetable mixture aside and allow to cool enough to handle.

❖ Lightly oil a cookie sheet. Wet your hands and form the mixture into golf ball–size croquettes.

❖ Place them an inch apart on the cookie sheet and flatten slightly.

❖ Bake 20 minutes.

❖ Serve with Carrot-Leek Glaze with Thyme (page 203).

Entrées:
Daily Seasonal
Creations

Five-Grain Croquettes with Carrot-Leek Glaze with Thyme

chickpea tart with potatoes and onions

YIELD: 6 servings   COOKING TIME: 1³/4 hours

Chickpeas are a staple of Angelica-style cuisine. Panisse is the polenta-like mixture that comes from the region around Nice, on the French Riviera. It's a chickpea flour gruel that's poured into a pan, cooled until firm, then cut into the desired shapes and fried. Here is one way to make use of this regional specialty without the fat associated with frying.

Serving suggestion: For a luncheon or a light supper, serve either hot or cold with Sea Caesar Salad (page 146) and a soup.

For the tart:
2 cups chickpea flour
6 cups cold water
2 tablespoons olive oil
1 teaspoon sea salt
1 large pinch saffron
¹/2 teaspoon freshly ground white pepper
1 10-inch glass pie pan

For the filling:
1 pound waxy potatoes such as Red Bliss or Yukon Gold, sliced into
    ¹/2-inch-thick rounds
1 pound onions, sliced 1¹/2-inch thick
3 tablespoons olive oil
White wine vinegar
Sea salt and freshly ground black pepper
Paprika for garnish

For the rosemary glaze:
1 cup thinly sliced shallots
1 cup thinly sliced mushrooms, button or fresh shiitake
2 tablespoons olive oil
2 tablespoons mirin
1¹/2 teaspoons shoyu or tamari
3 cups Kombu Vegetable Bouillon (page 131)
2 teaspoons finely chopped fresh rosemary
1¹/2 teaspoons arrowroot
3 tablespoons cold water
Sea salt and freshly ground black pepper to taste
¹/2 teaspoon freshly squeezed lemon juice, strained

(continued)

Chickpea Tart with Potatoes and Onions.

Sculpture "La Vendeuse" by Bill King. See profile on page 123.

(continued)

To prepare the tart:

❖ Whisk all the ingredients together in a heavy-bottomed 3-quart saucepan. Bring to a boil, lower the flame, and cook, stirring constantly, for about 25 minutes. Puree with a handheld mixer to smooth out any lumps.

❖ Lightly oil a 10-inch pie pan. Pour in the chickpea polenta.

To make the filling:

❖ Place the potatoes in a 3-quart saucepan equipped with a steamer basket and tight-fitting lid and steam for 10 to 15 minutes or until cooked through. Toss with 2 tablespoons oil, a splash of vinegar, and salt to taste.

❖ Meanwhile, steam the onions 10 minutes and toss with the remaining olive oil and salt to taste.

To make the glaze:

❖ Place the shallots, mushrooms, and olive oil in an 8- to 10-inch sauté pan over high heat and cook, stirring constantly, until lightly browned.

❖ Add the mirin, shoyu, and bouillon and bring to a boil. Add the rosemary and continue to cook until the mixture is reduced by half.

❖ Dissolve the arrowroot in 3 tablespoons of water. Stir into the sauce, reduce the heat to low, and simmer for 1 minute or until lightly thickened.

NOTE: You must bring the sauce (with the arrowroot) back to a simmer or the thickening properties of the arrowroot will not take effect.

❖ Add salt and freshly ground pepper to taste. Stir in the lemon juice.

To assemble the tart:

❖ Preheat the oven to 375°F.

❖ Arrange the potato slices on top of the polenta. Spread the onions over the potatoes. Drizzle with the remaining 2 tablespoons of olive oil.

❖ Dust the tart with paprika and allow to rest for 1 hour or until the tart is set.

❖ Bake for 45 minutes.

❖ Cut into wedges and serve warm with rosemary glaze on the side.

Entrées:
Daily Seasonal
Creations

quinoa and jasmine rice risotto with spring vegetables and gremolata

YIELD: 4 servings   COOKING TIME: 20 to 30 minutes

Here's a good example of a seasonal recipe that can easily be adapted. If you don't have the spring vegetables, try substituting an equal volume of roasted mushrooms, winter squash, and sun-dried tomatoes. Julienned zucchini, carrots, and fennel also work well.

Try this: Substitute 2 globe artichokes (pared to hearts and simmered until tender in water to cover with the juice of 1 lemon, then diced) for the asparagus.

> *5 to 6 cups vegetable stock*
> *2 tablespoons extra virgin olive oil*
> *1 cup finely sliced scallions*
> *3/4 cup quinoa*
> *3/4 cup white jasmine rice*
> *1 cup asparagus sliced into inch-long diagonals, approximately*
>   *1/4-inch thick*
> *1 teaspoon fresh thyme*
> *1 cup shelled peas*
> *Sea salt and freshly ground black pepper to taste*
>
> *For the gremolata:*
> *Mix the following ingredients in a small bowl:*
>   *4 tablespoons minced fresh parsley*
>   *2 teaspoons minced garlic*
>   *1 1/2 teaspoon grated lemon zest*

* Bring the vegetable stock to a simmer in a 2-quart saucepan.

* Heat the oil in a wide, heavy-bottomed 3-quart sauté pan over medium heat, add scallions, and sauté 3 minutes.

* Add quinoa and rice to the oil and scallion mixture and stir to coat, 2 minutes.

* Add thyme and pinch of salt.

* Add 1/2 cup hot stock and cook, stirring until absorbed. Continue adding stock 1/2 cup at a time and stirring until the grains are firm to the bite or "al dente" in center and creamy on the outside (about 20 minutes).

* Add asparagus and peas, along with the remaining stock, and simmer until almost absorbed.

* Serve the risotto sprinkled with the gremolata.

Sauces and Marinades

aduki bean sauce

YIELD: 4 cups   COOKING TIME: 1 hour, 15 minutes

Aduki beans are relatively petite, and they provide an interesting texture when left somewhat firm. They also cook up quite a bit quicker than their larger counterparts, and adukis do not need pre-soaking.

Serving suggestion: Serve over Basic Brown Rice or Three-Grain Pilaf (pages 94, 107) and top with Kimchee (page 111) and a sprinkle of Gomasio (page 90). Also good with Five-Grain Croquettes (page 194) and Millet, Angelica Style (page 92).

> *1 cup aduki beans*
> *6 cups cold water*
> *6 slices fresh ginger, each about the size of a quarter*
> *3 plump cloves garlic*
> *2 cloves*
> *1 small red onion, peeled*
> *1 bay leaf*
> *2 tablespoons mirin*
> *1 tablespoon toasted sesame oil*
> *Sea salt*

❖ Sort through the beans, discarding any broken ones or stones. Rinse in a strainer under cold running water and drain.

❖ Place the beans and 6 cups cold water in a heavy 3-quart saucepan over high heat. Bring to a boil.

❖ Lower the heat and add the ginger and garlic.

❖ Stick cloves into the onion and add it to the pot along with the bay leaf and mirin.

❖ Cover the pan and allow to simmer for 1 hour.

❖ Uncover the pan and season with salt to taste. Remove the onion, bay leaf, and ginger slices.

❖ Continue to cook 15 to 20 minutes longer until the sauce thickens.

❖ Stir in sesame oil and serve.

Sauces &
Marinades

béchamel with basil and garlic

YIELD: 4 cups COOKING TIME: 30 to 40 minutes

Béchamel is one of the basic French sauces, made by stirring milk into a roux of flour and butter. Here is the Angelica version, which we're convinced is better than the original. Serving suggestions: You can substitute it for the carrot-beet No-mato Sauce (page 206) in lasagna; you can serve it over root vegetables or steamed greens. Experiment—this is a hugely versatile item.

Try this: Make a gratin by pouring the béchamel over potatoes, or pasta, sprinkling them with breadcrumbs, and baking them in oven until the topping turns crispy.

> ^{1}/$_4$ *cup garlic cloves*
> *3 cups chopped onions*
> ^{1}/$_3$ *cup olive oil*
> *2 bay leaves*
> *1 teaspoon sea salt plus additional for seasoning*
> ^{1}/$_3$ *cup unbleached white flour*
> *2 cups vegetable stock or water*
> *2 cups plain soy milk*
> ^{1}/$_2$ *teaspoon freshly ground white pepper plus additional for seasoning*
> *2 tablespoons minced fresh basil*
> *Sea salt and freshly ground black pepper*

* Place garlic, onion, oil, and bay leaves in a heavy 2- to 3-quart saucepan over medium heat.
* Stirring, cook until the vegetables sizzle.
* Add 1 teaspoon sea salt. Reduce heat to low.
* Cover and cook gently for 30 minutes. Stir frequently. Do not allow onions or garlic to brown.
* Remove the bay leaves, stir in the flour, and cook, stirring, for 5 minutes or until the flour becomes fragrant and toasty.
* Add the stock, soy milk, and white pepper.
* Raise the heat to high and bring to a boil.
* Lower the heat and simmer for 10 minutes.
* Stir in the basil and cook 2 to 3 minutes longer.
* Puree the sauce until smooth.
* Season with additional salt and pepper to taste.

Beans as Sauce

Beans make surprisingly good sauces, which is why there are three bean-sauce recipes in this chapter. Bean sauces complement all kinds of other flavors well and they're fun, practical, and economical to make. The recipes are straightforward, without a lot of complicated steps. Once the beans and other ingredients are prepped and in the pot, you can let them simmer away while you go about your other tasks. In general, when you cook beans for a little less time, they retain their firmness and texture, which is what you want for a salad. If you simmer them longer, they begin to melt into a smooth consistency for a sauce. Thin them down and the bean sauces can double as soups. Add chunks of vegetables and they become stews.

A roux is a thickening, flavor-enhancing base that gives body and complexity to sauces and other dishes. To make a roux, fat or oil is heated over low to medium heat in a saucepan and then flour is stirred in. The flour is toasted in the fat for up to an hour, whisking often to keep the mixture from turning lumpy. The longer the flour is toasted, the darker and more flavorful it becomes. Louisiana Cajun and Creole cuisines use fairly dark roux for dishes like gumbo. If you're making a large batch of roux, you can make it in the oven using a roasting pan.

brown rice gravy

YIELD: 4 cups   COOKING TIME: 20 minutes

On the menu, our basic gravies are Brown Rice Gravy and Brown Rice Gravy with Mushrooms. (For the latter, all you have to do is follow both steps of this recipe.) They are roux-based sauces, utilizing brown rice flour to accommodate people who are wheat sensitive. These gravies are finger-licking good on potatoes and grains. However you use them, be sure to have a good piece of bread handy to mop up.

¹/₃ cup plus 1 tablespoon brown rice flour
3¹/₂ tablespoons olive oil
3 cups hot water or vegetable stock
5 tablespoons shoyu or tamari
1 to 2 tablespoons minced fresh herbs such as thyme, sage, rosemary, or tarragon, leaves only, stems removed

❖ Heat the 3 cups of vegetable stock or water in a small saucepan.
❖ Place the flour and oil in a heavy-bottomed 2-quart saucepan over low heat.
❖ Cook, stirring constantly with a wooden spoon, until the flour is lightly browned, about 5 minutes.
❖ Whisk in the hot water, shoyu, and herbs and bring to a boil.
❖ Lower the flame and simmer gently for 20 minutes or until the sauce thickens.

roasted mushroom variation

YIELD: 5 cups total   COOKING TIME: 30 minutes

10 ounces mushrooms of choice (shiitake, white cremini, and chanterelle are all suitable)
1 tablespoon olive oil
Pinch of sea salt
Pinch of freshly ground black pepper
Tablespoon of minced garlic

❖ Preheat the oven to 400°F.
❖ Rinse the mushrooms, drain well, and pat dry.
❖ Slice the mushrooms into thin pieces and toss them with the oil, salt, pepper, and garlic.
❖ Spread the mushrooms on a baking sheet large enough to hold them in a single layer and roast for 20 minutes, stirring occasionally.
❖ Stir the roasted mushrooms into the gravy.

carrot-leek glaze with thyme

YIELD: approximately 2 cups   COOKING TIME: 20 minutes

This is a shiny, translucent sauce, which is why we call it a glaze. It has clear, bright colors with beautiful flecks of carrot pulp running throughout. It's a light, delicate sauce that offsets hefty dishes such as the various casseroles and the Five-Grain Croquettes (page 194). Freshly pressed carrot juice is a must here. Juice 'em and use 'em or don't bother with this recipe.

Serving suggestions: Try this glaze with a three-grain mix or with baked, marinated tofu. It can also work well on the Chickpea Tart with Potatoes and Onions (page 196).

¹/₄ cup finely sliced leeks, white part only
2 teaspoons extra virgin olive oil
¹/₄ teaspoon sea salt
Pinch of cayenne pepper
1 teaspoon finely chopped fresh thyme, leaves only
2 teaspoons freshly squeezed lemon juice, strained
2 cups freshly made organic carrot juice, strained
2 tablespoons kuzu or arrowroot
Thinly sliced scallions or chopped parsley for garnish

❖ Place the leeks, oil, salt, cayenne, and thyme in a heavy 2-quart saucepan over the lowest possible heat.

❖ Cover and cook for 10 to 15 minutes. Do not allow the leeks to brown.

❖ Add lemon and carrot juices.

❖ Raise the heat and bring to a boil; reduce the heat to low and simmer for 2 minutes.

❖ In a small bowl, dissolve the kuzu or arrowroot in 3 tablespoons cold water.

❖ Whisk it into the simmering juice and continue to cook for 1 to 2 minutes longer or until the sauce thickens. Add a little water if the sauce becomes too thick.

❖ Serve over Five-Grain Croquettes (page 194), garnished with thinly sliced scallions or chopped parsley.

french lentil sauce

YIELD: 6 cups   COOKING TIME: 40 minutes

For such a simple, easy-to-make sauce, this one is remarkably savory. It goes great with the Greek Phyllo Casserole (page 184). It also makes a nice pasta sauce as is—or you could add a cup of peeled, seeded, diced tomatoes.

1 cup dried French lentils, sorted and rinsed
6 cloves garlic
1 bay leaf
1 teaspoon minced fresh thyme
1 teaspoon minced fresh rosemary
2 tablespoons extra virgin olive oil
1 tablespoon mirin
5 cups water
2 teaspoons red wine vinegar
Sea salt and freshly ground black pepper

❖ Place the lentils, garlic, bay leaf, thyme, rosemary, oil, mirin, along with 5 cups of water in a heavy-bottomed 2- to 3-quart saucepan.

❖ Simmer gently, uncovered, for 40 minutes or until the lentils are tender and the sauce has thickened.

❖ Add vinegar, salt, and pepper to taste.

❖ Remove the bay leaf before serving.

herbed mushroom gravy

YIELD: 5 cups   COOKING TIME: 30 minutes

This recipe is more sophisticated, light, and delicate than the Brown Rice Gravy. It is bound by arrowroot or kuzu, has a delightful shine to it, and features fresh herbs and a variety of mushrooms.

Serving suggestions: Recommended for roasted or baked polenta squares or on tempeh. Works well as a pasta sauce since it doesn't have any flour in it and you get plenty of starch from the pasta.

Try this: Pour the sauce over sliced seitan and braise in a 350-degree oven for 30 minutes.

Note: This sauce will keep refrigerated for three days or frozen up to three months.

1¹/2 ounces dried porcini mushrooms
3 cups hot water or Kombu Vegetable Bouillon (page 131)
1 cup sliced button mushrooms

Sauces &
Marinades

¹/₂ cup sliced fresh shiitake mushroom caps
3 tablespoons olive oil
1 cup diced onions
Pinch of salt
1 teaspoon minced garlic
1 tablespoon finely chopped fresh thyme leaves
3 tablespoons tamari
2 tablespoons mirin
1 quart water or vegetable stock
2 tablespoons kuzu or arrowroot
Sea salt and freshly ground black pepper

- Preheat the oven to 400°F.
- Soak porcini mushrooms in 3 cups hot water for 30 minutes or until soft.
- Toss button and shiitake mushrooms in a bowl with 2 tablespoons oil.
- Spread on a pan and roast for 20 minutes or until nicely browned.
- While the mushrooms roast, place 1 tablespoon olive oil, onions, and a pinch of salt in a 2- to 3-quart saucepan over medium heat and cook, stirring occasionally, for 10 minutes or until the onions are lightly browned.
- Add garlic and thyme, remove pan from heat, and allow ingredients to cook 1 to 2 minutes in the pan.
- Carefully remove porcini from soaking liquid without disturbing the grit on the bottom of the bowl.
- Coarsely chop porcini and add them to the saucepan.
- Line a strainer with a double layer of cheesecloth and strain the porcini liquid into the saucepan.
- Add the roasted mushrooms, tamari, mirin, and the water to the saucepan and bring to a boil over high heat.
- Reduce the heat to low and simmer, uncovered, for 20 minutes.
- In a small bowl, dissolve the kuzu or arrowroot in 2 tablespoons of cold water. Stir into the sauce and continue to cook for 1 to 2 minutes or until the sauce thickens.
- Season the sauce with sea salt and freshly ground black pepper to taste.

no-mato sauce

YIELD: 8 cups   COOKING TIME: 1 hour

Despite the cute name, we don't really think of it as a substitute for
tomato sauce. It stands on its own, with an assertive vegetable flavor and
a color vaguely reminiscent of tomato sauce but much more orange.

We use it as a layer for lasagnas or a backdrop for seitan wheatballs.
It can also be thinned with water or stock to create a satisfying soup—
or used as a flavorful addition to most simply prepared whole grains.

> 4 cups chopped onions
> ¹/₄ cup olive oil
> 4 cups peeled, chopped carrots
> 2 cups peeled, chopped beets
> 2 tablespoons minced garlic
> 1 quart water
> 3 tablespoons finely chopped fresh herbs such as thyme, tarragon,
>   sage, basil, or rosemary
> 2 tablespoons red wine vinegar
> 2 teaspoons sea salt
> Freshly ground black pepper

* Place the onions and olive oil in a heavy 3-quart saucepan over
  medium heat. Sauté for 7 to 8 minutes.
* Add the carrots, beets, and garlic to the pan.
* Lower the heat, cover, and cook for 30 minutes, stirring occasionally.
* Raise the heat, add 1 quart water, and the herbs.
* Bring to a boil, lower heat, stir in the vinegar, cover and simmer for
  20 minutes.
* Puree until smooth.

   NOTE: When using a food processor to puree very hot liquids, allow
   mixture to cool before beginning. Hot liquids in a covered processor
   or blender are very dangerous.

* Season with salt and pepper to taste.

*Sauces &
Marinades*

onion glaze

YIELD: 6 cups   COOKING TIME: 40 minutes

At Angelica Kitchen, we go through two tons of onions a month—that's 48,000 pounds per year! Needless to say, onions are one of the great pillars of our cuisine and this super-savory sauce is one of the most popular uses for them. It's an excellent all-purpose item that turns up on many of our daily specials. Use it to lend flavor to casseroles, croquettes, and grains of all sorts.

Try this: Turn this sauce into a delicious onion soup by adding only 1 tablespoon of kuzu and serving it in bowls over toasted sourdough bread.

2 tablespoons extra virgin olive oil
6 cups peeled, finely sliced onions (about 3 pounds)
*1 tablespoon finely chopped fresh herbs (a combination of rosemary,
    sage, and thyme works well)*
1 bay leaf
Pinch of sea salt
1 quart water
¹/₄ cup shoyu or tamari
2 tablespoons mirin
2 tablespoons kuzu
3 tablespoons cold water
1 tablespoon finely minced fresh parsley, leaves only

❖ Place the oil, onions, minced herbs, bay leaf, and salt in a heavy 3-quart saucepan over high heat and cook until the onions sizzle.

❖ Reduce the heat to low, cover the pan, and cook 30 minutes. Uncover and stir occasionally to prevent sticking.

❖ Add 1 quart water, shoyu, and mirin, raise the heat, bring to a simmer, then cook for 5 minutes (the heat having been reduced by the addition of the liquids).

❖ In a small bowl, dissolve the kuzu in 3 tablespoons cold water and whisk into the pan. Cook 2 minutes more.

❖ Stir in the parsley and serve.

ragout of white beans with gremolata

YIELD: 4 to 6 servings   COOKING TIME: 1¹/₂ hours

Gremolata is an Italian garnish consisting of lemon zest, mint and/or parsley, and finely minced garlic. It's traditionally sprinkled over heavy dishes such as boiled or braised meats to add a light touch. Of course, it must be made within an hour of serving, using the freshest possible ingredients. In this case, it adds a refreshing twist to the smooth, substantial consistency of the beans.

Like most of our sauces, this one is delicious over pasta or polenta and it can double as a soup.

1 cup dried cannelini or Great Northern beans sorted, presoaked
    overnight
3 tablespoons extra virgin olive oil
1 cup finely diced red onion
4 cloves garlic, minced
¹/₂ cup finely diced celery
¹/₂ cup finely diced carrots
¹/₄ teaspoon chili flakes
1 teaspoon salt
2 cups peeled, chopped fresh or canned tomatoes
1 tablespoon minced fresh sage

For the Gremolata:
3 tablespoons minced fresh mint, leaves only
2 tablespoons minced fresh parsley, leaves only
2 teaspoons minced lemon zest
2 teaspoons minced garlic

To prepare the ragout:

❖ Drain the beans and rinse.

❖ Place the beans with 4 cups of water in a 3-quart saucepan and bring to a boil over high heat.

❖ Reduce the heat to low and simmer about 1 hour or until tender.

❖ While the beans cook, place the oil, red onion, garlic, celery, carrots, red pepper flakes, and salt in a sauté pan and cook, covered, over low heat until the vegetables soften, about 15 minutes.

❖ Once beans are done, drain them in a strainer, reserving the cooking liquid.

❖ Add the cooked beans, tomatoes, sage, and enough of the bean cooking liquid to the sautéed vegetables to create a thick sauce.

❖ Simmer 10 minutes more. Season with salt to taste.

Sauces &
Marinades

❖ Serve over polenta (page 93) and garnish with gremolata.

To prepare gremolata:

❖ Combine all the ingredients in a small bowl.

❖ Cover tightly with plastic wrap until ready to use.

soba sensation sauce

YIELD: 3 cups   PREPARATION TIME: 15 minutes

Here is the Angelica Kitchen version of a classic soba sauce: rich and satisfying. Its distinguishing trait is that it contains mustard. An all-purpose sauce, it can be served with steamed vegetables, tofu, or whole grains—or even used as a sandwich spread. We serve it cold over soba or udon noodles (see Soba Sensation Sidebar).

Note: The Sensation Sauce will keep refrigerated for a week in a well-sealed container.

> 1 clove garlic, crushed
> 2 to 3 tablespoons peeled and minced ginger
> 2 tablespoons prepared mustard of your choice, Dijon or English style
> $^1/_3$ cup brown rice vinegar
> $^1/_3$ cup natural soy sauce
> $^1/_3$ cup brown rice syrup
> 2 tablespoons toasted sesame oil
> $1^1/_3$ cups tahini
> $^1/_3$ cup hot water
> pinch of cayenne pepper

❖ Vigorously whisk all the ingredients together in a bowl. Alternately, pour them into a food processor and puree until creamy.

spicy black bean sauce

YIELD: 4 cups   COOKING TIME: Approximately 1 hour

This delicious sauce, based on the Mexican classic, is simple to make and loves to play with other food.

Serving suggestions: On any kind of grain or with burritos or other Mexican-style dishes. Make a complete main course by serving it over rice and topping it with Hijiki-Cucumber Salsa (page 109), diced avocadoes, fresh tomatoes, and corn chips on the side.

Try this: Drain the sauce, puree and chill it, then use it as a dip.

(continued)

Soba Sensation

To enjoy our famous Soba Sensation:

• Cook one package of soba noodles al dente.

• Drain the noodles and refresh under cold running water until thoroughly chilled.

• Serve topped with Soba Sensation Sauce and garnished with sliced scallions and one of the following: Ruby Kraut, Kimchee, or Hijiki-Cucumber Salsa (pages 122, 111, 109).

(continued)

> 1 cup dried black beans
> 1 cup chopped onion
> 1 tablespoon olive oil
> 1 teaspoon ground coriander
> 1 teaspoon ground cumin
> 2 cloves garlic, minced
> 1 dried chipotle pepper, rinsed
> 1 dried pasilla pepper, rinsed
> 6 cups water or vegetable stock
> Sea salt

* Sort through the beans, discarding any stones or broken ones.
* Rinse them under cold running water in a strainer.
* Place the beans in a bowl and pour enough boiling water over them to cover by 2 inches. Soak for 1 hour.
* Drain the beans and discard the soaking water.
* Place the onions, oil, coriander, and cumin in a heavy 3-quart saucepan over medium heat and sauté until the onions are softened, about 8 to 10 minutes.
* Add the garlic and cook 2 minutes longer.
* Add the beans and chile peppers plus 6 cups of water or stock, raise the heat, and bring to a boil.
* Reduce heat to low and simmer, uncovered, for 1 hour or until the beans are soft.
* Remove the chile peppers.
* Season with sea salt to taste and continue to simmer until the sauce thickens.

spicy sun-dried tomato sauce

YIELD: 7 to 8 cups   COOKING TIME: 30 minutes

When I tasted this sauce for the first time, it went right on the list for the book—no questions asked, no discussion. It's a real knockout, with a medium-spicy flavor, great tangy tomato taste, and a bright, sweetish accent from the touch of orange and the cinnamon stick.

Serving suggestions: Try it on pasta or toss it together with some plain beans. It would also make a phenomenal pizza sauce.

> 4 cups sun-dried tomatoes, dry packed
> 6 cups water
> 1/4 cup extra virgin olive oil

Sauces &
Marinades

3 cups diced onions
1/2 cup peeled, diced carrots
6 cloves garlic
1 cinnamon stick, about 2 inches long
1 strip orange peel, *1/2* inch by 3 inches, pith removed
1/2 teaspoon freshly ground black pepper
1 teaspoon cayenne pepper
2 teaspoons sea salt plus additional for seasoning
2 to 3 tablespoons chopped fresh basil
1 tablespoon balsamic vinegar

* Bring 6 cups of water to a boil in a 3-quart sauce pan. Add the tomatoes and simmer for two minutes. Remove the pan from the heat and set aside.

* In another 3-quart saucepan, soften the onions in the oil over medium heat for 5 to 7 minutes, then add the carrots, garlic, cinnamon, orange peel, black pepper, cayenne, and salt.

* Reduce the heat to low, cover the pan, and simmer for 20 minutes.

* Drain the tomatoes and add them to the pot along with 6 cups of fresh water. Raise the heat to high and bring the sauce to a boil.

* Reduce the heat to low and simmer, uncovered, for 10 minutes.

* Remove the cinnamon stick and orange peel. Add the basil and balsamic vinegar.

* Puree the sauce in batches in a blender until smooth.

NOTE: When using a food processor to puree very hot liquids, allow mixture to cool before beginning. Hot liquids in a covered processor or blender are very dangerous.

* Season with additional sea salt to taste.

charmoula (for tempeh)

YIELD: 2¹/2 cups, enough for 2 pounds of tempeh

PREPARATION TIME: 20 minutes

This traditional North African marinade is used for cooking vegetables or fish. It's spicy and it's zesty, with a real jolt of lemon. Peter was looking for a way to jazz up some tempeh one day and got the inspiration for this recipe from Joyce Goldstein's wonderful book *Mediterranean Cooking*.

Serving suggestion: Accompanied by the Carrot-Mint Salad (page 142) or with minted cucumber and basmati rice.

(continued)

Marinated Sun-Dried Tomatoes

You can make your own oil-marinated sun-dried tomatoes by cooking the dried ones in water until tender, patting them dry, and then packing them in a jar with your favorite olive oil and herbs. This product is available in specialty markets but it's very expensive. It's a lot more fun—and economical—to make your own. The tomatoes will keep up to a year refrigerated.

(continued)

> 6 tablespoons freshly squeezed lemon juice, strained
> $^1/_2$ cup water
> 4 cloves garlic, minced
> 6 tablespoons chopped fresh cilantro
> 2 teaspoons ground cumin
> 2 teaspoons paprika
> $^1/_2$ teaspoon cayenne pepper
> 2$^1/_2$ teaspoons sea salt
> $^1/_2$ cup extra virgin olive oil

❖ Whisk all the ingredients together in a bowl.

❖ Proceed with directions for Baked Tempeh with Soy-Mustard Marinade (page 102), substituting the Charmoula for the soy-mustard mixture.

barbecue marinade (for tempeh)

YIELD: 8 servings, enough for 2 pounds of tempeh   PREPARATION TIME: 20 minutes

This marinade gets its zing from smoked jalapeños, otherwise known as chipotle chiles. Our chiles come to us in a whole dried state from a farmer in New Mexico.

> 1$^1/_2$ cups sun-dried tomatoes, dry packed
> 1 dried jalapeño pepper (chipotle)
> 1 quart water
> $^1/_2$ cup apple cider vinegar
> $^1/_2$ cup shoyu or tamari
> $^1/_2$ cup maple syrup
> $^1/_2$ cup olive oil
> 2 cloves garlic, minced

❖ Combine tomatoes, jalapeño, and 1 quart water in a 2-quart saucepan.

❖ Bring to a boil over high heat.

❖ Reduce heat to low and simmer 4 or 5 minutes or until tomatoes are plumped.

❖ Drain.

❖ Combine with all other ingredients in a food processor and puree until smooth.

❖ Proceed with directions under Baked Tempeh with Soy-Mustard Marinade (page 102), substituting the Barbecue Marinade for the soy-mustard mixture.

*Sauces &
Marinades*

sweet ginger marinade (for tofu)

YIELD: 1¹/₂ cups, enough for
1 pound of tofu

PREPARATION TIME: 10 minutes

> ¹/₄ cup shoyu or tamari
> ¹/₄ cup rice vinegar
> ¹/₄ cup apple cider or mirin
> 2 tablespoons sesame oil
> 2 tablespoons maple syrup
> 1 clove garlic, minced
> 1 tablespoon peeled, minced ginger

❖ Whisk all ingredients together in a bowl.

❖ Proceed with directions for Baked Tofu with Lemon-Rosemary
  Marinade (page 105), substituting the Sweet Ginger Marinade for
  the lemon-rosemary mixture.

orange-balsamic marinade (for tofu)

YIELD: 1¹/₂ cups, enough for
1 pound of tofu

PREPARATION TIME: 20 minutes

Try this one on a baguette with sun-dried tomatoes and fresh basil for a
stupendous sandwich.

> ²/₃ cup freshly squeezed orange juice, strained
> ¹/₂ tablespoon freshly squeezed lemon juice, strained
> ¹/₂ teaspoon orange zest
> 3 tablespoons balsamic vinegar
> 1 clove garlic, minced
> 1 teaspoon sea salt
> ¹/₄ cup olive oil

❖ Combine all ingredients in a mixing bowl and whisk until emulsified.

❖ Proceed with directions for Baked Tofu with Lemon-Rosemary
  Marinade (page 105), substituting Orange-Balsamic Marinade for
  lemon-rosemary mixture.

Desserts

We frequently use light olive oil in our desserts. Virtually without flavor and less dense than extra virgin oil, light olive oil is very different in character and more suitable to baking. See sidebar about olive oil on page 88.

apple pie

YIELD: **6 to 8 servings**   COOKING TIME: **1 hour, 15 minutes**

Not overly sweet, the Angelica version of this classic is a pie-lover's paradise. The crust has about half the fat of a non-vegan version. We include baking powder, which is not a traditional crust ingredient, to keep it tender. When you blend the crust ingredients, it's important to use a delicate hand and avoid overmixing so it stays light and flaky. It's a good idea to use, say, three varieties of apples: Northern Spy, Jonathan, Cortland, Golden Delicious, Pippen, Gala, Winesap, and Mutsu all work well. Don't skip the barley malt glaze: it's the finishing touch that makes this pie a real showpiece.

For the filling:
3 1/2 pounds apples
1 teaspoon freshly squeezed lemon juice, strained
2 teaspoons cinnamon
1/2 cup maple syrup
1/4 cup maple sugar
1/4 cup arrowroot

For the crust:
2 cups whole wheat pastry flour
2 cups unbleached white flour
2 tablespoons maple sugar
1 1/2 teaspoons baking powder
1/2 teaspoon sea salt
3/4 cup olive oil

For the glaze:
2 tablespoons barley malt
2 tablespoons water

❖ Preheat the oven to 325°F.

❖ Peel, core, and slice the apples into 1/4-inch-thick wedges. Toss the apple slices with the lemon juice, cinnamon powder, maple syrup, maple sugar, and arrowroot in a medium-size mixing bowl and set aside.

Desserts

* In a separate mixing bowl, whisk together the flours, maple sugar, baking powder, and sea salt. Drizzle in the oil and stir with a wooden spoon until just mixed. Do not overmix. Add $^1/_2$ cup cold water and stir lightly to form the dough into a ball. The dough should have a marbled appearance.

* Divide the dough in half and form into two balls. Place each ball between two pieces of wax paper (parchment paper can be substituted). Using a rolling pin, roll the dough into circles approximately 12 inches in diameter and $^1/8$ inch thick.

* Lightly oil a 10-inch pie plate. Place one circle of the dough in the plate and fill with the apple mixture. Place the second circle of dough on top. Crimp the edges and cut three or four slits in the top of the dough, approximately 2 inches in length.

* Place the pie plate on the middle rack of the oven on top of a cookie sheet. (This will help catch any drips.) Bake at 325°F for 35 minutes.

* To make the glaze, stir the barley malt and 2 tablespoons of water together in a small mixing bowl. After the pie has been baking for 35 minutes, remove it from the rack and brush it with glaze.

* Return pie to oven and bake for 15 to 25 minutes more or until the crust is golden brown and the apples are bubbling.

* Remove pie from oven and cool for 30 minutes before slicing.

chocolate layer cake with chocolate frosting

YIELD: 12 servings   COOKING TIME: 1¹/2 hours

Once a month, when the moon is full, a luscious chocolate dessert such as this one appears on the menu at Angelica Kitchen. If you're looking for a delightfully rich cake that satisfies even the most hardcore chocolate lovers every time and yet has very little fat in the icing, stop here. The cake itself is moist and delicious; the icing provides a good wallop of chocolate flavor. It is definitely our top chocolate dessert and among the most popular items on the menu.

For the batter:
2 cups whole wheat pastry flour
2 cups unbleached white flour
1 tablespoon plus 1 teaspoon baking powder
2 teaspoons baking soda
1 cup cocoa powder
2 teaspoons cinnamon
1 teaspoon sea salt
1 cup olive oil
3 cups maple syrup
2 teaspoons apple cider vinegar
4 teaspoons vanilla extract
2 cups water

For the frosting:
6 tablespoons agar flakes
1¹/2 cups water
3/4 cup cocoa powder
2¹/4 cups maple syrup
¹/4 teaspoon sea salt
1¹/2 teaspoons vanilla extract
4¹/2 tablespoons arrowroot
6 tablespoons plain soy milk

To prepare the cake:

❖ Preheat the oven to 350°F.

❖ Lightly oil and flour two 9-inch springform pans.

❖ Whisk together the flours, baking powder, baking soda, cocoa, cinnamon, and salt in a medium-size mixing bowl.

❖ In a separate mixing bowl, whisk together the oil, maple syrup, vinegar, vanilla, and water until emulsified.

(continued)

Chocolate Layer Cake
with Chocolate Frosting

(continued)

❖ Using a wooden spoon, stir the wet and dry ingredients together; do not overmix.

❖ Divide the batter equally between the two cake pans and bake on the middle rack of the oven for 35 minutes or until a toothpick comes out clean.

❖ Do not open the oven door for the first 30 minutes or the cake could collapse.

❖ Cool for 30 minutes before frosting.

To prepare the frosting:

❖ Place the agar flakes and $1^1/2$ cups of water in a small saucepan over medium heat. Simmer and occasionally stir for 5 minutes or until the agar is dissolved.

❖ Whisk in the cocoa powder, maple syrup, sea salt, and vanilla extract.

❖ In a small mixing bowl, dissolve the arrowroot in the soy milk.

❖ Add this mixture to the agar mixture, raise the heat to medium, and simmer for 1 minute.

❖ Pour the frosting into an ovenproof glass pie plate and refrigerate until it becomes firm, approximately 20 minutes.

❖ Cut the frosting into squares and puree in a food processor until creamy.

To finish the cake:

❖ Remove each of the layers from the springform pans. Spread frosting on top of one layer, then place second layer on top. Frost the top and sides.

date-pecan coffee cake

YIELD: 10 to 12 servings   COOKING TIME: 1 hour, 15 minutes

This is a recommended midday pick-me-up with a steaming cup of tea or grain coffee. It's also good for breakfast, although it may be too sweet for some palates. Don't limit yourself; test the versatility of this recipe by experimenting. Try substituting fresh fruit for the dried fruit; try any other kind of nut; try out different combinations—banana-walnut, peach-pecan, strawberry-almond—or opt for pear or apple without the nuts.

For the crumb topping:
1 cup whole wheat pastry flour
$^1/_3$ cup maple sugar (or maple sprinkles)
1 teaspoon cinnamon

Desserts

¹/₂ teaspoon baking powder
Pinch of sea salt
5 tablespoons olive oil

For the filling:
1 cup pecans (any other nut can be substituted)
¹/₂ cup dried dates (apricots or other dried fruit can be substituted)
2 tablespoons olive oil
¹/₄ cup maple sugar
2 tablespoons cinnamon
Pinch of sea salt

For the batter:
1¹/₂ cups whole wheat pastry flour
1¹/₂ cups unbleached white flour
1 tablespoon baking powder
1 tablespoon baking soda
¹/₂ cup olive oil
1¹/₄ cups maple syrup
1 tablespoon plus 1 teaspoon apple cider vinegar
3 tablespoons vanilla extract
1³/₄ teaspoons salt dissolved in 1 cup water

To prepare the crumb topping:
❖ Combine pastry flour, maple sugar, cinnamon, baking powder, and salt in a bowl. Slowly drizzle in the oil, mixing with your fingers until the oil is incorporated and the mixture has the consistency of wet sand with pebbles. Set aside.

To prepare the filling:
❖ Preheat the oven to 350°F.
❖ Spread pecans on a baking sheet, place in the oven on the middle rack, and toast until golden, about 9 minutes.
❖ Pulse toasted pecans in a food processor with dried fruit and remaining ingredients until coarsely chopped. Set aside.

To prepare the batter:
❖ Oil a 9-inch springform pan.
❖ Sift flours, baking powder, and baking soda together in one bowl.
❖ In another bowl, whisk together wet ingredients, until emulsified.
❖ Fold wet into dry ingredients and mix to form a smooth batter.
❖ Cover the bottom of the springform pan with batter, about 2 cups worth.

(continued)

(continued)

❖ Evenly distribute date-pecan filling on top of the batter.

❖ Cover the filling with the remaining batter and sprinkle with crumb topping.

❖ Bake 50 to 60 minutes or until a toothpick comes out clean.

❖ Remove the cake and cool for $1/2$ hour before unmolding.

date-nut cookies

YIELD: 2 dozen   COOKING TIME: 30 minutes

These cookies are chewy and rich, another classic fixture on the menu. They're equally delicious with walnuts, pecans, pistachios, almonds, or macadamia nuts.

> *1 cup rolled oats*
> *1^2/$_3$ cups walnuts (pecans can be substituted)*
> *1^1/$_3$ cups brown rice flour*
> *1 teaspoon sea salt*
> *1^1/$_2$ teaspoons cinnamon*
> *6 tablespoons olive oil*
> *^{1}/$_3$ cup brown rice syrup*
> *^{1}/$_2$ cup maple syrup*
> *1 cup pitted, finely chopped dates*

❖ Preheat oven to 325°F.

❖ Spread the oats and walnuts on a cookie sheet (side by side without mixing the two). Toast in the oven for 10 minutes.

❖ Place the rice flour, half the oats, and half the walnuts in a food processor fitted with a steel blade. Process to a fine meal. Add remaining walnuts and pulse a few times to coarsely chop them.

❖ Pour the mixture into a medium-size mixing bowl. Add remaining oats, sea salt, and cinnamon. Mix well, with a wooden spoon.

❖ Mix the olive oil, rice syrup, and maple syrup together in a separate bowl.

❖ Combine the wet mixture with the oat mixture. Mix well, then fold in the chopped dates.

❖ On a lightly greased cookie sheet, drop rounded tablespoons of batter approximately 2 inches apart.

❖ Bake for 15 to 18 minutes until lightly golden around the edges.

❖ Allow the cookies to cool on the cookie sheet before serving.

Desserts

ginger snaps

YIELD: 2 dozen   COOKING TIME: 40 minutes

These cookies offer a powerful hit of ginger with a wonderful, crunchy, "snappy" texture.

1 cup rolled oats
1 cup blanched, slivered almonds
1 cup whole wheat pastry flour
1¹/₂ tablespoons powdered ginger
1 teaspoon cinnamon
¹/₂ teaspoon sea salt
¹/₂ teaspoon mace
¹/₄ cup maple syrup
¹/₄ cup molasses
1 teaspoon vanilla extract
¹/₃ cup olive oil

❖ Preheat oven to 325°F.

❖ Spread the oats and almonds on a baking sheet and toast in the oven for 10 minutes.

❖ Place the oats, flour, almonds, ginger, cinnamon, salt, and mace in a food processor and grind to a very fine meal.

❖ Pour the dry mix into a bowl. In a separate bowl, whisk together the maple syrup, molasses, vanilla, and oil, and then stir into the dry mix until a thick dough is formed.

❖ With moist hands, roll pieces of the dough into walnut-sized balls.

❖ Place the balls 2 inches apart on a lightly oiled cookie sheet and flatten into 2-inch circles.

❖ Bake 18 minutes. Remove from oven and cool completely before serving.

ELIZABETH RYAN,
BREEZY HILL ORCHARD AND CIDER MILL

For many years now, Breezy Hill, run by dynamo Elizabeth Ryan, has supplied Angelica Kitchen with a large selection of apples as well as cider. The farm's products are an integral part of many of our recipes including kanten, chutneys, pies, buckles, coffee cakes, and juices.

(continued)

(continued)

Breezy Hill is located in Clinton Corners, New York. The farm produces organic vegetables such as heirloom tomatoes, mesclun greens, edible flowers, and extraordinary pears, but the real attraction is the orchard with fifty different varieties of

apples grown for eating and cider. Elizabeth's farm stand has been a fixture at the Union Square Greenmarket for many years. It used to sell just cider and apples, then jellies, jams, and salsas were added, and before long a whole assortment of baked goods was offered, including apple pies and brownies, as well as various vegetables grown on the farm. In 1995, after visiting hard cider makers in England, where hundreds of old varieties of apples are grown without resorting to chemicals, Elizabeth founded the Hudson Valley Draft Cider Company, which produces traditional farmhouse hard cider.

Elizabeth comes from several generations of farmers—her great-grandparents were home-steaders who emigrated from Europe in the late nineteenth century, and her mother grew up on a farm in Iowa where Elizabeth spent summers as a child. Of the fifty-odd grandchildren, she was the only one to make a conscious choice to farm.

In the late 1970s, Elizabeth worked with Responsible Agriculture, a Washington-based nonprofit organization that promoted what has since become known as sustainable agriculture. But rather than stay in the city talking farming, she and husband Peter Zimmermann bought Breezy Hill and in 1984 began building the business.

"When I first started doing this," she explains, "it was really about returning to my roots. Part of it was I love fruit. In my fantasies I'd be growing red raspberries, yellow raspberries, white peaches, blood peaches, different kinds of plums. There's an art to growing fruit that I find really wonderful.

"Another part of it was political. When I was in Washington I worked on the Family Farm Development Act. But it didn't seem right to me to be living in D.C. and talking about agriculture. I decided I wanted to farm for a living, and if I wanted to work on policy issues I'd do it from inside the community, not outside.

"Then there's the lifestyle part. Nowadays no one would put up with me. I'm sure I'd be fired in a week from any corporate job

Desserts

222

because I'm used to being able to go for a walk in the orchard even if I'm putting in an eighteen-hour day. There are certain perks."

Elizabeth finds selling to her customers at the Union Square Greenmarket to be one of the most rewarding aspects of the business. She never tires of the ritual. "Every single Saturday is like a festival, a celebration of life. It becomes a personal thing. There's a real sense of community at Union Square." Meanwhile, true to her word, Elizabeth continues her activism, working from inside the farm community. She has worked with the Eastern Migrant Healthcare Alliance to make health care available to farmworkers, and she has won grants from the New York State Council for the Arts to create oral histories of farming. She serves on the advisory board of the Cornell University College of Agriculture and Life Sciences, lectures, and makes her farm available to groups as diverse as chefs and schoolchildren. Her talks focus on the human side of farming, the need to sustain people and farm communities as well as the land. "Real sustainable agriculture is not just about food, it has to reward every hand that touches the food. It's a very inclusive concept. We're not just saving landscapes, we're supporting people."

kanten parfait with nut cream

YIELD: 8 servings   COOKING TIME: 2 hours

The kanten parfait is one of our most popular desserts. It consists of layers of seasonal fruit kanten, nut cream, and cookie crumbs. It is wheat-free, very light, and the sum is much more beautiful and delicious than each of the parts. If you don't want to bother making cookies especially for this dessert, any store-bought crumbled cookies will do.

The parfait is one of those wonderful accidents. We were making desserts one day and something didn't work out. Not wanting to toss out the ingredients and needing to fill a hole on the day's menu, we ended up building a parfait. Customer requests immediately began pouring in.

(continued)

(continued)

The parfait became a daily theme. We make different nut creams: almond, cashew, hazelnut—and include different fruits in the kanten—apples, pears, apricots, raisins. Cookies are baked every morning and any broken ones are just crumbled up for the parfait.

For the kanten:
1 pint fresh strawberries, peaches, blueberries, apricots, or ripe pears
3 1/2 cups apple cider
4 tablespoons agar flakes
1 tablespoon arrowroot
2 tablespoons cold apple cider

❖ Wash and hull the strawberries.

❖ Liquify 1 cup of the strawberries with one cup of the cider in a blender. Strain through a fine mesh strainer or cheesecloth. You should have 1 1/2 cups of strawberry juice.

❖ Place the strawberry juice, remaining cider, and agar flakes in a 2-quart saucepan over high heat. Bring to a boil, lower flame, simmer, and stir until agar dissolves.

❖ Meanwhile, dissolve the arrowroot in the cold cider. Whisk it into the agar mixture and simmer 1 additional minute.

❖ Remove from heat, pour into a shallow pan, cool, then refrigerate until the kanten sets (20-30 minutes).

❖ While kanten is cooling, slice remaining strawberries in bite-size pieces.

❖ Remove kanten to a mixing bowl (a rubber spatula is handy for this) and beat with a wire whisk to smooth out any lumps.

❖ Fold in sliced strawberries.

For the nut cream (yields 2 cups):
2 cups blanched almonds
1/2 cup rice syrup
3/4 cup water
1 teaspoon vanilla extract
1/4 teaspoon almond extract
Pinch of sea salt

❖ Place all ingredients in a food processor fitted with a metal blade. Process until creamy and smooth.

To assemble the parfait:

❖ Spoon 2 tablespoons of nut cream in the bottom of a wine or parfait glass.

Desserts

❖ Top with $^1/_4$ cup kanten and 2 tablespoons of cookie crumbs. Any favorite cookie will work here. Try crumbled Ginger Snaps or the recipe below.

❖ Repeat layers and garnish with extra cookie crumbs or mint leaf.

almond anise cookies

YIELD: 20 cookies   COOKING TIME: 30 minutes

$^1/_2$ cup rolled oats
1 cup whole unsalted almonds
1 tablespoon anise seeds
1 cup brown rice flour
$^1/_2$ cup sliced almonds
$^1/_3$ cup olive oil
5 tablespoons maple syrup
3 tablespoons rice syrup
1 tablespoon vanilla extract
1 teaspoon almond extract
$^1/_4$ teaspoon sea salt

❖ Preheat the oven to 325°F.

❖ Spread the oats and almonds on a baking sheet and toast in the oven for 10 minutes.

❖ Dry-toast the anise seeds in a small skillet over medium heat, stirring frequently until fragrant, about 1 minute. Grind to a powder in a spice mill.

❖ Place oats, whole toasted almonds, and rice flour in a food processor and grind to a fine meal.

❖ Combine the fine meal, ground anise, and almond slices in a bowl.

❖ In another bowl, whisk together olive oil, maple syrup, rice syrup, vanilla extract, almond extract, and salt.

❖ Combine the syrup mixture with the dry mixture. Mix well until all ingredients are incorporated.

❖ Drop tablespoonfuls of batter onto an oiled or parchment-covered baking sheet.

❖ Bake 18 minutes until lightly golden around the edges.

❖ To use in the Kanten Parfait with Nut Cream, grind 1 dozen Almond Anise Cookies in a food processor to yield about 2 cups of crumbs.

lemon-almond tart with raspberry sauce

YIELD: 6 to 8 servings   COOKING TIME: 1 hour

This is a special dessert, perfect for special occasions. Take a look at the picture.

Try this: Substitute pistachios for the almonds in the crust.

For the crust:
1 cup slivered almonds
1 cup whole wheat pastry flour
1/4 teaspoon sea salt
1/4 cup olive oil
1/4 cup maple syrup

For the filling:
1 agar bar
2 cups apple juice
1/8 teaspoon turmeric
Pinch of sea salt
1 cup rice syrup
1/4 cup maple syrup
1 cup freshly squeezed lemon juice, strained
1/4 cup kuzu
1/2 cup soy milk
2 teaspoons vanilla extract
1 pint fresh raspberries or strawberries (optional for garnish)

To prepare the crust:

❖ Preheat the oven to 350°F.

❖ Spread the almonds on a cookie sheet and toast in the oven for 8 minutes.

❖ Combine the almonds, flour, and salt in a food processor and grind to a fine meal.

❖ Whisk the oil and maple syrup together in a mixing bowl.

❖ Add the almond-flour meal and stir to form a dough.

❖ Lightly oil a 9-inch tart pan with a removable bottom.

❖ Place the dough in the center of the pan with a piece of plastic wrap on top of it. Using your hands, smooth and press the dough evenly across the bottom and up the sides of the pan. Using a rolling pin, trim away any excess dough. There shouldn't be much.

❖ Bake the crust for 20 minutes. Remove from the oven and allow to cool completely before filling.

(continued)

Lemon-Almond Tart
with Raspberry Sauce

Zesting a Lemon

The true fragrance or essence of a lemon comes from its oil, which is contained in the peel. This applies only to the vivid yellow of the peel; the white pith is bitter and should be avoided. In contrast, lemon flesh, which is mostly juice, is totally dominated by the sour taste of citric acid; it really has very little of that wonderful "lemony" essence.

There are three ways to zest a lemon:

1. Use a lemon zester, a small tool that has tiny holes designed to scrape thin strands of the outer layer of the lemon peel.

2. Use a swivel-style vegetable peeler to remove strips of lemon peel by dragging the peeler across the lemon surface with a sawing motion. Then remove any white pith lining the lemon peel with the tip of a sharp knife.

3. Grate the lemon with the finest holes of a box grater.

(continued)

(continued)

Note: Citrus fruit, unless organically grown, is a sponge for synthetic chemicals sprayed on during the growing season. The highest concentration of toxins is of course in the peel and pith, so please, always use organic when zesting.

(continued)

To prepare the filling:

❖ In a small saucepan over medium heat, dissolve the agar in the apple juice.

❖ Add turmeric and a pinch of salt.

❖ Stir in rice syrup, maple syrup, lemon juice, and lemon zest and bring to a boil.

❖ In a small bowl, dissolve kuzu in soy milk, making sure there are no lumps. Add the soy milk to the agar mixture and continue to cook, stirring, until the mixture has cleared and thickened, 1 to 2 minutes.

❖ Remove pan from heat and stir in vanilla.

❖ Pour filling into prebaked tart shell and place in the refrigerator, allowing it to set for approximately thirty minutes or until chilled.

❖ Garnish tart with fresh raspberries or strawberries (optional) and serve over a pool of raspberry sauce.

> *For the raspberry sauce:*
> *1 pint raspberries*
> *2 tablespoons maple syrup*
> *1/2 teaspoon vanilla extract*

❖ Puree raspberries in a blender.

❖ Use a rubber spatula or back of spoon to push them through a strainer to remove seeds.

❖ Stir in the remaining ingredients and serve with the tart.

lemon-tofu cheesecake with strawberry topping

YIELD: 10 to 12 servings   COOKING TIME: 1¹/₂ hours

In a vegan diet, it is a challenge to create those rich, smooth, creamy taste sensations for desserts without resorting to dairy products. Here is the Angelica solution, showcasing the tremendous versatility and potential of vegan ingredients such as tofu.

For years, I discouraged the use of tofu in desserts because in combination with the sugars it can become dense and difficult to digest. Frankly, these are not everyday dishes and they are not for everybody, but then neither are traditional cheesecakes. They are treats made from multistep recipes that are appropriate for special occasions and all-out feasts.

Variations: There are two main cheesecake recipes here, Lemon-Tofu and Mocha. Since tofu absorbs all kinds of flavors successfully, there are also many possible variations. For example, you can substitute orange zest for the lemon. You can also try adding nuts, carob, ginger, or orange zest to the crust.

Desserts

For the crust:
1¹/₂ cups pastry flour
¹/₂ teaspoon baking powder
¹/₂ teaspoon cinnamon
6 tablespoons olive oil
6 tablespoons maple syrup
Pinch of sea salt

For the filling:
2 pounds firm tofu
¹/₃ cup olive oil
1¹/₂ cups maple syrup
¹/₂ teaspoon sea salt
¹/₄ cup freshly squeezed lemon juice, strained
¹/₂ teaspoon minced lemon zest
2 tablespoons vanilla extract
3 tablespoons plus 1 teaspoon agar flakes
1 cup water
2 tablespoons arrowroot powder
3/4 cup plain soy milk

For the strawberry topping:
2 pints fresh strawberries
2 tablespoons maple syrup
1 tablespoon freshly squeezed lemon juice, strained
¹/₂ teaspoon vanilla extract

To prepare the crust:

❖ Preheat oven to 350°F.

❖ Combine pastry flour, baking powder, and cinnamon in one bowl and oil, maple syrup, and salt in another.

❖ Mix the wet and dry ingredients together to form a smooth dough.

❖ Press the dough into the bottom of an oiled, 9-inch springform pan.

❖ Bake until crust is golden, about 15 minutes.

To prepare the filling:

❖ Place the tofu, oil, maple syrup, salt, lemon juice, lemon zest, and vanilla in a food processor and process until the mix is very creamy.

❖ Place the agar with 1 cup water in a small saucepan over low heat. Bring to a simmer and continue to cook on low heat until flakes have completely disappeared.

❖ In a small bowl, dissolve arrowroot in soy milk. Pour into the agar solution, stirring continuously until mixture begins to bubble and has thickened considerably, about 1 to 2 minutes.

(continued)

Succanat (Dehydrated Cane Juice)

Dehydrated cane juice is a form of whole, unrefined dark brown sugar. All of its vitamins and minerals are left intact, as opposed to commercial brown sugar, which has been refined and to which coloring and molasses have been added. Succanat is one recommended brand of dehydrated cane juice; if it's unavailable, try to find another organic supplier.

In order to digest and process refined sugars, the body has to draw on its own reserves of minerals whereas unrefined sugars still contain those minerals. This is why refined sugars are considered "empty calories"—they provide calories but no nutritional value.

(continued)

❖ Add the agar mixture to the tofu mixture and process until completely smooth.

❖ Pour the filling into a springform pan and place in the refrigerator to set, about 1 hour.

❖ Run a knife around the cheesecake before releasing the springform.

❖ To serve, ladle strawberry topping over the cheesecake.

To prepare the strawberry topping:

❖ Slice strawberries thin. Stir together with maple syrup, lemon juice, and vanilla.

mocha cheesecake with chocolate brownie crust

YIELD: 10 to 12 servings   COOKING TIME: 1¹/2 hours

This recipe is a little involved, but definitely worth the extra effort to mark a special celebration or as a surprise to spice up a workday evening.

For the brownie crust:
¹/4 cup whole wheat pastry flour
¹/4 cup unbleached white flour
¹/2 teaspoon baking powder
6 tablespoons Succanat
¹/4 cup cocoa powder
¹/4 cup olive oil
¹/4 cup maple syrup
1 teaspoon vanilla extract
2 tablespoons plain soy milk
¹/4 teaspoon sea salt

For the chocolate sauce:
¹/2 cup maple syrup
2 tablespoons pure cocoa powder
2 teaspoons arrowroot
¹/2 cup plain soy milk
¹/4 teaspoon vanilla extract

For the mocha filling:
2 pounds firm tofu
¹/4 cup Yannoh or other grain coffee
¹/3 cup olive oil
1¹/2 cups maple syrup
¹/2 teaspoon sea salt
3/4 teaspoon freshly squeezed lemon juice, strained
2 tablespoons vanilla extract

Desserts

3 tablespoons agar flakes
1 cup water
3/4 cup plain soy milk
2 tablespoons arrowroot

To prepare the brownie crust:

❖ Preheat the oven to 350°F.

❖ Oil a 9-inch springform pan and set aside.

❖ Combine pastry flour, unbleached white flour, baking powder, Succanat, and cocoa powder in a mixing bowl.

❖ In another bowl, whisk together the oil, maple syrup, vanilla, soy milk, and salt. Make sure liquids are well combined, then proceed to pour wet ingredients into the dry, mixing until all ingredients are incorporated.

❖ Pour into the pan, distributing the batter evenly along the bottom, and bake until cake has begun to separate from the sides and springs back when touched, about 15 to 20 minutes.

❖ Set aside to cool.

To prepare the chocolate sauce:

❖ Place the maple syrup and cocoa powder in a small saucepan over low heat and stir until cocoa is dissolved.

❖ In a small bowl, dissolve arrowroot in soy milk.

❖ When cocoa mix begins to boil, add soy milk mixture, stirring continuously until bubbles appear on surface and liquid has thickened. Remove from heat and stir in vanilla extract.

❖ After sauce has cooled, about 15 minutes, pour into squeeze bottle for ease in decorating top of cheesecake.

To prepare the mocha filling:

❖ Place tofu between 2 plates with a weight on top and press for about ¹/₂ hour. Drain off the water that has been squeezed out of the tofu

❖ Combine pressed tofu, grain coffee, oil, maple syrup, salt, lemon juice, and vanilla in a food processor and blend until completely smooth.

❖ Place the agar flakes and 1 cup cold water in a small saucepan over medium heat. Cook, stirring from time to time, until agar has dissolved, 5 to 8 minutes.

❖ In a small bowl, dissolve arrowroot in soy milk.

❖ When agar reaches a boil, add soy milk–arrowroot mixture and stir until bubbles start to form and liquid has thickened.

❖ Pour the agar mixture into the tofu cream and process until completely smooth.

(continued)

(continued)

To finish the cake:

- ❖ Pour the tofu mixture immediately into the pan containing the brownie crust.
- ❖ To form a decorative top, squeeze straight lines of chocolate sauce across the top of the filling while it is still unset. Run a toothpick or a knife through the lines.
- ❖ Place the cheesecake in the refrigerator for about 1 hour to set.
- ❖ Run a knife around the side of the cheesecake before releasing the springform. Unmold and serve.

orange-poppyseed layer cake

YIELD: 12 servings   COOKING TIME: 2 hours

Here is a moist, delicious cake that happens to be my favorite. The orange flavor comes from a combination of orange zest and orange juice and the icing is velvety.

For the batter:
2 cups whole wheat pastry flour
2 cups unbleached white flour
1 tablespoon plus 1 teaspoon baking powder
2 teaspoons baking soda
¹/₃ cup poppy seeds
²/₃ cup freshly squeezed orange juice, strained
1 cup water or apple juice
4 teaspoons freshly squeezed lemon juice, strained
1²/₃ cups maple syrup
²/₃ cup olive oil
2 teaspoons vanilla extract
4 tablespoons orange zest
1 teaspoon sea salt

- ❖ Preheat the oven to 350°F.
- ❖ Lightly brush 2 (9-inch) springform pans with oil. Add several table-spoons of flour to each pan and shake to coat evenly. Invert pans and knock against the counter to rid them of excess flour.
- ❖ Whisk the flours, baking powder, baking soda, salt, and poppy seeds together in a medium-size mixing bowl.
- ❖ In a separate bowl, whisk together the orange, apple, and lemon juices, maple syrup, oil, vanilla, and zest.
- ❖ Using a wooden spoon, stir the wet mixture into the dry to form a batter. Do not overmix.

Desserts

* Divide the batter equally between the two cake pans and bake on the middle rack of the oven for 25 minutes or until a toothpick comes out clean.
* Cool for 30 minutes before removing from the cake pans.

> *For the frosting:*
> *1 pound firm tofu*
> *3 tablespoons olive oil*
> *3/4 cup maple syrup*
> *1 1/2 tablespoons freshly squeezed orange juice, strained*
> *2 tablespoons orange zest*
> *1 teaspoon vanilla extract*
> *5 tablespoons agar flakes*
> *1 1/3 cups water*
> *4 teaspoons arrowroot*
> *2 tablespoons plain soy milk*

* Combine the tofu, oil, maple syrup, orange juice, zest, and vanilla in a food processor and blend until creamy.
* Dissolve the agar in 1 cup water in a small saucepan over medium heat. Slowly simmer, stirring frequently, until the flakes have completely disappeared.
* In a small bowl, dissolve the arrowroot in the soy milk. Pour the arrowroot into the agar solution. Continue to cook, stirring continuously, until the mixture begins to bubble and has thickened considerably.
* Add the agar mixture to the tofu mixture in the processor and process again to blend.
* Pour the frosting into an ovenproof pan or bowl and refrigerate until firm, about 20 minutes.
* Cut the frosting into pieces and process once more until creamy.

To assemble the cake:
* Remove the cake sections from the pans. Spread frosting on top of one layer and place the other layer on top. Frost top and sides.

lemon poppy seed variation

For the batter:
* Substitute 1/3 cup strained lemon juice for the 2/3 cups orange juice.
* Substitute an equal amount of lemon zest for orange zest.
* Add 1/3 cup water.

For the frosting:
* Substitute lemon juice for orange juice and lemon zest for orange zest.

pear-cranberry crisp

YIELD: **8 servings**　　　　　　　　　　COOKING TIME: **1 hour**

A crisp like this one is the quintessential homey dessert. It fills the kitchen with heavenly aromas. It's easy to prepare and delicious. What could be more enticing than bubbling fruit beneath a blanket of maple-scented pecan crumbles? This crisp also has a good hint of vanilla and a lot of rustic charm.

For the filling:
2¹/₂ to 3 pounds firm pears, Bosc or Bartlett
1 heaping teaspoon kuzu or arrowroot
¹/₂ cup apple juice
¹/₂ cup cranberries
2 to 3 tablespoons maple syrup
1 teaspoon vanilla extract
1 teaspoon fresh ginger juice
Pinch of sea salt

For the topping:
1 cup rolled oats
1 cup whole wheat pastry flour
1 cup chopped pecans
¹/₃ cup olive oil
¹/₃ cup maple syrup
1 teaspoon vanilla extract
¹/₂ teaspoon sea salt

❖ Wash, halve, and core the pears. Quarter lengthwise and cut cross-wise into ¹/₄-inch-thick slices.

❖ Preheat the oven to 375°F.

❖ Dissolve kuzu or arrowroot in apple juice.

❖ Combine remaining filling ingredients, then toss lightly with pears.

❖ Combine all the topping ingredients in a separate bowl. Mix well.

❖ Fill baking dish with pear mixture, sprinkle topping on top, cover with foil, and bake for 40 minutes.

❖ Uncover and bake for another 15 minutes or until topping is golden brown and filling is bubbling.

Variations with fruit or nuts:

❖ Apple can replace pear in the same amounts.

❖ Cinnamon can replace ginger in the filling (1 tsp. dried).

Desserts

- Replace cranberries with raisins or currants (add 2 tablespoons juice to fruit).
- Walnuts, pine nuts, sunflower seeds, and cashews are a great replacement for pecans.

poached pears with cider sauce

YIELD: 6 servings   COOKING TIME: 1 hour

This dessert is elegant, simple, and fat free. The cider is reduced to a gleaming syrup with a heady mix of cinnamon and ginger, a delightful combination of flavors.

Serving suggestions: Position a sprig of mint in place of the stem of the pear. Serve Ginger Snaps or Date-Nut Cookies (pages 221, 220) as an accompaniment.

> 6 firm pears, stems intact
> Freshly squeezed juice of $1/2$ lemon, strained
> $1/2$ gallon apple cider
> 1 cinnamon stick
> 1 vanilla bean, split
> 2 slices ginger root, size of a quarter
> Mint leaves for garnish

- Peel the pears and core them from the bottom. Slice a small section off the bottom of each pear so it can stand upright.
- Place the pears in a bowl of cold water with the lemon juice.
- Place the cider, cinnamon, vanilla bean, and ginger in a 4-quart saucepan over medium heat and bring to a simmer. Reduce the heat to low.
- Add the pears, cover, and simmer for 15 minutes or until pears are just tender.
- Gently remove pears to a platter with a slotted spoon.
- Raise heat to high and bring cider mixture to a boil. Continue to cook until mixture is reduced to a syrupy consistency, about $1^1/2$ cups. Discard cinnamon stick, vanilla bean, and ginger.
- Plate the pears and pour $1/4$ cup syrup over each.
- Allow to cool to room temperature and garnish each pear with fresh mint leaves.

strawberry shortcake with maple tofu whip

YIELD: **8 servings**   COOKING TIME: 1 hour

This is a dish we featured at the Full Moon Party at the Cathedral of St. John the Divine to raise money for the Whole Foods Project AIDS relief fund. Among dishes presented by twenty other restaurants, the Strawberry Shortcake with Maple Tofu Whip was the hit. The maple tofu whip used in this recipe is our all-purpose dessert cream. It goes extremely well with just about any cake or crisp or with brownies.

Note: Tofu whip takes 1 hour to chill before serving; therefore, recipe total is 2 hours.

For the shortcake:
6 tablespoons plus 1 teaspoon maple sugar
¹/₄ teaspoon cinnamon
1 cup whole wheat pastry flour
1 cup unbleached white flour
1¹/₂ teaspoons baking powder
¹/₂ teaspoon baking soda
¹/₄ cup freshly squeezed lemon juice, strained
6 tablespoons plain soy milk
3 tablespoons water
¹/₂ teaspoon sea salt
6 tablespoons olive oil

For the strawberry sauce:
1 pint fresh strawberries
2 to 3 tablespoons maple syrup, depending on how sweet the strawberries are
1¹/₂ teaspoons freshly squeezed lemon juice, strained
1¹/₄ teaspoon vanilla extract
Pinch of sea salt

For the topping:
1 pint fresh strawberries
1 tablespoon maple sugar (or sprinkles)

To make the shortcake (biscuits):

❖ Preheat the oven to 350°F.

❖ Mix 1 teaspoon maple sugar with ¹/₄ teaspoon cinnamon. Set aside in a small bowl.

❖ Combine the flours, baking powder, baking soda, and remaining maple sugar in a mixing bowl.

(continued)

Desserts

Strawberry Shortcake
with Maple Tofu Whip

(continued)

❖ In another mixing bowl, whisk together the lemon juice, soy milk, 3 tablespoons of water, salt, and olive oil.

❖ Pour liquid ingredients into the dry mixture and stir lightly to combine. Do not overmix.

❖ Scoop out $^1/_3$-cup portions of batter and place them onto a lightly oiled cookie sheet to make 8 biscuits. (As an alternative to oiling the cookie sheet, you can use parchment paper.) Place each dollop 3 inches apart. Sprinkle with maple sugar cinnamon mix.

❖ Bake until toothpick comes out clean, about 15 to 20 minutes.

❖ Remove from oven and allow to cool.

To make the strawberry sauce:

❖ Remove stems from strawberries.

❖ Combine all ingredients in a food processor and process until smooth.

To make the strawberry topping:

❖ Remove stems from strawberries.

❖ Thinly slice strawberries lengthwise.

❖ Toss with maple sugar and set aside.

For the Maple Tofu Whip:
1 pound soft tofu
$^1/_2$ cup maple syrup
$^1/_2$ cup olive oil
2 tablespoons vanilla extract
1 tablespoon freshly squeezed lemon juice, strained
$^1/_4$ teaspoon sea salt
4 tablespoons agar flakes
1 cup cold water
2 tablespoons arrowroot
1 cup plain soy milk

❖ Combine tofu, maple syrup, oil, vanilla, lemon juice, and salt in a food processor.

❖ Place agar flakes and 1 cup cold water in a heavy-bottomed saucepan over medium heat. Cook, stirring, until mixture reaches a boil.

❖ In a separate bowl, combine arrowroot with soy milk, then add to boiling liquid. Cook, stirring continuously, until mixture begins to bubble. Remove from heat.

❖ Pour hot mixture gradually into food processor and process until smooth.

Desserts

* Pour into a clean container and allow to set in refrigerator until firm, about 1 hour.
* Whip again just prior to serving.

To assemble:
* Pour about 2 tablespoons of strawberry sauce onto each plate.
* Slice each biscuit in half horizontally and place bottom half on top of the sauce.
* Place a dollop of Maple Tofu Whip on top of each biscuit bottom, along with a tablespoon more of sauce. Cap each with the corresponding biscuit top; add another dollop of tofu whip and a couple of spoonfuls of sliced strawberries. Garnish with mint leaf and serve.

rice pudding

YIELD: 4 to 6 servings   COOKING TIME: 50 minutes

Another classic homey dessert, rice pudding is among the tastiest and also the fastest and easiest to make. Here is our non-dairy, vegan version. The world is divided into two types of people: those who like our rice pudding and those who don't. If you find yourself among those who do, you can have a lot of fun experimenting with different variations of this recipe. Dress it down (serve plain) or dress it up (with strawberries and pralines) to create a sophisticated dessert.

Serving suggestion: Layer the rice pudding with fresh berries in a parfait glass and serve chilled, sprinkled with cinnamon and maple sugar. Omit the raisins and serve the pudding topped with sliced fresh fruit such as strawberries, peaches, plums, nectarines, or blueberries; sprinkle with almond pralines (see page 240).

> $4^1/2$ cups water
> $3/4$ cup maple syrup
> $1^1/2$ cups plain soy milk
> $1/4$ teaspoon sea salt
> 1 vanilla bean
> 1 cinnamon stick
> $1^1/3$ cup white basmati rice
> $1/2$ cup raisins

* Preheat the oven to 300°F.
* Place $4^1/2$ cups of water, maple syrup, soy milk, and salt in a heavy 3-quart saucepan over high heat. Bring to a boil.

(continued)

(continued)

❖ Meanwhile split the vanilla bean in half lengthwise and scrape out the seeds using the back of a knife.

❖ Add the seeds, the vanilla pod, and the cinnamon stick to the cooking liquid.

❖ Rinse the rice in a strainer and add to pot after cooking liquid comes to a boil.

❖ Stir in the raisins.

❖ Place on the middle rack of oven. Bake for 45 minutes.

❖ Remove the pot from the oven. Discard the vanilla pod and cinnamon stick.

❖ Serve warm or cold.

variation with strawberries and pralines

For the strawberries:
2 pints fresh strawberries, hulled and sliced
1/4 cup maple syrup
Freshly squeezed juice of 1/2 lemon, strained
1/2 teaspoon vanilla extract

❖ Combine maple syrup, lemon juice, and vanilla extract. Toss lightly with strawberries.

❖ Let the berries macerate for 10 minutes.

For the pralines:
1 cup slivered almonds, (pecans, walnuts, or hazelnuts can be substituted)
2 tablespoons maple syrup
2 tablespoons maple sugar

❖ Preheat oven to 350°F.

❖ In a small bowl, combine the nuts, maple syrup, and maple sugar. Mix well.

❖ Spread the maple-nut mixture on a cookie sheet and bake for 30 minutes, stirring occasionally.

❖ Scrape the pralines onto a plate and cool until crunchy.

❖ Serve pudding topped with strawberry sauce and pralines.

Desserts

It's a Sweet Life:
Sugaring with Ozzie and Gary

Once upon a time way up in the Northeast Kingdom of Vermont lived two sugarers named Ozzie and Gary. Each year as winter gave way to spring, the sap would rise in the thousands of maple trees that covered the hills of this lovely kingdom. Ozzie and Gary would tap into those trees to extract the sap, thus beginning the long, laborious process that ended when jars of pure, sweet maple syrup were set on the tables of homes throughout the land.

In the realm of Angelica, maple syrup is one of our favorite sweeteners, and we use lots of it, so it's important that we know exactly who produces it and how. Gary Johnson and Ozzie Henchel, our suppliers for nearly ten years, are sugarers we can trust. And their playful spirit makes doing business with them special. Gary started the business, Sweet Life, fourteen years ago out of his garage in Barton, Vermont. Despite the operation's small size, their syrup is shipped far and wide, across the United States and even to Europe.

The British colonists learned sugaring from the Indians, who had been at it for hundreds if not thousands of years. It's a relatively simple though labor-intensive process. Simply cutting the wood that feeds the fire used to boil the sap into syrup is a year-round occupation. As Ozzie says, sugarers really do it for love, because if they were paid what it was worth the syrup would cost twenty-five dollars a cup.

(continued)

(continued)

In the old days, sugarers would drill a hole in the tree, insert a spout, and hang a bucket on it. Buckets would be checked regularly, emptied when full, and rehung, and the sap would be taken in a horse-drawn sleigh to the evaporator for boiling. Later

some sugarers installed a system of interconnected iron pipes so the sap would flow downhill to a collection point. Today the sap flows through a network of surgical tubing instead of pipe.

Sap runs for about three weeks or so beginning in late winter and ending in early spring. Perfect sap weather consists of warm days and cold nights, when the temperature drops below freezing. Just a degree or two of variation can stop the flow. Exactly when the season starts depends on the orientation of the sugarbush, how far north it's located, and, of course, the weather. Ozzie and Gary usually start sugaring between March 10 and March 15, but it could be as early as March 1, as late as April 1. Budding trees indicate the end of the season.

Unlike many sugarers who place several taps in each tree, Ozzie and Gary take a conservative approach, placing one tap per tree, possibly two if the tree is very large. They figure on one quart of syrup per tap per season. On average, it takes forty gallons of sap to make one gallon of syrup. A minimum of 600 gallons of sap are boiled down at a time, and it's done quickly. Sweet Life's total annual production of syrup averages about 600 gallons.

Vermont maple syrup comes in six grades: fancy, or Grade A light amber, grade A medium amber, grade A dark amber, grade B, grade C ("mud" according to the locals), and commercial grade. True Vermont connoisseurs prefer the lighter grades of syrup, while folks "down country," that is in places like New York City, like the heavier, darker kind. We use grade B at Angelica Kitchen because it conveys the maple flavor better in our baked goods. Maple syrup is also produced in Maine, New Hampshire, New York, Connecticut, Massachusetts, and

Desserts

Quebec, and while some of these areas produce excellent syrup, Vermont's syrup is generally considered the crème de la crème due to superior soil and climate conditions.

In addition to sugaring, Ozzie is involved in two other enterprises: fiddlehead ferns and Circus Smirkus. For years Ozzie was known as the fiddlehead king in New York City, supplying farmers markets and top restaurants with up to three-quarters of a ton of the hand-picked ferns per week in season. The fiddlehead season begins shortly after the sugaring season ends.

Fiddleheads are the tops of forest ferns, picked before they have matured. They grow primarily by riverbeds, and the season lasts for two to five weeks in the spring. Fiddleheads taste like a cross between an artichoke and asparagus. They're often used as a garnish or in salads, but they are best blanched, shocked with cold water, and sautéed. Caution: Don't go picking unless you know exactly what you're after. There are many different kinds of ferns in the woods, the fiddlehead being the only edible one.

Ozzie is also the general manager and assistant CEO (Clown Executive Officer) of Circus Smirkus, a traveling circus academy for young people. He and founder Rob Mermin process applications and interview applicants during the winter, run a training program for two weeks in the beginning of the summer, then take Circus Smirkus on the road for six weeks. Look for its graduates starring in all the top circuses—Ringling Brothers, Cirque du Soleil, and Big Apple Circus.

Beverages

At the restaurant, we do not serve drinks iced or very cold, because that chill numbs the organs and glands that are charged with digesting your food. Their job is to produce digestive juices and they operate at body temperature. Therefore, we prefer to offer beverages at or just above room temperature.

Ideally, the juices generated by chewing should be the only liquid you have during the meal. These juices actually begin to break down your food much before it hits your stomach. Washing food down with water or other liquids interferes with this digestive process. If you're going to drink vegetable or fruit juice, do it on an empty stomach, giving your body some time to digest it before eating solid food.

Always have vegetable juice fresh, never packaged or pre-juiced. In the restaurant, we offer freshly made carrot and mixed vegetable juices and apple cider. For a savory beginning to a meal or as a soothing elixir, we serve a Kombu Vegetable Bouillon (page 131). I recommend the bouillon, described on the menu as "a warm invigorating cup of broth, rich in minerals, delicately seasoned with ginger and thyme," to stimulate digestive juices before eating or to help boost the body and spirit when feeling out of sorts.

If you like to have an after-dinner beverage, we recommend kukicha tea, which aids digestion. Other hot drinks we serve are hot apple cider (in autumn and winter); green tea; grain coffee, and Mu #16 tea, which is a blend of sixteen Oriental, nonstimulating herbs. Our preferred brand of grain coffee is Yannoh, made from barley, rye, malted barley, chicory, and acorns.

In summer, we offer a refreshing cooler served chilled. It consists of two herbal teas—Eater's Digest from Yogi Tea and Zesty Lemon Drop from Long Life Herbal Teas—blended with cider and kukicha tea.

Kukicha tea, a.k.a. twig tea, is made from the roasted twigs of mature Japanese tea bushes. (Kukicha means "twigs" in Japanese.) The terms bancha and kukicha are often incorrectly interchanged. Bancha is composed of leaves as well as twigs, while kukicha consists of twigs only. The caffeine in kukicha is 18.6 milligrams per eight-ounce cup compared with 80 milligrams per eight-ounce cup of black tea.

Beverages

Resources

Suggested Reading

Books

Ableman, Michael. *On Good Land: The Autobiography of an Urban Farm*. San Francisco: Chronicle Books, 1998.

Ausubel, Kenny. *Seeds of Change, the Living Treasure*. San Francisco: Harper, 1994.

Berry, Wendell. *Another Turn of the Crank: Essays*. Washington, D.C.: Counterpoint, 1995.

———. *The Gift of Good Land: Further Essays Cultural and Agricultural*. San Francisco: North Point Press, 1981.

———. *Home Economics: Fourteen Essays*. San Francisco: North Point Press, 1995.

———. *The Unsettling of America: Culture and Agriculture*. San Francisco: Sierra Club Books, 1986.

Berthold-Bond, Annie. *The Green Kitchen Handbook*. New York: HarperPerennial, 1997.

Colbin, Annemarie. *Food and Healing*. New York: Ballantine Books, 1996.

Demuth, S. *Community Supported Agriculture: An Annotated Bibliography and Resource*. Beltsville, Md.: National Agriculture Library, 1993.

Erasmus, Udo. *Fats That Heal, Fats That Kill*. Burnaby, B.C., Canada: Alive Books, 1995.

Fallon, Sally, with Mary G. Enig, Ph.D. *Nourishing Traditions*. San Diego: ProMotion Publishing, 1995.

Garland, Anne Witte, with Mothers and Others for a Livable Planet. *The Way We Grow*. New York: Berkeley Books, 1993.

Groh, Trauger, and Steven S. H. McFadden. *Farms of Tomorrow— Community Supported Farms, Farm Supported Communities*. Kimberton, Pa.: Bio-Dynamic Farming and Gardening Association, 1990.

Gussow, Joan Dye. *Chicken Little, Tomato Sauce and Agriculture: Who Will Produce Tomorrow's Food?* New York: Bootstrap Press, 1991.

Henderson, Elizabeth. *Sharing the Harvest: A Guide to Community-Supported Agriculture* / by Elizabeth Henderson with Robyn Van En. White River Junction, Vermont: Chelsea Green Publishing Company.

Kimbrell, Andrew. ed. *Fatal Harvest: The Tragedy of Industrial Agriculture.* Sausalito, Calif.: Foundation for Deep Ecology.

Lappé, Frances Moore. *Hope's Edge* / by Frances Moore Lappé and Anna Lappé. New York: Penguin Putnam Inc.

Lappé, Francis Moore, and Joseph Collins, with Cary Fowler. *Food First: Beyond the Myth of Scarcity.* Boston: Houghton-Mifflin, 1977.

Pitchford, Paul. *Healing with Whole Foods: Oriental Traditions and Modern Nutrition.* Berkeley: North Atlantic Books, 1993.

Schumacher, E. F. *Small Is Beautiful: Economics As If People Mattered.* New York: Perennial Library, 1973.

———. *People, Land, and Community: Collected E. F. Schumacher Society Lectures.* Edited by Hildegarde Hannum, with the assistance of Nancy Jack Todd. New Haven: Yale University Press, 1997.

Wood, Rebecca. *The New Whole Foods Encyclopedia.* New York: Penguin, 1999.

———. *The Splendid Grain.* New York: William Morrow and Company 1997.

Periodicals

Food & Water

Food & Water's monthly publication, *Wild Matters,* is a national publication of politics, ecology, news, and views. With hard-edged, no-nonsense journalism, they aim to create a contagious activist ethic in all forms of social and environmental justice. Food & Water publish on a monthly schedule (except January and July), without any advertising. As a nonprofit, they often rub two pennies together to maintain our steady stream of muckraking, informative, bigger picture news. Their donors and subscribers remain our lifeblood. Subscribe now and help Food & Water educate, motivate, and campaign for lasting change.

Wild Matters
c/o Food & Water, Inc.
P.O. Box 543
Montpelier, VT 05601
Tel: 802-229-6222
Toll free: 800-328-7233
Fax: 802-229-6751
www.foodandwater.org

The GreenMoney Journal

Socially and environmentally responsible investing and business information since 1992.

The GreenMoney Journal
P.O. Box 67
Santa Fe, NM 87504
Tel: 505-988-7423
Email: info@greenmoneyjournal.com
www.greenmoneyjournal.com

The Ecologist

Established in 1970, *The Ecologist* is the world's longest running environmental magazine. Published in London, the magazine is read in over 150 countries by people with an interest in environmental, social, and economic issues.

> The Ecologist
> Ecosystems Ltd
> Unit 18 Chelsea Wharf, 15 Lots Road
> London SW10 OQJ, UK
> Tel: +44 (0)20 7351 3578
> Fax: +44 (0)20 7351 3617
> www.theecologist.org

Orion People & Nature

Since 1982, *Orion* has worked to reconnect human culture with the natural world, blending scientific thinking with the arts, engaging the heart and mind, and striving to make clear what we all have in common.

> The Orion Society and The Myrin Institute
> 187 Main Street
> Great Barrington, MA 01230
> Tel: 413-528-4422
> Email: orion@orionsociety.org
> www.oriononline.org

Natural Home

Natural Home offers today's health-conscious, environmentally concerned homeowners the information they need to practice earth-inspired living. Since their first issue in May 1999, *Natural Home* has brought together the best in home design, earth-friendly décor and natural living. Their bimonthly magazine and dynamic website feature sustainable, healthy homes, decorating tips, and the latest green products and services.

> Natural Home
> 201 East Fourth Street
> Loveland, CO 80537
> Tel: 800-272-2193
> www.naturalhomemagazine.com

Resurgence

Resurgence not only offers a critique of the old paradigm, it also gives working models for an emerging new paradigm. *Resurgence* is packed full of positive ideas about the theory and practice of good living: permaculture, community-supported agriculture, local economics, ecological building, sacred architecture, art in the environment, small schools, and deep ecology.

> Resurgence
> Ford House, Hartland,
> Bideford, Devon, EX39 6EE, U.K.
> Tel: +44 (0) 1237 441293
> Fax: +44 (0) 1237 441203
> Email: mail@resurgence.org
> www.resurgence.gn.apc.org

Organizations

50 Years Is Enough Network

50 Years Is Enough builds partnerships to overcome global economic injustice. They work toward people's greater control over the resources, structures, and economic policies and processes that affect their lives.

> 50 Years Is Enough Network
> 3628 12th St. NE
> Washington, DC 20017
> Tel: 202-IMF-BANK (202-463-2265)
> Email: 50years@50years.org
> www.50years.org

The Alliance for Sustainable Jobs and the Environment (ASJE)

A network of environmental organizations, ASJE includes environmental justice groups, labor unions, and individuals dedicated to holding corporations accountable to strong environmental and labor standards.

> The Alliance for Sustainable Jobs and the Environment
> 1125 SE Madison
> Portland, OR 97214
> Tel: 503-736-9777
> Fax: 503-736-9776
> Email: asje@asje.org
> www.asje.org

Bioneers operates as an entrepreneurial not-for-profit organization, promoting understanding of the human-nature relationship and to revitalize our cultural and spiritual connection with the natural world. Developing model economic strategies for ecological agriculture, environmental restoration, and community self-reliance that conserve biological and cultural diversity, and strengthen traditional, indigenous, and restorative farming practices, Bioneers conducts public education through conferences, workshops, and the media.

Collective Heritage Institute
901 West San Mateo Rd., Suite L
Santa Fe, NM 87505
Tel: 505-986-0366
Toll free: 877-246-6337
Fax: 505-986-1644
www.bioneers.org

The Center for Food Safety

The Center for Food Safety provides leadership in legal, scientific, and grassroots efforts to address the increasing concerns about the impacts of our food production system on human health, animal welfare, and the environment.

The Center for Food Safety
660 Pennsylvania Ave, SE, Suite 302
Washington, DC 20003

West Coast Office:
Bldg. 1062, Fort Cronkhite
Sausalito, CA 94965
Tel: 202-547-9359
Fax: 202-547-9429
Email: office@centerforfoodsafety.org
www.centerforfoodsafety.org

CETOS

CETOS is committed to protecting vulnerable populations from harmful toxicants, and to assuring a toxic-free world for our children and our children's children.

CETOS
P.O. Box 673
39120 Ocean Dr., Suite C-2-1
Gualala, CA 95445
Tel: 707-884-1700
Fax 707-884-1846
Email: cetos@cetos.org
www.cetos.org

Community-Supported Agriculture (CSA)

To find a CSA in your area and obtain further information, contact:

Alternative Farming Systems Information Center
10301 Baltimore Ave, Room 132
Beltsville, MD 20705-2351
Tel: 301-504-6559
Fax: 301-504-6409
Email: afsic@nal.usda.gov
www.nal.usda.gov/afsic

Earth Island's Project Network consists of more than 30 projects worldwide. Through innovative education and activist campaigns, they are addressing many of the most pressing social and environmental issues, such as protecting rain forests, marine mammals, sea turtles, and indigenous lands, promoting organic and sustainable agriculture, ecological paper alternatives, and the emerging Russian environmental movement, and pursuing community-based habitat restoration, reduction of marine pollution, and development of urban multicultural environmental leadership.

> Earth Island Institute
> 300 Broadway, Suite 28
> San Francisco, CA 94133
> Tel: 415-788-3666
> Fax: 415-788-7324
> www.earthisland.org

E.F. Schumacher Society

The E. F. Schumacher Society, named after the author of *Small Is Beautiful: Economics As If People Mattered,* is an educational non-profit organization founded in 1980. Their programs demonstrate that both social and environmental sustainability can be achieved by applying the values of human-scale communities and respect for the natural environment to economic issues.

Building on a rich tradition often known as decentralism, the society initiates practical measures that lead to community revitalization and further the transition toward an economically and ecologically sustainable society.

> E. F. Schumacher Society
> 140 Jug End Road
> Great Barrington, MA 01230
> Tel: 413-528-1737
> E-mail: efssociety@aol.com
> www.schumachersociety.org

Farm Aid

The mission of Farm Aid is to provide assistance to poor and needy families in rural farming communities and to conduct a musical concert to draw attention to the needs of such families and to raise funds to relieve those needs. Farm Aid brings together the common interests of family farmers, consumers, and people who care about the environment. Farm Aid's goal is to keep family farmers on their land and to restore a strong family farm system of agriculture.

"The fight to save family farms isn't just about farmers. It's about making sure that there is a safe and healthy food supply for all of us. It's about jobs, from Main Street to Wall Street. It's about a better America."

WILLIE NELSON, President, Farm Aid

> Farm Aid
> 11 Ward Street, Suite 200
> Somerville, MA 02143
> Tel: 617-354-2922
> Toll free: 800-FARM-AID
> Fax: 617-354-6992
> Email: info@farmaid.org
> www.farmaid.org

Food First

The Institute for Food and Development Policy–better known as Food First–studies root causes and value-based solutions to hunger and poverty around the world, with a commitment to establishing food as a fundamental human right. A "people's" think tank, Food First produces books, reports, articles, films, and electronic media, plus interviews, lectures, workshops, and academic courses.

> Food First/Institute for Food and Development Policy
> 398 60th Street
> Oakland, CA 94618
> Tel: 510-654-4400
> Fax: 510-654-4551
> Email: foodfirst@foodfirst.org
> www.foodfirst.org

Global Exchange

Global Exchange is a human rights organization dedicated to promoting environmental, political, and social justice around the world. Since their founding in 1988, they have been striving to increase global awareness among the U.S. public while building international partnerships around the world.

> Global Exchange
> 2017 Mission Street #303
> San Francisco, CA 94110
> Tel: 415-255-7296
> Fax: 415-255-7498
> Email: info@globalexchange.org
> www.globalexchange.org

The International Forum on Globalization (IFG)

The International Forum on Globalization is an alliance of sixty leading activists, scholars, economists, researchers, and writers formed to stimulate new thinking, joint activity, and public education in response to economic globalization.

> The International Forum on Globalization
> 1009 General Kennedy Avenue #2
> San Francisco, CA 94129
> Tel: 415-561-7650
> Fax: 415-561-7651
> Email: ifg@ifg.org
> www.ifg.org

Just Food

> 307 7th Avenue, Suite 1201
> New York, NY 10001
> Tel: 212-645-9880
> Fax: 212-645-9881
> Email: info@justfood.org
> www.justfood.org

The Land Institute

The Land Institute seeks to develop an agriculture that will save soil from being lost or poisoned while promoting a community life at once prosperous and enduring.

"When people, land, and community are as one, all three members prosper; when they relate not as members but as competing interests, all three are exploited."

> The Land Institute
> 2440 E. Water Well Road
> Salina, KS 67401
> Tel: 785-823-5376
> Fax: 785-823-8728

The National Campaign for Sustainable Agriculture

The National Campaign for Sustainable Agriculture is a not-for-profit organization created in 1994 to coordinate unified action within the sustainable agriculture system that is economically viable, environmentally sound, socially just, and humane.

> National Campaign for Sustainable Agriculture
> P.O. Box 396
> Pine Bush, NY 12566
> Tel: 845-744-8448
> Fax: 845-744-8477
> Email: campaign@sustainableagriculture.net
> www.sustainableagriculture.net

The National Family Farm Coalition (NFFC)

The NFFC was founded in 1986 to serve as a national link for grassroots organizations working on family farm issues. Their membership currently consists of 33 grassroots farm, resource conservation, and rural advocacy groups from 33 states.

NFFC brings together farmers and others to organize national projects focused on preserving and strengthening family farms.

They strongly oppose the vertical integration of agriculture, and serve as a network for groups opposing corporate agriculture. Over the past fourteen years, NFFC has worked to promote the safety of the food supply and the security of those who make it possible.

National Family Farm Coalition
110 Maryland Ave., N.E.
Suite 307
Washington, DC 20002
Tel: 202-543-5675
Fax: 202-543-0978
Email: nffc@nffc.net
www.nffc.net

Organic Farming Research Foundation

The Organic Farming Research Foundation is a nonprofit foundation founded to sponsor research related to organic farming practices, to disseminate research results to organic farmers, and to growers interested in adopting organic production systems, to educate the public and decision-makers about organic farming issues.

Organic Farming Research Foundation
P.O. Box 440
Santa Cruz, CA 95061
Tel: 831-426-6606
Fax: 831-426-6670
Email: research@ofrf.org
www.ofrf.org

The Pesticide Action Network is a network of over 600 participating nongovernmental organizations, institutions, and individuals in over 60 countries working to replace the use of hazardous pesticides with ecologically sound alternatives. Its projects and campaigns are coordinated by five autonomous Regional Centers.

> Pesticide Action Network
> 49 Powell St., Suite 500
> San Francisco, CA 94102
> Tel: 415-981-1771
> Fax: 415-981-1991
> Email: panna@panna.org
> www.panna.org (North American site)
> www.pan-international.org (international site)

The Small Planet Fund

A project founded to support movements addressing the root causes of hunger and showing—through food, farming, and economic innovation—how we can re-embed economic life in the community, ensure we all eat healthyfully, and heal our relationship with the earth.

> Small Planet Fund
> c/o The Funding Exchange
> 666 Broadway, Suite 500
> New York, NY 10012
> Tel: 212-529-5300
> Fax: 212-982-9272
> Email: anna@smallplanetfund.org
> www.smallplanetfund.org

Mail-Order Resources

Great Eastern Sun
92 McIntosh Road
Asheville, NC 28806
Tel: 828-665-7790
Fax: 828-667-8501
www.great-eastern-sun.com

Natural Import Company
9 Reed Street
Biltmore Village, NC 28803
Tel: 828-277-8870
Toll free: 800-324-1878
Fax: 828-277-8892
www.naturalimport.com

Global Environmental Technologies, Inc.
P.O. Box 8839
1001-1003 S. 10th Street
Allentown, PA 18105-8839
Tel: 610-821-4901
Fax: 610-821-5507
www.terraflo.com

Gold Mine Natural Food Co.
7805 Arjons Drive
San Diego, CA 92126-4368
Tel: 858-537-9830
Toll free: 800-475-FOOD
Fax: 858-695-0811
Email: sales@goldminenaturalfood.com
www.goldminenaturalfood.com

Jaffe Bros. Natural Foods
28560 Lilac Road
Valley Center, CA 92082
Tel: 760-749-1133
Fax: 760-749-1282
Email: JB54@worldnet.att.net
www.organicfruitsandnuts.com

(continued)

(continued)

Native Seeds/SEARCH
526 N. 4th Ave.
Tucson, AZ 85705-8450
Tel: 520-622-5561
Fax: 520-622-5591
Email: info@nativeseeds.org
www.nativeseeds.org

Ocean Harvest Sea Vegetable Company
P.O. Box 1719
Mendocino, CA 95460
Tel: 707-937-0637; 707-937-1923
Email: ohveggies@pacific.net
www.ohsv.net

Index

Page numbers given in *italics* indicate illustrations
Page numbers given in **bold** indicate profiles.